Hiding Politics in Plain Sight

Hiding Politics in Plain Sight

Cause Marketing, Corporate Influence,
and Breast Cancer Policymaking

PATRICIA STRACH

OXFORD
UNIVERSITY PRESS

OXFORD
UNIVERSITY PRESS

Oxford University Press is a department of the University of Oxford. It furthers
the University's objective of excellence in research, scholarship, and education
by publishing worldwide. Oxford is a registered trade mark of Oxford University
Press in the UK and certain other countries.

Published in the United States of America by Oxford University Press
198 Madison Avenue, New York, NY 10016, United States of America.

Library of Congress Cataloging-in-Publication Data
Names: Strach, Patricia, author.
Title: Hiding politics in plain sight : cause marketing, corporate influence,
and breast cancer policymaking / Patricia Strach.
Description: New York, NY : Oxford University Press, 2016. | Includes
bibliographical references and index.
Identifiers: LCCN 2016001446 (print) | LCCN 2016013619 (ebook) |
ISBN 9780190606848 (hardcover : alk. paper) | ISBN 9780190606855 (pbk. : alk. paper) |
ISBN 9780190606862 (Updf) | ISBN 9780190606879 (Epub)
Subjects: LCSH: Social marketing—United States. | Social responsibility of
business—United States. | Breast—Cancer—Political aspects—United States. |
Breast—Cancer—Social aspects—United States.
Classification: LCC HF5414 .S77 2016 (print) | LCC HF5414 (ebook) | DDC 658.8—dc23
LC record available at http://lccn.loc.gov/2016001446

To Jerry, Joe, and Lily

CONTENTS

Acknowledgments ix

1. Introduction 1

2. Foundations: Cause Marketing, Breast Cancer, and Framing in America 22

3. Cooperative Market Mechanisms 56

4. Telling Stories 75

5. Effects 117

6. Defining Issues: Breast Cancer and the Creation of Consensus Politics 138

7. Hiding Politics in Plain Sight 174

Appendix A: Model Details for Chapter 3 185
Appendix B: Regression Results for Chapter 5 190
Appendix C: Notes on Methodology and Sources 199
Appendix D: Citizen Consumer Survey 206

References 221
Index 233

ACKNOWLEDGMENTS

"Is this a project about an interesting phenomenon or is this political science?" a senior professor once asked me. I sat there momentarily stunned. Although intended as a criticism of this work, it came off as a damning of the discipline as a whole. Do we really have to choose between doing interesting work and doing political science? I am fortunate to have had the help of so many people who answer that question no and who have pushed me to do both.

For financial support that enabled me to pursue this project, I am deeply grateful to the University at Albany, State University of New York (FRAP B), for seed money to get started; the Robert Wood Johnson Foundation Scholars in Health Policy Research for two years at Harvard University to pursue my research as well as generous support for many of the best authors in this area; and the National Science Foundation (SES-0912666) for a grant that enabled me to conduct a national survey and hire a graduate student. The Rockefeller Institute of Government served as a second home, where I revised much of this book. Any opinions, findings, and conclusions or recommendations expressed in this material are mine and do not necessarily reflect the views of the National Science Foundation, the Robert Wood Johnson Foundation, the University at Albany, or the Rockefeller Institute of Government.

For detailed and constructive advice I thank Virginia Eubanks, Hahrie Han, Susan Moffitt, Julie Novkov, Elizabeth Pérez-Chiqués, and Ed Walker. For comments, I thank Dan Carpenter, Elizabeth Clemens, Laura Evans, Erika Franklin Fowler, Colin Jerolmack, Anna Levine, Christine Percheski, Travis Ridout, David Rousseau, Deb Schildkraut, and Dara Strolovitch. For helpful discussions, I thank Tom Burke, Andrea Campbell, Erzsebet Fazekas, Nancy Folbre, Alethia Jones, Paul Manna, Peter Marsden, Eileen McDonagh, David Pellow, Mark Peterson, Alisa Rosenthal, Kathleen Sullivan, and Priscilla Yamin. Thank you, David Canon, for teaching me the classics; E. E. Schattschneider never goes out of style. And for being great mentors, I thank John Coleman, Carol Nackenoff, Julie Novkov, and Kathy Swartz.

I've been lucky to have really wonderful research assistants: Heather Bennett, Na'ama Nagar, Elizabeth Pérez-Chiqués, Marcus Schultzke, and Katie Zuber. And I have been fortunate to have people who navigated the various bureaucracies for me and made my life so much easier: Dawn Guinan, Sage Kochavi, Barbara Mathews, Joan Nellhaus, and Lois Brando Pownall. Angela Chnapko at Oxford University Press helped me tighten the manuscript and make it more readable to a broader audience.

I would like to thank the men and women affiliated (past and present) with governmental agencies and nonprofit groups who generously shared their time and stories with me. To say I learned a lot from them is an understatement. For those people who are not here to tell their stories in person, I thank the men and women who archived their papers so researchers like me could get to know them and their contributions.

I'd like to thank my family—especially Walter and Carol Strach, Joyce and Gerald Marschke—for everything they do. I am grateful for each one of you.

Finally, if you're reading this book, thank you, dear reader! If you find it too interesting, too (political) scientific, or problematic in any other way, I alone am to blame.

Hiding Politics in Plain Sight

Introduction

More Americans know a pink ribbon is the symbol of breast cancer than know the name of the vice president of the United States. They more often identify the nonprofit Susan G. Komen (Komen) as a funder of breast cancer research than they do the National Institutes of Health—the single largest funder of breast cancer research. Yet, as late as the 1980s, breast cancer was a stigmatized disease not discussed openly, so much so that local reporters avoided using the word *breast* in their stories and early breast cancer organizations steered clear of it in their names. How did breast cancer transform from a "non-issue" that couldn't be mentioned in public to a household name?

Quite simply, breast cancer activists with corporate backgrounds marketed it. They branded breast cancer as "pink": feminine, hopeful, and uncontroversial. They created visible activities like corporate-sponsored walks and runs and paired with industry to create cause-marketing campaigns where a portion of the sale of specially marked products benefits breast cancer research, treatment, and support. Groups like Komen, which pioneered market-based strategies, saw them as the mechanisms in a broader movement for large-scale social change. Americans are exposed to pink products, from breakfast cereal to running shoes to circular saws, on trips to supermarkets, shopping malls, and big box stores. When they bring these products home, the pink picture of breast cancer is embedded and reinforced as a part of their daily routines: at breakfast, in their work-outs, and during their household chores.

Breast cancer activists have had an enormous impact on how Americans understand breast cancer and, in turn, how the policy process has addressed the disease. Cause-marketing campaigns are ubiquitous, and they portray breast cancer as largely symbolic. As a result, the over-whelming majority of Americans are more familiar with breast cancer symbols, like the pink ribbon, than with facts, like the lifetime risk of the disease. On labels of consumer packaged goods, cause marketing gives the impression that cancer is tractable and fixing it is easy and conve-nient. Therefore, people who participate in breast cancer cause-marketing campaigns (even when they did not intend to participate) feel good about what they do. Because breast cancer is pink—skirting political contro-versy associated with other women's issues like equal pay—policymakers in Congress have embraced the disease, significantly increasing fund-ing for existing programs in the National Institutes of Health and creat-ing new programs in the Department of Defense and the US Post Office (breast cancer stamp).

Yet success has come at a price. Reliance on cooperative market mech-anisms, like cause marketing and corporate-sponsored walks, has shifted issue definition away from the contentious processes in the political sphere to industry–nonprofit partnerships in the market, in which adver-tising campaigns portray complex issues along a single dimension with a simple solution: breast cancer research will find a cure, and Americans can participate easily by purchasing specially marked products.

Market mechanisms do more than raise awareness of issues or money to support charities. This book suggests they also give industry a key role in selecting and framing issues and activists with ties to business a mo-nopoly over its definition, shifting power in American society in largely uncharted ways. Industry's direct effect on the policy process—through lobbying, for example—may pale in comparison with the more pervasive *indirect* effect it exercises when it shapes how Americans think about indi-vidual issues and, more broadly, the right way to address public problems. Industry and corporate-connected individuals market issues, like breast cancer, widely, shaping public understanding. But framed as consensus-based social issues rather than contentious political issues, they essentially hide politics in plain sight.

A DEMOCRATIC DILEMMA

The more we value participatory or representative self-governance, the more the marketing of breast cancer problems and solutions should alarm or at least concern us. Corporate-connected breast cancer activists achieved stunning success (changing the way Americans talk about breast cancer) at daunting costs (dominating how the disease is framed). The case of breast cancer illustrates how ideas generated through market mechanisms become embedded in American culture and then get translated into public policy. Market processes, more than policy processes, shape the debate about the disease, determine winners and losers, and create stable coalitions. Market actors, more than policy actors, determine what issues are important and how we think about them. But policy scholars know a lot more about how policy processes work than market processes and more about how policy actors frame issues and set the agenda than market actors. In short, even though cause marketing and corporate-sponsored walks and runs are widespread, there are more questions than answers about how market mechanisms work and what effect they have. Which activists are most likely to have relationships with industry? With regard to what issues? What impact does corporate involvement have on how Americans understand issues? What effect does broad attention in the marketplace have on how issues fare in policy processes and, more broadly, on democratic politics?

I answer these questions by examining cooperative market mechanisms, or instances when industry partners with nonprofits to raise awareness about and resources for a cause. In particular I focus on two mechanisms: cause marketing, where a portion of the purchase price of goods or services supports a designated cause, and, to a lesser extent, corporate-sponsored walks and runs, where organized, sponsored athletic events raise awareness of and resources for a designated cause. In both cases industry works cooperatively with activists. For example, New Balance (athletic shoes) has partnered with Komen to sponsor the Race for the Cure since 1991, underwriting the costs of the event. New Balance also has a cause-marketing partnership with Komen, donating 5 percent of the suggested retail price of athletic shoes to Komen.[1] In both of these partnerships, New Balance is perceived to be doing a good deed, Komen receives more resources, and breast cancer gets more attention. Cooperative partnerships like these look very different from contentious forms of activism directed against industry, such as African American boycotts in Don't Buy Where You Can't Work campaigns in the 1930s and 1940s or contemporary student boycotts of college athletic wear produced in sweatshops. In contentious cases like these, activists attract public attention to their cause when individuals perceive industry as harming others.

Cooperative market mechanisms can be powerful forces in framing issues, or how issues are portrayed, potentially shaping the way that Americans think about a problem. Public policy scholars show that framing determines the issues policymakers examine and the institutions and politics around those issues. But cause-marketing stories are often different from stories generated in the policy arena, with which scholars are more familiar.[2] By selecting, analyzing, and comparing cause-marketing issues with policy issues across the full spectrum of topics they address, I show that cause-marketing campaigns overwhelmingly address social welfare concerns like disease, education, and humanitarian causes. These are tangible issues that Americans can see, feel, and easily understand. Not only do cause-marketing campaigns focus on a distinct set of issues,

---

1. Susan G. Komen: http://ww5.komen.org/MeetPartners.aspx, accessed March 16, 2015.

2. Barbara Nelson, *Making an Issue of Child Abuse: Political Agenda Setting for Social Problems* (Chicago: University of Chicago Press, 1984); Frank R. Baumgartner and Bryan D. Jones, *Agendas and Instability in American Politics* (Chicago: University of Chicago Press, 1993); Deborah A. Stone, *Policy Paradox: The Art of Political Decision Making*, rev. ed. (New York: Norton, 2002).

they also tell a qualitatively different story. Cause-marketing stories emphasize awareness over information. They promote individual over collective solutions. They enable and empower individuals. They frame issues around marketable emotions (like hope). And they are consensual, positive, and seemingly apolitical.

These stories are also highly visible. Cause marketing is employed for a wide range of products and services, from BMWs to real estate. But it occurs most frequently with consumer packaged goods, items like groceries, clothing, and cleaning products. Americans see these products when they go to the supermarket or shopping mall. When they buy these products and bring them into their homes, consumers integrate them into their daily routines: eating breakfast, getting dressed, or cleaning up. They also learn from them.

Survey evidence presented in this book shows that exposure to cause-marketing products changes how Americans *think* and *feel* about issues. Americans' understanding of breast cancer, for example, looks similar to the stories that cause marketing tells. Survey respondents are more familiar with awareness of an issue than with specific information about it, more likely to believe that consumer purchases have an effect on companies' behavior and personal satisfaction, more likely to believe their purchases make a difference, and more likely to feel good about doing so. These results hold for individuals who purchase cause-marketing products intentionally because they want to support a particular cause, such as breast cancer or the environment ("cause followers"). They hold for individuals who purchase cause-marketing products intentionally because they believe in supporting causes whenever they can, such as someone who chooses products that support causes over ones that do not ("lifestyle buyers"). But less intuitive—and more problematic for democratic politics—these results also hold for individuals who say they would purchase a product *regardless* of whether it supported a cause ("accidental activists"), for example, someone who always buys New Balance shoes.

In short, whether or not Americans choose to participate in cause marketing, they are exposed to its messages. Regardless of why they purchase these products, cause marketing changes how respondents think and feel. These results have implications for what we know about politically motivated consumption, the politics of breast cancer, and framing and agenda setting more broadly.

My results suggest, first, that *studies of politically motivated consumption actually understate who participates and why.* Scholars show that approximately half of all Americans engaged in some sort of political consumerism in the past year, buying products because they believe in the social and political values of the company that produces them or avoiding products because they disagree. This pattern is especially true for younger Americans.[3] Still, by looking at people who buy with *intent*, these studies undercount who actually participates and why they get involved. I find that just about every American is exposed to cause marketing. Most survey respondents remember seeing cause-marketing products. A majority of them actually buy these products and incorporate them into their daily routines. But many of them participate *unintentionally*, saying they would buy the product regardless of whether it supported a particular cause. Cause marketing, then, affects a much broader group of people than scholars have previously thought and in ways we have not yet analyzed.

Second, *scholars who have written about breast cancer demonstrate that the dominant framing of breast cancer as pink has wide-ranging cultural and social effects; I suggest that it also affects politics and policymaking.* Scholars show that pink framing shapes how Americans understand breast cancer and how individuals with breast cancer experience the disease. Pink framing leads to a disproportionate emphasis on mammography, even though scientists suggest this may have no benefit and may be harmful; and it gives greater voice to organizations that promote a pink understanding of breast cancer at the expense of other breast cancer organizations and movements, such as health social movements and the environmental breast cancer movement. I argue

---

3. See, e.g., Cliff Zukin et al., *A New Engagement: Political Participation, Civic Life, and the Changing American Citizen* (New York: Oxford University Press, 2006).

that it affects mainstream politics and policymaking too. Ideas framed through market mechanisms can become embedded in the policymaking process, generating broad support for an issue and encouraging particular types of symbolic policymaking at the expense of substantive policymaking on breast cancer, other women's health issues, or other issues altogether. Federal public policymakers have embraced breast cancer as a way to show support for women without taking on an issue steeped in overt controversy.

Third, my results *contribute to literature on framing and agenda setting, expanding it beyond the more traditional sources that policy scholars study—like the media and policy actors—to show that framing can also occur through market mechanisms.* Using a national survey, I show that exposure to breast cancer cause marketing has an effect on how respondents think and feel about the disease. I also demonstrate effects through a historical case study of breast cancer. Even though breast cancer can be framed in different ways—as a feminist issue of inequality, a medical issue of pain and suffering, or an environmental one about the need to regulate corporations—a view of breast cancer that is hopeful, positive, and uncontroversial dominates. Nonprofits and corporations reify this understanding through continued cause marketing of breast cancer with the pink ribbon. Policy actors support it through symbolic measures, such as covering the White House in a pink ribbon, lighting up the St. Louis arch in pink, and authorizing a semi-postal breast cancer stamp, where a portion of the price of the stamp is directed to cancer research. In short, market mechanisms that portray breast cancer as pink shape how Americans think about it and how policymakers act on it.

Taken together, these contributions support a broader argument about the indirect ways industry exercises influence in America. Because the logic and processes that generate cause-marketing stories and issues are often different from those generating policy stories and issues, who exercises influence, how they do so, and with what effect differ from what studies of framing and agenda setting in the federal policy process have shown.

CONSENSUS, POLITICS, AND POWER

Baumgartner and Jones argue that ideas are the core around which political institutions are built.[4] In the mid-twentieth century, for example, when nuclear energy was understood as "too cheap to meter," the agencies and congressional committees overseeing nuclear power saw their job as *promoting* this energy source, not regulating health and environmental effects (that came later). Actors who control how issues are understood, like nuclear power, influence the institutions and policies that are put in place. With cooperative market mechanisms, like cause marketing, industry and a select group of activists define issues as positive and consensual, stripping away negative associations, controversy, or discussion of alternative issues that may also be vying for attention.

Yet issues always have more than one side. As Samantha King explains, "[N]othing is inherently uncontroversial about breast cancer. Instead, the disease has been manufactured as such over two decades of organizing."[5] While nobody wants *more* breast cancer, within the breast cancer community there is debate about what to do: some people want more robust and effective healthcare for low-income Americans, while others want more environmental regulation to prevent carcinogens from entering the air, water, or commercial products. Further, resources are finite and there are debates about the best way to spend government dollars: within the women's health community some argue that there ought to be greater attention to heart disease or lung cancer, both of which are more deadly for American women, while individuals outside women's health prefer that resources be channeled into other areas, like education, defense, or foreign

4. Baumgartner and Jones, *Agendas and Instability in American Politics.*

5. Samantha King, "Pink Ribbons Inc.: The Emergence of Cause-Related Marketing and the Corporatization of the Breast Cancer Movement," in *Governing the Female Body: Gender, Health, and Networks of Power,* ed. Lori Reed and Paula Saukko (Albany, NY: SUNY Press, 2010), 108. See also Gayle Sulik and Edyta Zierkiewicz, "Gender, Power, and Feminisms in Breast Cancer Advocacy: Lessons from the United States and Poland," *Journal of Gender and Power* 1, no. 1 (2014): 111–45; Lori Baralt and Tracy A. Weitz, "The Komen–Planned Parenthood Controversy: Bringing the Politics of Breast Cancer Advocacy to the Forefront," *Women's Health Issues* 22, no. 6 (2012): e509–e512.

aid. Yet all of these debates are minimized when breast cancer is framed as pink. Americans see breast cancer as an issue about which people agree. Conflict—either within the breast cancer community or between breast cancer and other issues—is missing. But politics is fundamentally about the socialization of conflict, and power about suppressing it.

As E. E. Schattschneider explains, politics looks like a street rumble where the winners want to keep conflict contained and the losers want to expand it to the individuals watching the fight. In Schattschneider's imagery, cause marketing expands the scope of issue definition through market mechanisms to consumers in America and across the globe. But while Schattschneider contrasts private conflict, which takes place behind closed doors, with political conflict, which attempts to involve the larger public, companies engaged in cause marketing provide a third alternative: a public, nonconflictual, and seemingly nonpolitical way to address problems. By depicting issues as consensual and promoting them broadly through cause marketing, industry and select activists play a key role in defining issues and portraying them as apolitical, essentially hiding politics in plain sight.[6] Americans are familiar with breast cancer, but, when it is framed as pink, they understand it to be a consensus-based *social* issue, not a conflict-ridden *political* one.

When we cede authority to market mechanisms we are not merely expanding the scope of conflict; we may be *replacing* political conflict with market competition, trading democratic disagreement for a consensus built on preventing individuals "from having grievances by shaping their perceptions, cognitions, and preferences."[7] Every issue has more than one side. Defining and redefining issues is the fundamental basis of politics, determining who wins, who loses, and how.[8] With cooperative market

6. See also Vance Packard, *The Hidden Persuaders* (New York: Ig Publishing, 2007).

7. Steven Lukes, *Power: A Radical View*, 2d ed. (Hampshire: Palgrave Macmillan, 2005), 11.

8. Baumgartner and Jones, *Agendas and Instability in American Politics*; Deborah Stone, "Causal Stories and the Formation of Policy Agendas," *Political Science Quarterly* 104, no. 2 (1989): 281–300; Nelson, *Making an Issue of Child Abuse*; E. E. Schattschneider, *The Semi-Sovereign People* (New York: Holt, Rinehart, Winston, 1960).

mechanisms, *industry and key activists can exercise disproportionate influence* on what issues Americans are exposed to, how they think about those issues, and the kinds of actions they are likely (or not) to take.

Industry Influence in American Politics

Scholars have long shown that industry exercises undue influence by keeping contentious issues out of the political arena and effectively organizing and lobbying on issues that make it there.[9] Corporate packaged-food producers, for example, are better able to lobby against food standards that hurt their bottom line than are a diffuse group of consumers. But with cooperative market mechanisms, industry exercises influence as an unintentional by-product of contemporary business practices that stress "corporate social responsibility," defined as benefiting society beyond what laws and regulations require.[10] Although there is a long tradition of corporate philanthropy, since the 1980s and 1990s companies have adopted a range of practices, from Starbucks selling fair-trade coffee to Coca-Cola donating money for women's heart health when consumers purchase Diet Coke. While scholars argue that corporate social responsibility is beneficial because it brings social and ethical concerns into business practices,[11] the often overlooked other side is that market mechanisms also bring market biases into issue framing and public policymaking, which is inherently undemocratic.

---

9. Schattschneider, *The Semi-Sovereign People*; Mancur Olson, Jr., *The Logic of Collective Action: Public Goods and the Theory of Groups* (Cambridge, MA: Harvard University Press, 1965); Peter Bachrach and Morton S. Baratz, "Two Faces of Power," *American Political Science Review* 56, no. 4 (1962): 947–52.

10. David Vogel, *The Market for Virtue: The Potential and Limits of Corporate Social Responsibility* (Washington, DC: Brookings Institution Press, 2005), 2.

11. Sarah A. Soule, *Contention and Corporate Social Responsibility* (New York: Cambridge University Press, 2009); Brayden G. King and Nicholas A. Pearce, "The Contentiousness of Markets: Politics, Social Movements, and Institutional Change in Markets," *Annual Review of Sociology* 36 (2010): 249–67.

Industry's direct influence—through tactics like political lobbying—may pale in comparison with its more indirect influence—defining issues and options for the American public. Proctor & Gamble, for example, spent $4.4 million in 2012 to lobby the federal government on topics like corporate taxation and ingredient disclosure to protect its corporate privileges.[12] But Proctor & Gamble's market-based influence far exceeds its political lobbying. It is an 84-billion-dollar-a-year operation reaching 4.6 billion of the world's 7 billion people. It shapes both what Americans think is important (clean clothes, dry babies) and how to achieve it (Tide detergent, Pampers diapers). Americans are exposed to corporate messages directly and indirectly every day and, as a result, their familiarity with corporations and their products exceeds their familiarity with government and governmental actors. Survey data presented in this book reveal that while 62 percent of respondents know which party controls the House of Representatives and 66 percent know the name of the vice president, 77 percent of respondents know that Yoplait makes yogurt. Even more (82 percent) know that the pink ribbon is the symbol of breast cancer.

Nearly a century ago, Edward Bernays, one of the first public-relations experts, noted that those who manipulate the habits and opinions of the mass public "constitute an invisible government, which is the true ruling power of our country. We are governed, our minds molded, our tastes formed, our ideas suggested, largely by men we have never heard of."[13] Industry's influence in the political sphere extends well beyond lobbying government in cases where it has a clear stake in the outcome and shapes how Americans understand social issues, like the environment, health, and children's well-being, through market mechanisms. BMW manufactures cars, yet it influences public understanding of breast cancer; General Mills makes breakfast cereal but promotes K–12 education.

12. Center for Responsive Politics, http://www.opensecrets.org/lobby/clientsum.php?id=D000000485&year=2012, accessed June 6, 2013.

13. Edward Bernays, *Propaganda* (New York: Ig Publishing, 2004); but see Packard, *The Hidden Persuaders.*

Activists with Ties to Industry

If the turn to market mechanisms gives industry a powerful avenue for influence, it also privileges Americans with ties to industry over those without. Activists with corporate ties are able to exploit these relationships successfully to define and promote issues that are important to them because
they speak the language and have the skills to succeed in issue framing.[14]
Both Komen and the Breast Cancer Research Foundation, two organizations that use cause marketing extensively, were established by elite women
with corporate ties. Nancy Brinker, who founded Komen, trained with
Stanley Marcus (of Neiman Marcus) and Evelyn Lauder, who founded the
Breast Cancer Research Foundation, was a corporate executive at the cosmetics giant Estée Lauder. They branded breast cancer as pink, they chose
the pink ribbon as its symbol, and they pioneered cause marketing and corporate-sponsored walks and runs. As a result, they defined breast cancer as
pink for most Americans.

Before, during, and after Komen's Race for the Cure, the pink ribbon,
and cause-marketing products, there were organizations across the
United States that formed around breast cancer. Many of these organizations operated as support groups. But some of them with an activist orientation wanted to pursue a different set of tactics, from rejecting recon-
structive surgery to targeting corporations that put potential carcinogens
in products. Activists affiliated with the National Breast Cancer Coalition
and other relatively mainstream organizations that reject the pink ribbon
express frustration with Komen and the dominant framing of the disease
because they leave no room for alternative understandings. "[Komen]
partners with everything from maps to cars to prunes. The only slogan
I haven't seen is 'Fuck for the Cure,'" remarked one activist cynically.[15]
Notably, this framing affects not only how people see breast cancer but

14. Like Dara Strolovitch, who shows that interest groups represent their most advantaged
members, I find that market mechanisms benefit the most advantaged activists, exacerbating
inequality. See Dara Z. Strolovitch, *Affirmative Advocacy: Race, Class, and Gender in Interest
Group Politics* (Chicago: University of Chicago Press, 2007).

15. Interview with National Breast Cancer Coalition [henceforth NBBC] affiliate, 2009
(no. 90817).

how people see breast cancer activists; as another explained: "We don't want to be nice ladies dressed in pink."[16]

Many activists resent Komen and cause marketing because they shape how Americans think about breast cancer (as pink), how they think about people with the disease (as survivors), and how they think about breast cancer activists (nice ladies dressed in pink). Whether they want to go outside the mainstream by taking off their shirts to expose mastectomy scars or work inside the hallowed halls of Congress, disease activists who have other ideas about what breast cancer is and how to address it try, but have been unable, to shake breast cancer's pink framing.

Even though breast cancer is not the most deadly cancer (lung cancer is), the most common killer (heart disease is), or the fastest-growing killer (HIV/AIDS is), it is one of the most culturally and politically salient diseases. The disproportionate success of breast cancer cause marketing has pushed other disease activists and other cause advocates to follow the same market model. For example, the American Heart Association partners with Coca-Cola and Macy's in a Go Red for Women campaign to bring attention to heart disease, while the National Wildlife Foundation partners with Nickelodeon to promote endangered wildlife. Today, being an issue advocate means not merely framing and lobbying but *marketing* issues.

BREAST CANCER AND THE CREATION OF A *COMMERCIAL* SOCIAL MOVEMENT

I tell this story with a general overview looking at who participates in cause marketing, for what products, telling what stories, and with what effects. I employ aggregate survey data and content analysis. But to show how the logic of this works in practice, how these tactics came about, and the effects they have, I rely on the case of breast cancer. I chose breast cancer because breast cancer activists were early pioneers of cause marketing and, today, the breast cancer campaign is the largest and most successful cause-marketing campaign. One common explanation for breast cancer's meteoric rise as an

16. Interview with NBCC affiliate, 2009 (no. 90814).

issue is that it is a natural fit for cause marketing: it is "noncontroversial" and it appeals to many people. Unlike debates on universal healthcare or tax breaks, there are not two sides (pro and con) in breast cancer debates. Further, breast cancer has wide appeal for marketers and policymakers. As a disease that primarily affects women across socioeconomic groups, it creates a large and potent constituency for change. Industry and political officials can take a stand on an important issue and/or support women by publicizing their support for breast cancer research or treatment.

But thinking of breast cancer as noncontroversial and its cause as appealing broadly confuses cause with effect. Americans today are so steeped in a particular understanding of breast cancer as pink—feminine, hopeful, and uncontroversial—that it is hard for many to remember the disease any other way. Yet, for most of its history, breast cancer was stigmatizing and saying the word *breast* in public was taboo. Even into the 1980s, men and women with breast cancer did not talk about their diagnoses. Local media and organizations avoided using the word *breast*. Many women considered breast cancer treatment, which involved radical surgery to remove the breast, lymph nodes, and chest muscle walls, to be worse than the disease, and some chose to forgo treatment altogether. Rather than a natural fit, the first attempts at cause marketing for breast cancer failed miserably because, as one Komen executive recalled, companies asked, "Why would we want to do that? Why would we want to associate a female product with death and dying?"[17] Breast cancer is both painful and deadly. It is one of the *least likely* cases for market-based mechanisms. So why did activists choose market-based strategies? How did market mechanisms have such a profound effect on how Americans understand breast cancer? What social and political effects have market-based issue understandings had? What can we learn about using the market as a vehicle for broad-based change?

Breast cancer provides a unique opportunity to see how activists with corporate backgrounds partnered with industry to create a *commercial social movement*. In a commercial social movement, activists

17. Interview with Komen executive, 2009 (no. 090820).

work cooperatively with industry rather than contentiously against it; they employ market mechanisms like cause marketing and corporate-sponsored runs rather than defiant protests or marches. A commercial social movement is necessarily conservative. It seeks change that is incremental, relying on existing institutions. It is a continuation of rather than a sharp break from the past. Although it is unorthodox to call elite leaders of a nonprofit without an overt political strategy and without contentious means *activists* and equally unorthodox to call their efforts a *movement*, I use both terms consciously. As Jennifer Myhre explains, "[S]ocial movements pursue their goals in arenas beyond formal political institutions" and their actions may not be contentious.[18] To employ the terms often used to describe contentious movements that seek more radical change is to recognize that significant and lasting change can come from conservative and incremental means.[19]

Understanding cause marketing and corporate-sponsored walks and runs as *mechanisms* in a commercial social movement that was designed for broad-based conservative (in means and ends) change allows me to spell out how the organizations in this movement have been successful, the influence they have exercised in politics and policymaking, and the diverse avenues for change that activists engage. But it also makes sense of the palpable frustration that other breast cancer activists in other movements feel and gives scholars and activists alike a language to speak about what it is that groups like Komen do.

18. Jennifer Myhre, *Medical Mavens: Gender, Science, and the Consensus Politics of Breast Cancer Activism* (PhD dissertation, University of California Davis, 2001) p. 7; see also John D. McCarthy and Mark Wolfson, "Consensus Movements, Conflict Movements, and the Cooptation of Civic and State Infrastructures," in *Frontiers in Social Movement Theory*, ed. Aldon D. Morris and Carol McClurg Mueller (New Haven, CT: Yale University Press, 1992), 273–92; Marc Michaelson, "Wangari Maathai and Kenya's Green Belt Movement: Exploring the Evolution and Potentialities of Consensus Movement Mobilization," *Social Problems* 41, no. 4 (1994): 540–61.

19. Wolfgang Streek and Kathleen Thelan, "Introduction: Institutional Change in Advanced Political Economies," in *Beyond Continuity: Institutional Change in Advanced Political Economies*, ed. Wolfgang Streek and Kathleen Thelan (New York: Oxford University Press, 2005).

Nancy Brinker, of Komen, and Evelyn Lauder, of the Breast Cancer Research Foundation, created a commercial social movement that worked for broad-scale cultural change in the way Americans understand breast cancer. The goals of their movement were to take away the stigma associated with breast cancer, to encourage men and women to talk about the disease, and to promote treatment rather than avoidance. They saw the market as a platform for broad-based change, and they used their elite business backgrounds in and connections with large American companies to rebrand breast cancer as pink. They marketed the pink ribbon as its symbol.

Although these groups may be at odds with other organizations, they work cooperatively with industry. Brinker explained, "We weren't creating another charity; we were creating a movement. That meant Komen needed a mechanism to carry its message to every town and city in the nation."[20] Though social movement scholars associate movements with contentious politics, Komen executives see a movement of a different kind, mobilizing men and women through partnerships with industry. Like traditional social movements, Komen officials seek change. But they do so in a much more limited (less radical) fashion: they seek to change the way Americans think about, talk about, and act on breast cancer by partnering with corporations and utilizing market mechanisms like cause marketing and corporate-sponsored walks and runs.

They have been remarkably successful in changing the face of breast cancer. In contrast to the image of death and dying that breast cancer had in the past, today breast cancer is seen as pink: breast cancer water bottles carry slogans like "No one fights alone," and Wilson sells "Hope" tennis balls and rackets. The American Cancer Society promotes Stories of Hope, where one woman writes, "What finding the 'can' in cancer means to me is there's something good even around all of the terrible things."[21]

20. Nancy G. Brinker, *Winning the Race: Taking Charge of Breast Cancer* (Irving, TX: Tapestry Press, 2001), 75.

21. American Cancer Society: http://www.cancer.org/treatment/survivorshipduringandaftertreatment/storiesofhope/breast-cancer-survivor-finds-the-can-in-cancer, accessed April 18, 2014.

These very public, though seemingly apolitical, mechanisms of change mean that Americans in all walks of life are exposed to the message, even without watching the news or reading a newspaper. As a result, Americans now think about the disease differently than they did in the past. According to survey data I collected, two-thirds of American respondents report having seen products that benefit breast cancer research or treatment, 60 percent report having seen media stories, nearly 50 percent saw walks or runs, and 30 percent bought products that benefit breast cancer research or treatment in the past week.

Being pink—a women's issue, not a feminist issue—has given breast cancer a leg up in federal politics. Like many other diseases, breast cancer research is supported by the National Institutes of Health. But it was the first disease to receive funding from the Congressionally Directed Medical Research Programs in the Department of Defense and a semipostal stamp issued by the US Post Office. Both men and women running for Congress and in Congress tout their support for breast cancer as a way of showing support for women more generally, even though breast cancer is not the most deadly cancer, most deadly disease, or fastest-growing killer of women.

MAKING A CASE ABOUT CAUSE MARKETING

To be clear, this book is about cooperative market mechanisms (particularly cause marketing and corporate-sponsored walks and runs) that are employed across a broad spectrum of social welfare issues and a host of consumer products. It is an investigation into what these practices are, who participates in them, and what effect they have. I generate the bird's-eye analysis of individual participation—who participates, for what causes, when, and why—from data about cause marketing using a national survey. I generate the analysis about the types of cause-marketing issues and stories from content analysis of media and policy sources across all types of issues. These two pieces, which establish how individuals participate and what they see and hear, are generalizable to cause-marketing campaigns more broadly. To understand the ground-level processes for organizations and effects, however, I focus on the breast cancer case. The results are suggestive (rather than definitive) of the influence that industry and corporate-connected actors have.

The chapters that follow incorporate both the bird's-eye view of cooperative market mechanisms and an in-depth examination of the case of breast cancer. While the focus at the beginning is on the bird's-eye view in order to lay the groundwork for a discussion of practices that are often murky and understudied, it gives way to more emphasis on the ground-level processes illustrated by the case of breast cancer as the book progresses.

In Chapter 2, "Foundations," I further develop the argument laid out here by asking four key questions. What is cause marketing? Why is breast cancer a good case for examining it? What can an in-depth look at cause marketing and a case study of breast cancer tell us about framing and agenda setting? What are the implications of this study for understanding influence, power, and politics in America today? I discuss the methodology employed in this book before turning to the empirical work.

Few sources of data exist for studying who participates in cause-marketing campaigns, how often, and for what products, let alone the effects of these activities on broader social and political phenomena. To provide an overall picture, I created the Citizen Consumer Survey (CCS) that asked 1,500 Americans questions about their political and consumer practices in September and October 2010. The survey asks a number of questions about participation in market activism generally and about breast cancer in particular. In Chapter 3, "Cooperative Market Mechanisms," I use the survey data to provide a general introduction to cause marketing. Like other studies, mine shows that cause marketing is a very common part of American culture: 80 percent of Americans have seen cause-marketing products in the past month and 80 percent of people who have seen them have actually purchased one. But unlike other scholarly work, my own does not assume a motivation for participating, and I find that Americans participate for three distinct reasons: they are ideologically committed to making change through their purchases (lifestyle buyers); they believe in the cause the products support, like the environment or breast cancer (cause followers); or they would purchase the product even if it did not support a cause (accidental activists). Examining the effects of market activism for intentional participators (lifestyle buyers, cause followers) as well as unintentional participators (accidental activists) shows both that it is far more common and that the impact is more pervasive than other scholarly studies find.

Cause marketing is not just a watered-down version of what takes place in the policy process. It tells different stories. In Chapter 4, "Telling Stories," I analyze what issues cause marketing addresses and how market actors address them. I use issues in the federal policy process as a benchmark. Although cause marketing may have much in common with other elements of American politics, such as campaign advertising or sound bites from political speeches, I intentionally chose to contrast cause marketing with day-to-day elements of the policy process to provide snapshots of the issues that cause marketing addresses and how it addresses them, the issues the policy process addresses and how it addresses them, and how they differ. The snapshots lay the groundwork for understanding key features of both cause marketing and the policy process and, therefore, for understanding how policymaking around breast cancer incorporates both.

To form these snapshots, I created a database of cause-marketing issues by coding business-oriented publications between 1986 and 2010 for the presence of cause-marketing campaigns. I contrast the results of these large national campaigns (which are the focus of news articles) with data about congressional hearings (using the Policy Agendas Project database) to see what issues are addressed, how often they are addressed, and by whom. I show that cause marketing emphasizes different issues than the policy process does—social welfare over government regulation—and addresses those issues in fundamentally different ways, as simple, positive, and easily solved. Cause marketing removes the conflict at the center of American politics, essentially depoliticizing the subjects it addresses. I illustrate how this works in the case of breast cancer. I use the analysis in

Chapter 4 to generate expectations about potential effects that I test in Chapter 5.

When cause marketing emphasizes social welfare issues and portrays them differently than the policy process or media stories do, it can have real effects on Americans' issue understanding. In Chapter 5, "Effects," I show that Americans' issue understanding for breast cancer reflects the stories that cause marketing tells. Returning to the CCS, I exploit the survey's execution across September (control) and October (Breast Cancer Awareness Month) to look at the real-world impact of a cause-marketing campaign. I find that exposure to the breast cancer campaign leads to greater awareness: respondents are more likely to know that the pink ribbon is the symbol of breast cancer. But, like the stories cause marketing tells, awareness does not mean having more information about the disease; it does not make breast cancer a more important priority (like media stories do); and it does not lead to increased demands for collective solutions from government or industry officials. Instead, cause marketing makes individuals feel good. Though I would expect lifestyle buyers and cause followers—who buy products intentionally—to say that cause marketing feels good, even accidental activists—who say they would purchase a product regardless of whether or not it supported a cause—feel good about cause marketing.

While Chapter 5 uses survey data to examine effects, in Chapter 6, "Defining Issues: Breast Cancer and the Creation of Consensus Politics," I look at the long-term effects of cause marketing. Building on secondary studies and supplementing them with archival research and interviews, I show how cause marketing has changed the definition of breast cancer from a taboo disease to one that is very public and pink. Pink framing is not the only way to understand the disease, and market mechanisms are not the only means to address it. Comparing Komen (which emphasizes market-based mechanisms) and the National Breast Cancer Coalition, or NBCC (which emphasizes change working with and within government), I show how pink framing affects even mainstream lobbying organizations and public policy outcomes.

Finally, Chapter 7, "Hiding Politics in Plain Sight," returns to the themes central to this book and evaluates how corporate-marketing strategies, described by the business literature as responsible and ethical, influence change and have dramatic implications for democratic politics.

THE ROAD AHEAD

Although issue definition generated through political conflict is fraught with inequality, market mechanisms promote consensus issues and privilege even more specialized actors with connections to industry. In short, while the policy process gives elite actors (like doctors and lawyers) greater voice, market mechanisms privilege an even more specialized elite with corporate connections (e.g., vice presidents of marketing). While policy actors may wish to discuss "apple pie" issues that almost everyone can agree on, market actors necessarily must do so because conflict and controversy do not sell products. Americans may bemoan the constant conflict inherent in politics. Yet, as frustrating as it may be, conflict allows actors the opportunity to shape debate and win political battles by changing issue understandings.[22] Politics matters not just because it mediates conflict, but also because it generates it. This book shows what happens when conflict is replaced by consensus.

The chapters that follow tell a story of industry influence in American politics in a way that we do not usually think about it. Industry matters not only when it tries to shape debate on issues that directly affect it through lobbying, but also as a side effect of business practices associated with corporate social responsibility. Ideas generated through market processes frame issue understandings in American culture and are imported into the policy process, determining who gets what, when, and how. The next chapter provides a deeper look at the key questions underlying the study.

---

22. Schattschneider, *The Semi-Sovereign People*; Baumgartner and Jones, *Agendas and Instability in American Politics*.

Foundations

Cause Marketing, Breast Cancer,
and Framing in America

Since the 1990s, corporations have been adopting practices associated with "corporate social responsibility," often described as benefiting society in ways that go beyond what is legally required.[1] For example, Nike monitors the labor practices of its suppliers while Starbucks sells fair-trade coffee. Surveys show that most business leaders believe that it is *necessary* to act in socially responsible ways to maintain profitability, attract and retain employees, and enhance their company's image.[2] According to a Cone report, "[C]onsumers want companies to support relevant issues."[3] Companies are turning to corporate social responsibility to do well by doing good.

While corporate social responsibility motivates corporations to do more, it also offers activists additional avenues for change. Activists have long targeted corporate actors through *contentious* activism—from

---

1. Vogel, *The Market for Virtue*, 2.

2. Ibid.; see also Philip Kotler and Nancy Lee, *Corporate Social Responsibility: Doing the Most Good for Your Company and Your Cause* (New York: Wiley, 2005).

3. "Cone Research Report: Cause Evolution and Environmental Survey" (Boston: Cone LLC, 2007), 15.

throwing tea in the Boston harbor to boycotting clothing produced under apartheid—but activists also use expectations about responsible corporations as an opportunity to make change *cooperatively* by pairing their goals with corporate mechanisms. Companies partner with organizations to sponsor walks or runs and create cause-marketing products that raise attention to and money for their cause, while individual consumers can use their purchasing power to show their support for issues and practices with which they agree.

Socially engaged and responsible corporations may offer many benefits.[4] Such corporations may act more ethically and do more for social welfare, while markets give Americans another venue for seeking redress for their concerns and making their case to a much broader audience. But when businesses get involved with issues, from ethical treatment of animals to clean water, their actions may not stay contained in the market but bleed into other arenas, shaping public understanding and public policy. The result is increased public attention to issues and issue understandings that sell products—social welfare concerns over business regulation—and simple and consensual branding over complex and controversial framing. More broadly, I suggest that, with cause marketing, industry exercises a growing influence in American politics by creating the language with which Americans speak about problems, and, as a result, individuals with corporate training or business connections have the skills and vocabulary to succeed.

This chapter provides the background for the study that follows. It is organized around four key questions: What is cause marketing? Why is breast cancer a good case for examining it? What can an in-depth look at cause marketing and a case study of breast cancer tell us about framing and agenda setting? What are the implications of this study for understanding influence, power, and politics in America today? It also addresses the data and methods that I employ.

4. E.g., Soule, *Contention and Corporate Social Responsibility*; David P. Baron, "Private Politics, Corporate Social Responsibility, and Integrated Strategy," *Journal of Economics & Management Strategy* 10, no. 1 (2001): 7–45.

WHAT IS CAUSE MARKETING?

The focus of this book is specifically on cooperative market mechanisms, especially "cause-related marketing" or "cause marketing," which occurs when a "firm's contribution to a designated cause" is "linked to customers' engaging in revenue-producing transactions with the firms (exchange of goods and services for money)."[5] In cause marketing, companies align their products with particular issues, consumers are expected to make purchasing choices based upon those issues, and companies then donate money based on the number of products sold or the number of carton tops, package labels, or UPC codes that consumers clip and mail in.

Scholars of business and nonprofits show that cause marketing can benefit corporations by increasing sales, improving brand image, boosting customer attitudes, and spilling over to other brand products.[6] Additionally, cause marketing can benefit nonprofits by creating dedicated financial streams and raising awareness about an issue among the public.[7] But positive benefits are most likely when there is good fit between corporations and the causes they support, when relationships are sustained over time, when customers identify with the cause, and when the credibility of the corporation and cause are high.[8] Researchers caution

5. P. Rajan Varadarajan and Anil Menon, "Cause-Related Marketing: A Coalignment of Marketing Strategy and Corporate Philanthropy," *Journal of Marketing* 52, no. 3 (1988): 58–74.

6. Walter Wymer and Adrian Sargeant, "Insights from a Review of the Literature on Cause Marketing," *International Review on Public and Non Profit Marketing* 3, no. 1 (2006): 9–15; Brian D. Till and Linda I. Nowak, "Toward Effective Use of Cause-Related Marketing Alliances," *Journal of Product & Brand Management* 9, no. 7 (2000): 472–84; Aradhna Krishna and Uday Rajan, "Cause Marketing: Spillover Effects of Cause-Related Products in Product Portfolio," *Management Science* 55, no. 9 (2009): 1469–85.

7. Wymer and Sargeant, "Insights from a Review of the Literature on Cause Marketing"; see also Mary Runté, Debra Z. Basil, and Sameer Deshpande, "Cause-Related Marketing from the Nonprofit's Perspective: Classifying Goals and Experienced Outcomes," *Journal of Nonprofit & Public Sector Marketing* 21, no. 3 (2009): 255–70.

8. Paul N. Bloom et al., "How Social-Cause Marketing Affects Consumer Perceptions," *MIT Sloan Management Review* 47, no. 2 (2006): 49–55.

that consumers are wary when the corporate motivations are questionable or when the amount given to charities is low.[9]

Cause marketing is part and parcel of the turn to corporate social responsibility that also includes behavior change campaigns like Home Depot partnering with a public utility to promote water conservation tips (corporate social marketing); donating to charities that support a company's goals and philosophies (corporate philanthropy); encouraging employees to volunteer as tutors for children or to clean up beaches (community volunteering); or supporting social causes and community well-being, such as when Kraft ended all school marketing (socially responsible business practices).[10] Cause marketing looks different from contentious forms of activism.

How Cause Marketing Differs from Contentious Forms of Activism

When Americans expect industry to act in socially responsible ways, corporations are vulnerable to criticism of their practices, and they respond to the bright light of public scrutiny.[11] Organizations and individuals are

9. Michael Barone, Anthony D. Miyazaki, and Kimberly A. Taylor, "The Influence of Cause-Related Marketing on Consumer Choice: Does One Good Turn Deserve Another?," *Journal of the Academy of Marketing Science* 28, no. 2 (2000): 248–62; Bloom et al., "How Social-Cause Marketing Affects Consumer Perceptions"; Darren W. Dahl and Anne M. Lavach, "Cause-Related Markets: Impact of Size of Cause Related Promotion on Consumers Perception and Participation," in *1995 AMA Winter Educators Conference: Marketing Theory and Application*, ed. David W. Stewart and Naufel J. Vilcassim (Chicago: American Marketing Association, 1995), 476–81; but see John H. Holmes and Christopher Kilbane, "Cause-Related Marketing: Selected Effects of Price and Charitable Donations," *Journal of Nonprofit & Public Sector Marketing* 1, no. 4 (1993).

10. Examples from Kotler and Lee, *Corporate Social Responsibility*, 23–24.

11. Soule, *Contention and Corporate Social Responsibility*; Michael Yaziji and Jonathan Doh, *NGOs and Corporations: Conflict and Collaboration* (New York: Cambridge University Press, 2009); Baron, "Private Politics, Corporate Social Responsibility, and Integrated Strategy"; Timothy Werner, *Public Forces and Private Politics in American Big Business* (New York: Cambridge University Press, 2012). Examples in this paragraph and the next are drawn from Soule, *Contention and Corporate Social Responsibility*, except for cause marketing and where otherwise noted.

able to exert pressure through contentious forms of activism, such as *corporate campaigns* designed to harm corporate reputation, like Rainforest Action Network's campaign against Mitsubishi for poor lumbering practices; *advocacy/citizen science*, where organizations commission a scientific study to bring attention to an issue, such as Consumer Union's release of a study about the effect of hormones in milk to pressure the dairy industry to remove them; *protesting* against companies whose behavior activists find unacceptable, for example gay and lesbian organizations demonstrating against Cracker Barrel for anti-gay workplace policies.[12] Likewise, Americans are able to pressure companies to change by *boycotting* a product because they disagree with the social or political values of the company that produces it, such as refusing to buy Nike athletic apparel when unfair labor practices are involved.

Though Americans have a long and well-documented history of taking contentious actions against corporations, activists can also work *cooperatively* to reward companies for good behavior.[13] Organizations can partner with corporations in *corporate-sponsored promotions* such as races, walks, or runs and *cause marketing*, where a portion of the purchase price of goods and services goes to support a designated cause. Popular examples of promotions include Ford's long-term sponsorship of Komen's breast cancer run—Race for the Cure—and examples of cause marketing include Diet Coke's heart health campaign.[14] Furthermore, Americans may *buycott*, or buy a product because they believe in the social/political values of the company that produces it.[15] For example, consumers may

12. David Vogel, *Lobbying the Corporation: Citizen Challenges to Business Authority* (New York: Basic Books, 1978); Soule, *Contention and Corporate Social Responsibility*; Edward T. Walker, Andrew W. Martin, and John D. McCarthy, "Confronting the State, the Corporation, and the Academy: The Influence of Institutional Targets on Social Movement Repertoires," *American Journal of Sociology* 114, no. 1 (2008): 35–76.

13. Yaziji and Doh, *NGOs and Corporations*, ch. 7.

14. Maren Klawiter, *The Biopolitics of Breast Cancer: Changing Cultures of Disease and Activism* (Minneapolis: University of Minnesota Press, 2008); Kotler and Lee, *Corporate Social Responsibility*, ch. 3.

15. Zukin et al., *A New Engagement*.

purchase creams, soaps, and gels from the Body Shop because it does not test its products on animals.

Scholars show that the market provides additional venues, options, and choices for Americans. Market-based venues are particularly advantageous for people marginalized from traditional legislative politics, such as farmworkers who lacked state-mandated collective bargaining agreements,[16] and for individuals to whom elite politics is effectively closed, such as African Americans in Don't Buy Where You Can't Work campaigns.[17] It is advantageous (or at least not harmful) for actors who are shut out of governmental processes. Gay rights activists, for example, have found Fortune 500 companies to be more responsive to their cause than conservative governments in the early twenty-first century.[18] Sarah Soule, who has written a book on corporate activism (looking specifically at protest), concludes that we have reason for optimism: "[C]orporations *are* behaving in a far more ethical and responsible fashion than they once did."[19] But whether activism is contentious or cooperative, scholars look at forms of engagement that are *intentional*. Cause marketing may not be intentional on the part of individuals who engage in it.

16. King and Pearce, "The Contentiousness of Markets"; Werner, *Public Forces and Private Politics*; Marshall Ganz, "Resources and Resourcefulness: Strategic Capacity in the Unionization of California Agriculture, 1959–1966," *American Journal of Sociology* 105, no. 4 (2000): 1003–62.

17. Lizabeth Cohen, *A Consumers' Republic: The Politics of Mass Consumption in Postwar America* (New York: Knopf, 2003), 41–53; Lawrence Glickman, *Buying Power: A History of Consumer Activism in America* (Chicago: University of Chicago Press, 2009); Cheryl Greenberg, "'Don't Buy Where You Can't Work,'" in *Consumer Society in American History: A Reader*, ed. Lawrence Glickman (Ithaca, NY: Cornell University Press, 1999), 241–73.

18. Werner, *Public Forces and Private Politics*. Robert Reich has a more pessimistic view: "The upsurge of interest in 'corporate social responsibility' is related to the decreasing confidence in democracy. These days, reformers often say they find it easier to lobby corporate executives than to lobby politicians; they contend they can be more effective pushing certain large corporations to change their ways than trying to alter public policy." Reich, *Supercapitalism: The Transformation of Business, Democracy, and Everyday Life* (New York: Vintage Books, 2007), 169.

19. Soule, *Contention and Corporate Social Responsibility*, 27–28; see also Baron, "Private Politics, Corporate Social Responsibility, and Integrated Strategy."

How Cause Marketing Differs from Political Consumerism

Cause marketing is an organizational strategy employed by businesses and nonprofits. It provides options to consumers for purchasing products aligned with issues they support. However, in contrast to other types of activism, exposure to cause-marketing campaigns occurs regardless of an individual's interest in a cause and whether or not an individual is a media consumer who watches television, reads newspapers, or participates in social media. In fact, because messages appear on the labels of everyday consumer products, individuals often bring these products home without intending to support a particular issue or cause. This is very different from the literature on political consumerism, defined as "the *intentional* use of consumer choice over products and producers within the marketplace as a means of expressing policy preferences and achieving political objectives," where policy and political objectives include ethical and social concerns.[20] Political consumerism is an individual strategy to align consumer purchases with political, social, and ethical values.

Scholars of political consumerism have found that 72 percent of undergraduates buycotted, or based purchase decisions on personal ethical considerations (63 percent boycotted).[21] These trends were most pronounced for grocery purchases and less prevalent for the selection of banks. Shah et al.'s panel survey showed that "among the predispositions, only moral obligation was related to political consumerism, reinforcing the view that personal values and a sense of altruism underlie certain forms of political consumerism."[22] Zukin et al. ran the most comprehensive nationally

20. Benjamin J. Newman and Brandon L. Bartels, "Politics at the Checkout Line: Explaining Political Consumerism in the US," *Political Research Quarterly* 64, no. 4 (2011): 804; emphasis added.

21. Dietlind Stolle, Marc Hooghe, and Michelle Micheletti, "Politics in the Supermarket: Political Consumerism as a Form of Political Participation," *International Political Science Review* 26, no. 3 (2005): 255–56.

22. Dhavan V. Shah et al., "Political Consumerism: How Communication and Consumption Orientations Drive 'Lifestyle Politics,'" *Annals of the American Academy of Political and Social Science* 611, no. 1 (2007): 228.

representative survey—the National Civic Engagement Survey. They found that approximately half of Americans have engaged in some sort of political consumerism in the past year, but while political consumerism may be broadly practiced it is a "low bar of involvement."[23] Although critics find fault with both political consumerism and cause marketing when compared with more active forms of (political) engagement, these two forms of consumption have an important difference: political consumerism is an intentional act on the part of consumers, while cause marketing is not.

How Cause Marketing Differs from Historical Practices

If cause marketing, as part and parcel of corporate social responsibility, looks different from contemporary political consumerism, it also looks different from the politically motivated consumption that historians have described. Historically, consumption—either selecting or avoiding particular products—has been an important political act with broad consequences:[24] colonists protested the Stamp Act by refusing to buy British imports before the start of the American Revolution;[25] women used purchasing power to encourage progressive labor policies in the National Consumers' League as well as to fight inflation and support fair pricing during both the Depression and World War II rationing;[26] and African American activists engaged in Don't Buy Where You Can't Work campaigns to protest unfair and illegal labor practices for blacks.[27]

23. Zukin et al., *A New Engagement*, 62.

24. Glickman, *Buying Power*.

25. T. H. Breen, *The Marketplace of Revolution: How Consumer Politics Shaped American Independence* (New York: Oxford University Press, 2004).

26. Landon R. Y. Storrs, *Civilizing Capitalism: The National Consumers' League, Women's Activism, and Labor Standards in the New Deal Era* (Chapel Hill: University of North Carolina Press, 2000); Meg Jacobs, *Pocketbook Politics: Economic Citizenship in Twentieth-Century America* (Princeton, NJ: Princeton University Press, 2005); Cohen, *A Consumers' Republic*.

27. Cohen, *A Consumers' Republic*, 41–53; Glickman, *Buying Power*; Greenberg, "'Don't Buy Where You Can't Work.'"

In fact, historian Meg Jacobs argues that consumption "drove domestic politics" in the twentieth century.[28] Issues surrounding purchasing power were never far down on the governmental agenda, and citizens measured their well-being in large part by their ability to purchase goods and services. Jacobs demonstrates how the federal government responded to consumers through the creation of new federal agencies like the Food Administration, the Federal Trade Commission, the National Recovery Administration, and the Office of Price Administration. Economic citizenship, or participation in mass consumption, became essential "to the definition of modern liberalism itself."[29] Similarly, Lizabeth Cohen shows that competing visions of "consumer citizens," whose job it was to watch over the national interest by prodding government for protective consumer legislation, and "purchaser consumers," who aided society through their purchasing power, dominated domestic politics in the New Deal and World War II.[30] Postwar mass consumption, rather than detracting from a vision of politics and the greater good, "stood for an elaborate, integrated ideal of economic abundance and democratic freedom, both equitably distributed."[31]

As a whole, this historical research might suggest continuity of a long-held American tradition.[32] However, cause marketing looks very different from consumer activism described by Glickman as "collective, oriented toward the public sphere, grassroots, and conscious of the political impact."[33] Cause marketing may be explicitly disconnected from politics when industry is both the target of and vehicle for change.[34]

28. Jacobs, *Pocketbook Politics*, 2.

29. Ibid.

30. Cohen, *A Consumers' Republic*. See also Matthew Hilton, "Consumers and the State Since the Second World War," *Annals of the American Academy of Political and Social Science* 611 (2007): 66–81.

31. Cohen, *A Consumers' Republic*, 127.

32. E.g., Soule, *Contention and Corporate Social Responsibility*.

33. Glickman, *Buying Power*, 26.

34. Walker, Martin, and McCarthy, "Confronting the State, the Corporation, and the Academy"; Werner, *Public Forces and Private Politics*; Vogel, *Lobbying the Corporation*.

If cause marketing looks different from historical consumer activism, it is also distinct from traditional voluntary fundraising campaigns. Early-twentieth-century campaigns, like the sale of Christmas Seals (American Red Cross and later the National Tuberculosis Association), raised money for health-related issues. The sale of stamps (or seals) originated in Denmark, and stamps were first used in the United States by the Delaware Red Cross in 1907.[35] Given its unprecedented success, the national Red Cross took over seal sales and in 1909 raised $250,000 this way.[36] Voluntary organizations across the United States adopted the seals to raise funds, and Christmas Seals were a national symbol of the fight against tuberculosis: the Wisconsin Anti-Tuberculosis Association raised $8,000 selling Christmas Seals, dividing the proceeds between the association and local agencies;[37] the Arkansas Federation of Women's Clubs sold seals but netted only $10.98;[38] seals were the main source of funds for the Montana Tuberculosis Association, which used the funds to educate the public and finance projects.[39] Like cause marketing, early-twentieth-century fundraising—through seal campaigns—brought awareness and funds to a cause. But these campaigns were created by voluntary health organizations (e.g., the Red Cross and state-level tubercular organizations), and funds were used to support the organizations and aid the disease (through research or treatment). Corporations did not play a significant role, and if they did participate, their involvement was not part of their product marketing.

35. Mary Ellen Stolder, "Consumptive Citadel: The Crusade against Tuberculosis in Eau Claire County, 1903–1917," *Wisconsin Magazine of History* 77, no. 4 (1994): 272.

36. Esmond R. Long, "Development of the Voluntary Health Movement in America as Illustrated in the Pioneer National Tuberculosis Association," *Proceedings of the American Philosophical Society* 101, no. 2 (1957): 144; Kathleen Doyle, "Stamping Out Tuberculosis: The Story of Christmas Seals," *American History Illustrated* 24, no. 6 (1989): 68.

37. Stolder, "Consumptive Citadel," 273.

38. Clara B. Eno, "The First Tuberculosis Christmas Seal Sale in Arkansas," *Arkansas Historical Quarterly* 6, no. 3 (1947): 301.

39. Connie Staudohar, "'Food, Rest, & Happyness': Limitations and Possibilities in the Early Treatment of Tuberculosis in Montana, Part II," *Magazine of Western History* 48, no. 1 (1998): 49.

Unlike consumer activism, which seeks to make political change, and fundraising campaigns by voluntary health organizations, which use seals to solicit charitable donations, corporations often proactively generate cause-marketing campaigns as part and parcel of corporate social responsibility.

WHY BREAST CANCER?

Breast cancer activists mastered cooperative market-based strategies for change. They partnered with industry to hold fundraising and awareness-raising events—like walks and runs—and they created cause-marketing campaigns, where a portion of the sale price of a consumer purchase benefits breast cancer research, treatment, or support. Elite women with connections to business were able to brand breast cancer as pink, shutting out men and women with other issue understandings and other concerns.[40] Just as the existing literature suggests, market mechanisms (in this case races) gave breast cancer activists in the 1980s an alternative venue for making change when breast cancer was largely neglected in the policy process. But the women who took this route were not marginalized from policy channels. Instead, they had ready access to the policy process but chose another path. It is precisely the choice to work with industry and through market mechanisms to create a commercial social movement that makes breast cancer an important case to study.

There are hundreds of breast cancer organizations in the United States registered with the Internal Revenue Service and countless others that meet and provide support informally. Although I talked to representatives from many organizations, this book focuses on two groups: the National Breast Cancer Coalition (NBCC) and Komen. Both groups are nationally known. Both groups work within (rather than against) mainstream institutions. Although both address the issues surrounding breast cancer, the NBCC and Komen largely target different arenas and use different tactics.

40. See Chapter 6.

The NBCC is a national lobby organization that works to expand health-care options for women and research support for breast cancer. I compare the NBCC, whose tactical repertoire (writing letters, lobbying, synthesizing medical research) is familiar to scholars of politics, with Komen, whose repertoire includes market mechanisms that are not.

The National Breast Cancer Coalition wants to change how men and women experience breast cancer, how policymakers address the disease, and how agencies fund research. It makes change to existing institutions largely by working within them and through them. The NBCC is located in Washington, DC; it lobbies federal policymakers for increased funding for breast cancer research and for better access to healthcare. NBCC leaders push policy positions consistent with evidence-based practices. They train individuals to understand both the science of and advocacy strategies for breast cancer. From my interviews with NBCC affiliates, it was clear that the women who created the organization believed that a political voice was missing in breast cancer activism. They created a health social movement (although they do not use that term) to bring that voice to Washington.

Komen, on the other hand, seeks to make large-scale change: exactly the kind that interest-group scholars think ought to be accomplished via government (e.g., the NBCC) and social movement scholars via social dislocation. Komen works to change how Americans understand breast cancer and what it means to have breast cancer. But unlike interest groups, Komen works largely outside the Beltway. Unlike other "identity movements" seeking cultural change, Komen does not deal with traditional identity markers (cancer rather than sexual orientation), and it does not engage in the same types of expressive actions (walks and runs rather than marches or defiant "kiss-ins").[41] Why did Komen choose this alternative path, developing collaborative relationships with industry and creating novel market-based solutions as the primary vehicle for change?

---

41. Mary Bernstein, "Celebration and Suppression: The Strategic Uses of Identity by the Lesbian and Gay Movement," *American Journal of Sociology* 103, no. 3 (1997): 531–65.

Tactics and Strategies

Groups have options when they wish to make a change or defend the status quo: they can cultivate relationships, contact officials, testify, write policy, file suits or briefs, work with coalitions, encourage grassroots support, hold trainings and workshops, collect/participate in/disseminate research, buy advertisements, and hold events.[42] So how do they decide what they will do? Research suggests that the actions of any particular organization may be based on factors internal to the organization—such as structure, resources, or ideology—or the broader population of which the organization is a part.

Scholars know that group characteristics and resources are important for determining strategy and tactics. Groups with elite members, financial resources, and other groups as allies (such as business organizations) choose "insider" tactics associated with traditional lobbying, while groups with a large grassroots membership, local chapters, few resources, and that work in areas not characterized by conflict, use "outsider" tactics, such as mobilizing media or organizing letter-writing campaigns.[43]

Groups may adopt more radical means when they lack resources or efficacy, the belief that government is responsive to them.[44] Social movement

42. Kay Lehman Schlozman and John T. Tierney, *Organized Interests and American Democracy* (New York: Harper & Row, 1986); Jack L. Walker, *Mobilizing Interest Groups in America: Patrons, Professions, and Social Movements* (Ann Arbor: University of Michigan Press, 1991); Jeffrey M. Berry, *Lobbying for the People: The Political Behavior of Public Interest Groups* (Princeton, NJ: Princeton University Press, 1977); Frank R. Baumgartner and Beth L. Leech, *Basic Interests: The Importance of Groups in Politics and in Political Science* (Princeton, NJ: Princeton University Press, 1998); Ken Kollman, *Outside Lobbying and Interest Group Strategies* (Princeton, NJ: Princeton University Press, 1998); Marie Hojnacki, "Interest Groups' Decisions to Join Alliances or Work Alone," *American Journal of Political Science* 41, no. 1 (1997): 61–87; Vogel, *Lobbying the Corporation*.

43. Walker, *Mobilizing Interest Groups*; Anthony J. Nownes and Patricia Freeman, "Interest Group Activity in the States," *Journal of Politics* 60, no. 1 (1998): 86–112; Schlozman and Tierney, *Organized Interests and American Democracy*; Kollman, *Outside Lobbying and Interest Group Strategies*; Marie Hojnacki and David C. Kimball, "The Who and How of Organizations' Lobbying Strategies in Committee," *Journal of Politics* 61, no. 4 (1999): 999–1024.

44. John D. McCarthy and Mayer N. Zald, "Resource Mobilization and Social Movements: A Partial Theory," *American Journal of Sociology* 82, no. 6 (1977): 1212–41; Joe

organizations engage in more nontraditional forms of participation, such as rallies, protests, building takeovers, sit-ins, canvassing, boycotts, and acts of violence, when they are small, not highly professionalized, and decentralized.[45]

Groups' tactical repertoires are also affected by the ideology and culture of the organization.[46] For example, feminist groups promoting the Equal Rights Amendment (ERA) used a democratic structure that matched their political principles, while the STOP ERA movement relied on (in this case more effective) traditional hierarchy.[47] But it also matters who is in the constituent group and what their goals are.[48] Groups composed of subordinate actors take more radical positions, because they "have less to lose when faced with the costs or negative consequences of power."[49]

Group strategies are not only the result of organizational features, but may also be the result of population-level characteristics or the actions

Soss, "Lessons of Welfare: Policy Design, Political Learning, and Political Action," *American Political Science Review* 93, no. 2 (1999): 363–80; Deborah B. Gould, *Moving Politics: Emotion and ACT UP's Fight Against AIDS* (Chicago: University of Chicago Press, 2009).

45. Frances Fox Piven and Richard A. Cloward, *Poor Peoples' Movements* (New York: Vintage Books, 1977); Robert Michels, *Political Parties: A Sociological Study of the Oligarchical Tendencies of Modern Democracy* (Glencoe, IL: Free Press, 1949); Suzanne Staggenborg, "The Consequences of Professionalization and Formalization in the American Labor Movement," *American Sociological Review* 53, no. 4 (1988): 585–605.

46. Kathleen M. Blee, *Inside Organized Racism: Women and Men in the Hate Movement* (Berkeley: University of California Press, 2002); Francesca Polletta, *Freedom in an Endless Meeting: Democracy in American Social Movements* (Chicago: University of Chicago Press, 2002).

47. Jane Mansbridge, *Why We Lost the ERA* (Chicago: University of Chicago Press, 1986).

48. Daniel M. Cress and David A. Snow, "Mobilization at the Margins: Resources, Benefactors, and the Vitality of the Homeless Social Movement Organization," *American Sociological Review* 61, no. 6 (1996): 1089–109; "The Outcomes of Homeless Mobilization: The Influence of Organization, Disruption, Political Mediation, and Framing," *American Journal of Sociology* 105, no. 4 (2000): 1063–104; Edward T. Walker, "Contingent Pathways from Joiner to Activist: The Indirect Effect of Participation in Voluntary Associations on Civic Engagement," *Sociological Forum* 23, no. 1 (2008): 116–43.

49. Verta Taylor and Nella Van Dyke, "'Get Up, Stand Up': Tactical Repertoires of Social Movements," in *The Blackwell Companion to Social Movements*, ed. David A. Snow, Sarah A. Soule, and Hanspeter Kriesi (Malden, MA: Blackwell, 2007), 277.

and strategies of *other* players in the same area.[50] Debra Minkoff shows that organizational density matters, giving first-movers an advantage and allowing for the spread of new organizational forms.[51] As more groups fill a particular arena, newer organizations offer narrower strategies.[52]

Though groups have a range of options, scholars tend to study them by looking at the tactics and venues of one type of organization—interest group *or* nonprofit *or* social movement organization—operating in one type of arena, usually political. They find that interest groups (drawn from a sample of registered lobbies, political action committees, or PACs, or groups in the *Washington Information Directory*) engage in traditional forms of lobbying; nonprofits (drawn from 501(c)(3) organizations) engage in both lobbying and service provision; and social movement groups (drawn from content analysis of newspapers or case studies) engage in social protest, violence, and cultural expressions. But none of these studies adequately describe or explain what groups like Komen did and why.

Corporate-connected breast cancer organizations developed alongside (not prior to) the tactical repertoires they created. In many instances, organizational characteristics and resources were a *reflection* of the strategies they chose. For example, Komen pioneered cooperative market-based strategies. As it expanded, it held its signature event, Race for the Cure, in a growing number of cities. Komen's geographical spread had two

50. Debra C. Minkoff, "The Sequencing of Social Movements," *American Sociological Review* 62, no. 5 (1997): 779–99; McCarthy and Zald, "Resource Mobilization and Social Movements"; Debra C. Minkoff, "The Emergence of Hybrid Organizational Forms: Combining Identity-Based Service Provision and Political Action," *Nonprofit and Voluntary Sector Quarterly* 31 (2002): 377–401; Debra C. Minkoff and John D. McCarthy, "Reinvigorating the Study of Organizational Processes in Social Movements," *Mobilization: An International Journal* 10, no. 2 (2005): 289–308; Walker, *Mobilizing Interest Groups*; Virginia Gray and David Lowery, "Reconceptualizing PAC Formation: It's Not a Collective Action Problem, It May Be an Arms Race," *American Politics Quarterly* 25 (1997): 319–46; David Lowery and Virginia Gray, "Interest Organization Communities: Their Assembly and Consequences," in *Interest Group Politics*, ed. Allan J. Cigler and Burdett A. Loomis (Washington, DC: CQ Press, 2007), 130–56; Hojnacki, "Interest Groups' Decisions."

51. Minkoff, "The Sequencing of Social Movements"; see also Anthony J. Nownes, "The Population Ecology of Interest Group Formation: Mobilizing for Gay and Lesbian Rights in the United States, 1950–98," *British Journal of Political Science* 34 (2004): 49–67.

52. McCarthy and Zald, "Resource Mobilization and Social Movements."

particularly important consequences. First, tactics (races) determined organizational structure. Komen developed a federated structure because it wanted a more permanent presence in the cities where it held races. Second, as it expanded, Komen's market mechanisms defined the broader movement around breast cancer for every other organization. Future organizations were faced with the framing of breast cancer through market-based strategies and corporate actors that approached them for partnerships.

Komen works to change how Americans understand breast cancer and what it means to be diagnosed with breast cancer (e.g., "survivor" not victim). Komen has created what I call a commercial social movement, developing collaborative relationships with industry and creating novel market-based solutions as the primary vehicles for change.

Komen took these actions not because the political opportunity structure was closed or because it was marginalized from the policy process. On the contrary, the early 1980s were ripe for a political strategy to address breast cancer. Though it was largely a silent killer, high-profile political women had made their diagnoses public in the decade before: Shirley Temple Black (movie star and UN delegate) in 1973, Betty Ford (first lady) in 1974, Happy Rockefeller (wife of Vice President Nelson Rockefeller) in 1976, and Marvella Bayh (wife of Indiana Senator Birch Bayh) in 1979. Komen, in particular, would have been poised to lead a political charge. Like many breast cancer organizations, Komen included highly educated and well-resourced women. Komen was founded by Nancy Brinker, who was married to wealthy Texas businessman and Republican Party supporter Norman Brinker. Former first lady Betty Ford was the organization's first featured speaker and the future first lady Laura Bush was one of its first volunteers. Nancy Brinker testified before Congress about breast cancer in 1985 and was named to the President's Cancer Advisory Board in 1986.

Choosing Market Mechanisms, Creating a Commercial Social Movement

By every measure Komen had ready access to elite political actors at the highest levels of government and resources easily marshaled to target government through traditional lobby tactics. But it did not take that path. Contrary to existing theories about why activists pursue social movement strategies, Komen was not shut out of formal political channels and it was not averse to working with government;[53] it did not lack resources or efficacy, the belief that government is responsive to its leaders.[54]

Instead, *I suggest that groups like Komen pioneered market-based mechanisms not because political channels were closed but because market mechanisms were open to them.* For much of American history, breast cancer was scary and stigmatizing. Since its founding in 1913, the American Cancer Society has worked with government to change cultural understandings of cancer through public awareness campaigns, movies, and pamphlets.[55] But Komen was presented with a different opportunity and took a different path. Nancy Brinker and Komen capitalized on their backgrounds and relationships with industry.[56] The fear and stigma associated with breast cancer, which the American Cancer Society had tried for decades to change, could be addressed by a movement that encouraged Americans to think differently, to act differently, and to get involved. Komen created market mechanisms—corporate-sponsored runs and cause marketing—allowing companies to show their support for breast cancer not only with Komen but with any local or national group. As this movement has grown, its mechanisms have spread. Both local and national breast cancer organizations told me that they do not need to seek out corporate relationships (as Brinker and Komen originally did); instead *corporations regularly approach them.*

When deployed effectively, market mechanisms can be a powerful force in a *commercial* social movement. Researchers often study

---

53. Vogel, *Lobbying the Corporation*, 9.

54. McCarthy and Zald, "Resource Mobilization and Social Movements"; Soss, "Lessons of Welfare"; Gould, *Moving Politics*.

55. Barron H. Lerner, *The Breast Cancer Wars: Hope, Fear, and the Pursuit of a Cure in Twentieth-Century America* (New York: Oxford University Press, 2001).

56. Staff resources and skills play a role in group strategies. See, e.g., Berry, *Lobbying for the People*.

social movements that are radical in their aims and contentious in their means, movements that intentionally disrupt and alter institutions and authority. Scholars criticize the social movement literature for its overwhelming focus on contentious movements and failure to explain more mainstream movements that are consensual, like breast cancer education.[57] To remedy this problem, researchers have identified health social movements that challenge the authority of medical experts and work to include voices of patients and advocates in scientific inquiry, medical practice, and policymaking.[58] Unlike contentious movements, health social movements may work *within* medical and political institutions, for example putting patients and advocates on cancer panels to review research. The environmental breast cancer movement, which draws on men's and women's embodied experience with breast cancer, and the National Breast Cancer Coalition, which educates patients and activists, both fall under the social movement/ health social movement umbrella. But Komen and its brand of market-based activism does not.

Scholars do not define Komen's market-based mechanisms and branding of breast cancer as a social movement, and it is true that Komen's actions look very different from those of the social movements that scholars traditionally study. Komen's actions are both consensual and conservative, working *with* industry and *preserving* existing institutions and authority.

Yet, like social movements more generally, Komen officials engage in a "sustained series of interactions,"[59] they seek to make broad-based

57. Myhre, *Medical Mavens.*

58. Matthew E. Archibald and Charity Crabtree, "Health Social Movements in the United States: An Overview," *Sociology Compass* 4, no. 5 (2010): 334–43; Phil Brown and Stephen Zavestoski, "Social Movements in Health: An Introduction," *Sociology of Health & Illness* 26, no. 6 (2004): 679–94; Phil Brown et al., "Embodied Health Movements: New Approaches to Social Movements in Health," *Sociology of Health & Illness* 26, no. 1 (2004): 50–80.

59. Charles Tilly, "Social Movements and National Politics," in *Statemaking and Social Movements: Essays in History and Theory*, ed. Charles Bright and Susan Friend Harding (Ann Arbor: University of Michigan Press, 1984), 306.

cultural change,[60] and as I show in this book, they have political and policy impact. I call their actions a commercial social movement because I believe it is important to recognize what Komen does as a movement to underscore its organized behavior, its goals of broad-based change, and its political implications. Yet it is equally important to recognize it as commercial, and therefore unlike other movements (including health social movements). Commercial social movements seek large-scale incremental change *with* institutions, not *to* them or *within* them. They do not challenge authority. Instead, these movements accept existing political, market, and medical authorities and, through their market-based actions, preserve them.

To summarize, a commercial social movement is a distinct form of activism that (a) seeks broad-based cultural change, (b) works *with* industry through market mechanisms (like cause marketing and corporate-sponsored walks and runs) as its primary strategy, and (c) is conservative—preserving existing institutions and authority. Although these three components themselves are not unique—other movements have sought broad-based cultural change, other actors have worked with industry, and other forms of change have been conservative—the combination of all three distinguishes this form of activism from other forms of activism past and present.

Criticisms

Although they do not use the language of commercial social movement, scholars have been critical of the movement—specifically the pink ribbon, the pink branding of breast cancer, and the overwhelming presence of groups like Komen that market the disease. They argue that the commercial social movement's "success" has come at too steep a price. First, branding and marketing have created culture(s) of the disease that make uniform assumptions about what breast cancer is, how people with

60. Bernstein, "Celebration and Suppression."

the disease ought to feel, and how society sees the disease.[61] For example, Gayle Sulik demonstrates the "feeling rules" that structure how women with breast cancer ought to behave; women with breast cancer feel guilty when they are not positive and hopeful.[62] Additionally, the pink culture of breast cancer that is feminine, hopeful, and uncontroversial marginalizes cancer patients with deadly metastatic breast cancer, which has spread to other parts of the body (usually bone, brain, liver, and lungs); men with breast cancer, who are virtually invisible under the current framing; and those suffering from other types of cancer that are deadly and difficult but not as well known.[63]

Second, scholars argue that the movement has spillover effects on *other* movements, stifling the voices of more activist groups who prefer alternative framings and stories. Many scholars have criticized the commercial social movement for a conflict of interest, refusing to address the role of corporations in the rise of breast cancer.[64] At the same time, the movement limits the ability of activists in the women's health movement or environmental breast cancer movement to make headway.[65] Other organizations and other movements find it difficult to compete with the

61. Samantha King, *Pink Ribbons, Inc.: Breast Cancer and the Politics of Philanthropy* (Minneapolis: University of Minnesota Press, 2006); King, "Pink Ribbons Inc."

62. Gayle Sulik, *Pink Ribbon Blues: How Breast Cancer Undermines Women's Health* (New York: Oxford University Press, 2011), ch. 6; see also Marcy E. Rosenbaum and Gun M. Roos, "Women's Experiences of Breast Cancer," in *Breast Cancer: Society Shapes an Epidemic*, ed. Anne S. Kasper and Susan J. Ferguson (New York: St. Martin's Press, 2000), 153–81.

63. Gayle Sulik, "#Rethinkpink Moving beyond Breast Cancer Awareness SWS Distinguished Feminist Lecture," *Gender and Society* 28, no. 5 (2014): 655–78; Metastatic Breast Cancer Alliance, "Changing the Landscape for People Living with Metastatic Breast Cancer" (New York: Metastatic Breast Cancer Alliance, 2014).

64. Jane S. Zones, "Profits from Pain: The Political Economy of Breast Cancer," in *Breast Cancer: Society Shapes an Epidemic*, ed. Anne S. Kasper and Susan J. Ferguson (New York: St. Martin's Press, 2000), 119–52.

65. Barbara L. Ley, *From Pink to Green: Disease Prevention and the Environmental Breast Cancer Movement* (New Brunswick, NJ: Rutgers University Press, 2009); Sulik, "#Rethinkinpink"; Sulik and Zierkiewicz, "Gender, Power, and Feminisms in Breast Cancer Advocacy"; King, "Pink Ribbons Inc."; Sabrina McCormick, *No Family History: The Environmental Links to Breast Cancer* (Lanham, MD: Rowman & Littlefield, 2009); Sandra

dominant narrative that promotes individual solutions—like buying a product, donating money, or running a race—over more collective political ones. It is hard to have conversations about goals like expanded healthcare for low-income Americans or the regulation of corporations and the carcinogens that are in the air, water, and commercial products when breast cancer is treated as an individual problem rather than a collective issue about equality and/or the environment.

Third, the commercial social movement has also had an impact on the medical community and breast cancer treatment.[66] Just as it frames breast cancer as an individual problem with individual solutions, the commercial social movement promotes individual mammography as the best way to prevent and treat breast cancer. Yet scientists show that routine mammography is not the answer and, for women under the age of 50, may be problematic in that it overdiagnoses breast cancer.[67] For women with metastatic breast cancer, who are most likely to die from the disease, mammography will do little.

For all of the attention to breast cancer, there are few studies about the impact of market mechanisms on politics and policymaking. Scholars who look at national politics bracket breast cancer's commercial social

Steingraber, "The Environmental Link to Breast Cancer," in *Breast Cancer: Society Shapes an Epidemic*, ed. Anne S. Kasper and Susan J. Ferguson (New York: St. Martin's Press, 2000), 271–302.

66. Sulik and Zierkiewicz, "Gender, Power, and Feminisms in Breast Cancer Advocacy"; Sulik, "#Rethinkpink"; Gayle Sulik and Bonnie Spanier, "Time to Debunk the Mammography Myth," CNN.com (2014), http://www.cnn.com/2014/03/18/opinion/sulik-spanier-mammograms/, accessed March 20, 2016; Baralt and Weitz, "The Komen–Planned Parenthood Controversy; Christie Aschwanden, "Why I'm Opting out of Mammography," *JAMA Internal Medicine* 175, no. 2 (2014): 164–165; King, "Pink Ribbons Inc."; Anthony B. Miller et al., "Twenty Five Year Follow-up for Breast Cancer Incidence and Mortality of the Canadian National Breast Screening Study: Randomised Screening Trial," *British Medical Journal* 348 (2014): g366; Steven Woloshin and Lisa M. Schwartz, "How a Charity Oversells Mammography," *British Medical Journal* 345 (2012): e5132; Metastatic Breast Cancer Alliance, "Changing the Landscape"; Zones, "Profits from Pain"; Sue Rosser, "Controversies on Breast Cancer Research," in *Breast Cancer: Society Shapes an Epidemic*, ed. Anne S. Kasper and Susan J. Ferguson (New York: St. Martin's Press, 2000), 245–70; Carol S. Weisman, "Breast Cancer Policymaking," in *Breast Cancer*, ed. Kasper and Ferguson, 213–43.

67. Aschwanden, "Why I'm Opting out of Mammography."

movement as outside the scope of study. Maureen Hogan Casamayou explains the sudden increase in federal funding for breast cancer in the 1990s by pointing to the National Breast Cancer Coalition, which successfully lobbied for an expanded program in the Department of Defense, while Carol Weisman stresses the importance of timing.[68] Kendrowski and Sarow draw on framing and agenda-setting theory to show how grassroots survivors' organizations influence media attention and, ultimately, policymakers. The authors suggest that unlike prostate cancer groups, breast cancer organizations "benefit from the credibility [breast cancer] survivors provide and the sympathetic face its activists communicate," and the disease will "garner more media attention, enjoy more public awareness, and have more policy success than prostate cancer."[69] Their analysis focuses on how advocacy shapes media attention and ultimately policy, but they do not analyze market mechanisms.

In sum, cause marketing is an often-used corporate and organizational mechanism. The large body of social science literature on breast cancer focuses on how these strategies have created particular cultural understandings and an emphasis on individual prevention. Yet we do not know the political effects of breast cancer cause marketing or the policy outcomes of market-based mechanisms more generally. In addition to the numerous effects that scholars have found (listed earlier), I suggest that breast cancer cause marketing is a powerful mechanism of framing and agenda setting, which shapes public policy.

WHAT CAN CAUSE MARKETING AND BREAST CANCER TELL US ABOUT FRAMING AND AGENDA SETTING?

In their influential book, *Agendas and Instability in American Politics*, Baumgartner and Jones argue that institutions and policies are formed

68. Maureen Hogan Casamayou, *The Politics of Breast Cancer* (Washington, DC: Georgetown University Press, 2001); Weisman, "Breast Cancer Policymaking."

69. Karen M. Kendrowski and Marilyn Stine Sarow, *Cancer Activism: Gender, Media, and Public Policy* (Urbana: University of Illinois Press, 2007), 61.

around powerful motivating ideas.[70] In the 1950s, for example, when nuclear energy was "too cheap to meter," policymakers designed government institutions to encourage more nuclear production. But as ideas about nuclear energy changed in the 1960s and 1970s, so did government. Nuclear energy proponents, the Atomic Energy Commission and the Joint Congressional Committee on Atomic Energy, ceded authority and control to a greater number of critical congressional committees, state governments, and elected officials who pressed for increased regulation.[71]

Baumgartner and Jones call "structural arrangements that are supported by powerful ideas" *policy monopolies.*[72] Monopolies are based on dominant ideas, but they are not the *only* way to understand an issue. Quite the contrary. They are the prevailing way of defining an issue, and they confer status and power, bringing some people naturally to the table while leaving others out. Political insiders fight to retain the ideas that undergird monopolies in their favor, while outsiders fight to redefine issues.[73] In the case of 1950s-era nuclear energy, the policy monopoly included nuclear power companies, the Atomic Energy Commission, and the Joint Committee on Atomic Energy. But by the 1960s and 1970s, as ideas about nuclear energy turned negative, the monopoly shifted to include health and environmental advocates.

Following Baumgartner and Jones, a generation of policy scholars studied policy monopolies and traditional policy actors: public officials, interest groups, and media. What happens, however, when ideas are generated and maintained outside the policy process through market mechanisms? When market actors control the monopoly? Is the result then similar to (or the same as) the more familiar policy process?

The case of breast cancer illustrates how market actors have framed breast cancer, held on to a monopoly, and effectively silenced other ways

---

70. Baumgartner and Jones, *Agendas and Instability in American Politics.*

71. Ibid., ch. 4.

72. Ibid.

73. Ibid.

of thinking about and acting on the disease. We do not know what causes breast cancer and we do not have a cure. Still in the twenty-first century, breast cancer often results in disfigurement or even death.[74] Men and women with breast cancer face numerous problems: getting to work, finding appropriate healthcare, paying for medical care, and the long-term effects of the disease and its treatment. Americans with breast cancer assign blame for the disease and its resulting difficulties to industry, the medical establishment, employers, society, and government. Yet cause marketing defines breast cancer in cultural terms as pink. Pink is a color associated with traditional femininity, and breast cancer overwhelmingly affects women. But pink also reflects hope that there will be a cure; and pink is consensual, playing up the commonalities (rather than divisions) that people with breast cancer and their friends and families face.[75] As one breast cancer activist put it, pink puts "a happy face" on the disease.[76]

In framing breast cancer as pink and symbolizing it with a ribbon, cause marketing takes the emphasis away from disfigurement, death, and hardship and toward a progressive story of change. Colored ribbons, used first for soldiers (yellow) and people with AIDS (red), symbolize hope, solidarity, and awareness. Peggy Orenstein explains that the

74. In 2014 it was estimated that 232,670 Americans would be diagnosed with breast cancer, making it the second most common type of cancer. Roughly 40,000 would die from the disease, fewer than from lung cancer or colon cancer. See http://seer.cancer.gov/statfacts/html/breast.html, accessed November 23, 2015.

75. Lisa Belkin, "Charity Begins at . . . the Marketing Meeting, the Gala Event, the Product Tie-In: How Breast Cancer Became This Year's Cause," *New York Times*, December 22, 1996; Sulik, *Pink Ribbon Blues*; Barbara Ehrenreich, "The Pink Ribbon Breast Cancer Cult," Tomdispatch.com (2009), http://www.alternet.org/story/144320/ehrenreich%3A_the_pink-ribbon_breast_cancer_cult, accessed November 15, 2013; King, *Pink Ribbons, Inc.*; Maren Klawiter, "Racing for the Cure, Walking Women and Toxic Touring: Mapping Cultures of Action within the Bay Area Terrain of Breast Cancer," in *Ideologies of Breast Cancer: Feminist Perspectives*, ed. Laura K. Potts (New York: St. Martin's Press, 2000), 181–204; Klawiter, *The Biopolitics of Breast Cancer*; Peggy Orenstein, "Our Feel-Good War on Breast Cancer," *New York Times*, April 25, 2013; Jennifer A. Harvey and Michal Ann Strahilevitz, "The Power of Pink: Cause-Related Marketing and the Impact on Breast Cancer," *Journal of American College of Radiology* 6 (2009): 26–32.

76. Interview with National Breast Cancer activist, 2010 (no. 10012).

breast cancer ribbon "has come to symbolize both fear of the disease and the hope it can be defeated. It's a badge of courage for the afflicted, an expression of solidarity by the concerned. It promises continual progress toward a cure through donations, races, volunteerism. It indicates community."[77] This picture is certainly not the only way to understand breast cancer. Maren Klawiter, for example, describes the more radical environmental breast cancer Toxic Tours campaign as "not primarily an expression of solidarity with, or sympathy for, people with cancer. It is a collective expression of rage" at the cancer industry, including industry, public relations firms, and government actors that make cancer an individual problem.[78] Breast cancer as pink, however, is the dominant way to understand the disease.[79]

Although there are many aspects of politics (such as symbolic politics and political advertising) that are similar to marketing, market mechanisms share certain core features based on what they are trying to do (sell products, build brand image) and where their messages are located (often on packages). Market mechanisms privilege particular issue framings: feminine, hopeful, and uncontroversial over expressions of rage. Cause-marketing messages appear on consumer packaged goods: items like groceries, clothing, and paper goods.[80] Industry leaders that produce these goods are in the business of defining problems and selling solutions that are short, symbolic, and positive: Pampers keep babies dry or Diet Coke is a refreshing beverage. Companies that make consumer packaged goods define and package issues in the same way: issues are

---

77. Orenstein, "Our Feel-Good War on Breast Cancer."

78. Maren Klawiter, "Racing for the Cure, Walking Women, and Toxic Touring: Mapping Cultures of Action within the Bay Area Terrain of Breast Cancer," *Social Problems* 46, no. 1 (1999): 119.

79. King, *Pink Ribbons, Inc.*; Sulik, *Pink Ribbon Blues*; Barbara Ehrenreich, "Welcome to Cancerland: A Mammogram Leads to a Culture of Pink Kitsch," *Harper's Magazine*, November 2001, 43–53; Ehrenreich, "The Pink Ribbon Breast Cancer Cult"; Charlene Elliott, "Pink! Community, Contestation, and the Colour of Breast Cancer," *Canadian Journal of Communications* 32, no. 3 (2007): 521–36.

80. See Chapter 4.

portrayed as short and symbolic because packages have limited space and shoppers have limited time to make their choices; issues are necessarily positive and uncontroversial, because conflict and controversy do not sell products; and solutions are simple and convenient because consumers want to see that they make a difference. Cause marketing and corporate-sponsored runs are part and parcel of corporate marketing.[81]

Though policymakers like to address and promote similar kinds of consensus issues,[82] analysis of the policy process shows that while much of what federal policymakers do may be showmanship, it is not often short, symbolic, and uncontroversial. The analysis in Chapter 4 shows that in the federal policy process, government actors address different kinds of issues (government operations over social welfare) and address them in different ways: issues are big, complex, and messy. The full force of the federal government is necessary when local government, industry, and nonprofits cannot take up these concerns on their own. "Winning" in policy processes means destabilizing how Americans understand issues and replacing old frames with alternative frames in an attempt to change the shape of the debate and interest new actors.[83] Although public, designed to be persuasive and, at times, to appeal to a broader audience, policymaking is not the same as marketing. Policymaking takes place across many venues, it involves a different set of actors, and it creates binding outcomes (laws and regulations).

As much as we know about how the federal policy process works and how it can be manipulated, we know little of the effect of ideas generated

81. Barone, Miyazaki, and Taylor, "The Influence of Cause-Related Marketing"; Matthew Berglind and Cheryl Nakata, "Cause-Related Marketing: More Bank Than Buck?," *Business Horizons* 48, no. 5 (2005): 443–53; Steve Hoeffler and Kevin Lane Keller, "Building Brand Equity through Corporate Societal Marketing," *Journal of Public Policy & Marketing* 21, no. 1 (2002): 78–89; Xueming Luo and Chitra Bhanu Bhattacharya, "Corporate Social Responsibility, Customer Satisfaction, and Market Value," *Journal of Marketing* 70, no. 4 (2006): 1–18.

82. E.g., Nelson, *Making an Issue of Child Abuse*.

83. Ibid.; Schattschneider, *The Semi-Sovereign People*; John Kingdon, *Agendas, Alternatives, and Public Policies* (Boston: Little Brown, 1984); Baumgartner and Jones, *Agendas and Instability in American Politics*; Stone, *Policy Paradox*.

through market mechanisms. In fact, many scholars implicitly or explicitly agree with John Kingdon: "[T]he critical factor that explains the prominence of an item on the agenda is not its source, but instead the climate in government or the receptivity to ideas of a given type, regardless of source."[84] I argue, however, that it does matter where ideas come from. Ideas shape Americans' understanding of issues, the monopoly of actors that are relevant to an issue, and the institutional structures of public policy.[85] Ideas generated through market mechanisms look qualitatively different from ideas generated in policy processes. Yet we know less about who wins and who loses when issue framing takes place through market mechanisms, especially the cooperative forms I look at in this book.

WHAT ARE THE IMPLICATIONS FOR POWER, INFLUENCE, AND EQUALITY?

Cooperative market mechanisms fundamentally alter the public sphere by importing processes, values, and biases of market-based action. This means that individuals and groups with ties to business, like Brinker and Komen, have a louder voice, and issues that appeal to middle-class consumers, like breast cancer, are most likely to gain attention. This insight is particularly important because we know more about industry as an interest in the policy process than as a force that shapes it.

Existing research acknowledges the privileged place of industry as an interest in American policymaking.[86] Midcentury critics condemned the disproportionate influence that industry exercised, claiming that more powerful interests in society were better organized and better able to get

84. Kingdon, *Agendas, Alternatives, and Public Policies*, 76.

85. Baumgartner and Jones, *Agendas and Instability in American Politics*; Stone, *Policy Paradox*; Jal Mehta, *The Allure of Order: High Hopes, Dashed Expectations, and the Troubled Quest to Remake American Schooling* (New York: Oxford University Press, 2013).

86. Charles Lindblom, *Politics and Markets: The World's Political-Economic Systems* (New York: Basic Books, 1977).

what they wanted than other, less organized constituencies.[87] For example, as a small yet high-functioning coalition, tobacco companies lobbied more effectively than larger, more diffuse consumer interests. In addition to organizational advantages, scholars show additional mechanisms by which industry gains access to and influence in political processes: friendships with elites, campaign contributions to elected officials, a "revolving door" between officials in government and industry, appointments to key governmental positions, information sharing, and public opinion shaping through media and think tanks.[88]

If we are familiar with industry's privileged place as an interest in American politics, we know less about its much broader and more pervasive role in shaping and remaking the policy process.[89] While industry loses many political battles, it is winning the war because influence means not merely getting what one wants in a fight but shaping the political terrain so that no fight is necessary. As Steven Lukes explains, "[T]he most effective and insidious use of power is to prevent . . . conflict from arising in the first place."[90]

Today, ideas about and the language of American governance are taken from the private sector.[91] Industry's influence on politics is felt not only in the places where individual corporations or business leaders fight for or against policies that benefit or harm them, as when car manufacturers

87. Schattschneider, *The Semi-Sovereign People*; Olson, *The Logic of Collective Action*.

88. Soule, *Contention and Corporate Social Responsibility*, ch. 1; Schlozman and Tierney, *Organized Interests and American Democracy*; Mark A. Smith, *American Business and Political Power* (Chicago: University of Chicago Press, 2000); Edward T. Walker and Christopher M. Rea, "The Political Mobilization of Firms and Industries," *Annual Review of Sociology* 40 (2014): 281–304.

89. See, e.g., Daniel J. Boorstin, *The Image: A Guide to Pseudo-Events in America* (New York: Vintage Books, 2012); Murray J. Edelman, "Symbols and Political Quiescence," *American Political Science Review* 54, no. 3 (1960): 695–704; Jacques Ellul, *Propaganda: The Formation of Men's Attitudes* (New York: Vintage Books, 1973); John Gaventa, *Power and Powerlessness: Quiescence and Rebellion in an Appalachian Valley* (Urbana: University of Illinois Press, 1980).

90. Steven Lukes, *Power: A Radical View* (New York: Macmillan, 1974), 27.

91. See also Mehta, *The Allure of Order*.

lobby against fuel efficiency standards, or even in places where policies are kept off the agenda due to industry pressure, as illustrated by decades of support for (rather than regulation of) tobacco interests. Instead, industry's influence often comes as a by-product of business-as-usual in those places where industry may not have a direct stake in the fight, as in the case of breast cancer.

In this vein, Edward Walker's examination of firms dedicated to generating grassroots support shows how these organizations mobilize particular segments of the American population most likely to participate to begin with, exacerbating inequalities in political participation.[92] Paid to create support, these firms are not trying to win political battles that are in their direct interest (such as car manufacturers) but affect political outcomes indirectly as a consequence of their paid mobilization efforts. Walker's study of paid grassroots lobbying firms and my work on market mechanisms suggest that industry influences who is mobilized, how they get involved, and what issues are seen as important. Industry fosters growing political inequality in ways that are potentially pervasive but largely uncharted.

Although we know that industry exercises influence as a player, we know less about how it defines the rules of the game. Like Walker, this study develops the tools to understand that relationship and analyze its effects. To preview my argument:

1. Influential individuals with ties to industry are better able to negotiate market mechanisms and make their concerns the concerns of Americans more generally. On their face, these concerns may not appear to be either controversial or political. But this consensus framing diminishes other issues, alternative issue framings, and the solutions that may come with both.
2. Cooperative market-based mechanisms provide many opportunities for individuals to express themselves through consumption, but this alternative targets consumers with money to spend.

92. Edward Walker, *Grassroots for Hire: Public Affairs Consultants in American Democracy* (New York: Cambridge University Press, 2014).

3. Industry, generally, exercises disproportionate influence in cooperative market mechanisms by shaping public understandings—
   this may be a by-product (rather than the direct intent) of
   business-as-usual.
4. Ideas, or more specifically public understandings, are the basis
   on which powerful supporting institutions are created and maintained. In the case of market mechanisms, these institutions are
   located in *both* the private and public spheres.
5. Policy change, therefore, can come through private as well as
   public institutions (but see point 1).

The American policy process is far from perfect, and scholars have detailed the sources and effects of inequality.[93] However, when organizations turn to the market to define and solve problems, the biases inherent
in market processes take root within the policy process. Scholars know
little about how this happens and with what effect.

In this book, I show that cause marketing is pervasive and a part of
Americans' day-to-day lives, but campaigns overwhelmingly focus on
social welfare issues and frame them as simple, positive, and amenable
to an individual solution. As a result, Americans learn lessons about how
to think and feel about issues. In the case of breast cancer, industry and
activists with corporate ties framed breast cancer as pink and promoted
it widely through cause marketing and corporate-sponsored walks and
runs. As a result, Americans are very aware of breast cancer, but they see
it as a consensus-based social issue rather than a conflict-ridden political
one. The implications of my work are that industry and select activists
exercise undue influence in American politics. As Bachrach and Baratz,
Lukes, and Gaventa remind us, real influence quiets contention and un-
derlies the terms of debate, hiding politics in plain sight.[94]

93. E.g., Schattschneider, *The Semi-Sovereign People.*

94. Lukes, *Power*; Bachrach and Baratz, "Two Faces of Power"; Gaventa, *Power and Powerlessness.*

DATA AND METHOD

There are more questions than answers concerning cause marketing's relationship to individual, social, and political beliefs, behavior, and outcomes. I designed a mixed-methods study to learn more.

We do not have data on how, why, and with what effect Americans participate in cause marketing and corporate-sponsored walks and runs. Therefore, I created the Citizen Consumer Survey (CCS) to find out more. Generously funded by the National Science Foundation, the telephone survey reached a random and representative sample of 1,500 Americans through their landlines and cell phones. I designed the survey first and foremost to answer basic descriptive questions about the prevalence of cause-marketing campaigns generally: how often people are exposed to them, what the issues are, and what products are involved. I also want to know *why* Americans participate in this type of behavior, and the survey asks about motivation. Chapter 3 presents the results of this descriptive analysis. The striking finding from this chapter is that survey respondents see (and remember) cause-marketing campaigns for a range of social welfare issues on a wide variety of consumer packaged goods. Many of them participate in cause-marketing campaigns by buying products where a portion of the purchase price supports a designated cause. But survey respondents often said they participated unintentionally, and they would have bought the product even if it did not support a designated cause.

More than mapping the landscape of cause marketing, I want to know what effect it has. I relied on an analysis of cause-marketing stories (Chapter 4) to generate expectations to be tested in Chapter 5. Chapter 4 analyzes how issues are framed and stories are told in cause-marketing campaigns and benchmarks them against how issues are framed and stories are told in the federal policy process (using hearings). No doubt cause-marketing campaigns—which are a form of marketing—in many ways may be more similar to political advertising or political speech than to elements of the federal policy process. However, I am interested in creating snapshots of what issues are addressed and how in cause marketing, what issues are addressed and how in the policy process, and how cause marketing and the policy process differ. By detailing the typical features of cause marketing and the policy process, I lay the groundwork for showing how breast cancer policymaking adopts disproportionate (compared with general policy issues as well as other cancers) cause-marketing symbols and features.

To do this analysis, I created a database of cause-marketing campaigns drawn from media coverage and press releases in business-related publications and wires. The database is a proxy, however imperfect, for the universe of cause-marketing campaigns. I compare issues in the cause-marketing database with issues in the federal policy process, using data from Baumgartner and Jones's Policy Agendas Project.[95] The data provide quantitative measures of the landscape—what issues are addressed and how often—as well as qualitative analysis of the nature of framing in each source. Across a broad range of issues, cause-marketing framing tends to have certain core features: it promotes awareness, it provides individual solutions, it enables and empowers individuals, and it focuses on positive and marketable emotions, like hope. I show that breast cancer cause marketing shares many of the features of cause marketing more generally, and breast cancer policymaking reflects breast cancer cause-marketing features and symbols. Further, I use the analysis in Chapter 4 to generate expectations for potential effects to be tested using survey data on breast cancer cause marketing in Chapter 5.

The CCS was intentionally fielded across two months: September (control) and October (National Breast Cancer Awareness Month) to evaluate the effect of the largest and most concentrated cause-marketing campaign. If cause marketing has an effect, respondents in October ought to respond differently from those in September. However, simply by looking at blunt differences between months, I could not isolate the effect of cause marketing compared with that of media stories or other attention to breast cancer. So, in addition to the differences between months, I looked

---

95. Policy Agendas Project: http://www.policyagendas.org/, accessed June 10, 2011.

across months at those individuals who said they saw cause marketing, media stories, or walks and runs.

Consistent with the analysis of stories generated in Chapter 4, Chapter 5 shows that exposure to breast cancer cause marketing is associated with increased awareness of breast cancer, but not with an increase in specific knowledge about the disease. In this matter, I found that cause-marketing campaigns emphasize individual over collective (governmental) solutions and enable and empower individuals to think that their actions (through cause marketing) have an effect on corporate behavior, thereby encouraging consumers to feel good about participating.

Some critics may claim that cause marketing does not drive the way Americans think about breast cancer; rather it reflects what Americans already believe. In Chapter 6, I address the causal impact of cause marketing again, this time with a historical case study of breast cancer. I build on a number of secondary studies, but I also add original archival research and interviews. A history of breast cancer told in a single chapter must necessarily be limited. Here I focus on two key organizations: Susan G. Komen, a pioneer in partnerships with industry for cause marketing and corporate-sponsored walks and runs, and the National Breast Cancer Coalition, a highly effective organization that uses more traditional lobbying and political advocacy. For me, these organizations represent two different types of mainstream strategies that work within existing institutions. While sociologists and feminist scholars tend to look at Komen, political scientists tend to look at the NBCC.[96] I tie the two together intentionally because I want to know why Komen chose market mechanisms and what effect its strategies have on politics and policymaking.

A number of key secondary sources have established that breast cancer was, for most of its history, scary and stigmatizing.[97] I show that Komen deliberately turned to market-based mechanisms to change how Americans

96. But see Myhre, *Medical Mavens*.

97. Ellen Leopold, *A Darker Ribbon: Breast Cancer, Women and Their Doctors in the Twentieth Century* (Boston: Beacon Press, 1999); Kirsten E. Gardner, *Early Detection: Women, Cancer, and Awareness Campaigns in the Twentieth-Century United States* (Chapel Hill: Univeristy

think about, talk about, and act on breast cancer. Komen officials created what I call a commercial social movement. By that I mean they worked *with industry* to change broader cultural understandings: from fear to hope, from silence to visibility. By contrast, the NBCC, like many health social movements, worked *within more traditional policymaking channels* to change policymaking and medical research on breast cancer. Still, even as the pink ribbon frustrates NBCC activists, they, too, benefit from breast cancer's consensual framing by gaining political support from elected officials eager to do something for women that is not controversial.

CONCLUSION

Although my research describes and explains cause marketing in greater detail, the main contribution of this work is not specifying the circumstances in which cause marketing is more or less likely to be effective or even when, where, and why most organizations or individuals engage in it. Instead, I show the real-world effect of market mechanisms on American society and public policy. If something seemingly as nonpolitical as the marketing of disease has such a profound impact on ideas and the policy process, what might that tell us about the more embedded ways in which markets are used for public policy (e.g., education or healthcare)?[98] And, more important, what can it tell us about what twenty-first-century politics is and where it takes place? In this book, I return to the questions that the "classics" in American politics found so important: What is politics? Whose voices matter in it? By what processes do these voices exercise influence?

of North Carolina Press, 2006); Lerner, *The Breast Cancer Wars*; James Olson, *Bathsheba's Breast* (Baltimore: Johns Hopkins University Press, 2002).

98. Political scientists have started asking these questions, especially in regard to healthcare and the submerged state of policymaking. See, e.g., Jacob S. Hacker, *The Divided Welfare State: The Battle over Public and Private Social Benefits in the United States* (Cambridge: Cambridge University Press, 2002); Suzanne Mettler, *The Submerged State: How Invisible Government Policies Undermine American Democracy* (Chicago: University of Chicago Press, 2011).

Cooperative Market Mechanisms

While sociologists and historians have focused their attention on contentious market-based activity that *challenges* government and industry, such as protests and boycotts, and political scientists on political consumerism that is *intentional*, market activities are often cooperative, working with industry, not against it. People often participate in it *unintentionally*, benefiting a particular cause by taking actions they would have taken anyway. Therefore, most of what we know about historical and contemporary market-based activity does not apply to the common ways that activists and others use the market for change.

In this chapter, I look at cause marketing in general, and I show that companies create opportunities for Americans to learn about issues through cause-marketing products, a portion of the sale of which benefits a designated cause. More than three-quarters of survey respondents report seeing cause-marketing campaigns and more than half actually participate in them. Cause marketing is employed for products that Americans use daily, like food, soap, and clothing. Individuals are exposed to these items in stores, but when they buy them and bring them home, the products and the issues they promote become a part of their daily rituals: eating breakfast, washing clothes, or getting dressed.[1] In this

---

1. For more on the effectiveness of embedding message, see Archon Fung, Mary Graham, and David Weil, *Full Disclosure: The Perils and Promise of Transparency* (New York: Cambridge University Press, 2007).

way, cause marketing—and the issue understandings that it promotes—become part and parcel of Americans' everyday experiences. I show how this occurs with cause marketing generally and in the case of breast cancer specifically.

For some individuals who participate in cause marketing intentionally—because it allows them to express their ideological beliefs—these daily routines merely reinforce their existing beliefs. But for a significant portion of individuals who participate unintentionally, seeing these products in stores and in their homes provides effective lessons about the products and the issues they support, which I argue in this book has broader implications for democratic politics.

MARKET ACTIVISM AND COOPERATIVE
MARKET MECHANISMS

Though it has been used throughout American history, market-based activism has evolved over time: American revolutionaries transformed it from a local activity to a national one when they realized that refusing to buy British goods would pressure the colonizing nation across the Atlantic Ocean to heed their demands. Nineteenth-century consumer activists created boycotts when they connected purchasing and its broader political implications: Northerners boycotted slave-produced products, while Southerners refused to trade with the North. Twentieth-century activists used the market to challenge governments; for example, African Americans boycotted municipal transportation and American consumers boycotted Japanese silk products.[2]

Citizens' engagement with the market offers insight about social, political, and economic relationships of the time. Historian Lawrence Glickman explains:

Consumer activists in the Revolutionary era, for example, relied primarily on the agency of merchants' associations and political

2. Glickman, *Buying Power.*

elites. During the age of Jackson, as the politics of deference weakened, ordinary consumers became the chief political actors of activist campaigns. As workers began self-consciously identifying themselves as a class in society, they called for labor consumerism, a solidarity of working-class shoppers every bit as important as the producerist solidarity of the shopfloor or in the fields.[3]

Market activism seeks social ends by and through industry, and scholars generally examine it through contentious forms of activism: boycotts of British, slave-produced, Northern, Jim Crow, or Japanese goods and services. In these stories, market activism is political and democratic— offering Americans additional avenues for making their voices heard. Even scholars of cooperative market mechanisms see market activism as largely positive and beneficial for individuals who lack other options.[4] But for all of the attention on conflict and contention, we know little about how contemporary cooperative market mechanisms work. I suggest that they are both more common than contentious activism and more problematic because the mechanisms that encourage change for marginalized populations in contentious activism (publicity and reputation) work against these interests in cooperative market activism. In cause marketing, publicity about good deeds enhances a company's reputation, thereby encouraging cause marketing by other corporations, even when individuals affected by the issues cause marketing addresses disagree with the branding.

In this chapter, I examine cooperative market mechanisms, especially cause marketing. I show that people who participate in cause marketing do so both intentionally because they believe in making a difference through their purchases and unintentionally because they would purchase the product anyway. Though we know more about participating with intent from studies of buycotting and boycotting, participating

3. Ibid., 12–13.

4. Soule, *Contention and Corporate Social Responsibility*; King and Pearce, "The Contentiousness of Markets."

without intent is important too. Cause marketing is not something that consumers can easily opt out of unless they do not buy or use most consumer packaged goods. As I demonstrate in Chapters 4, 5, and 6, cause marketing *provides powerful lessons about issues and shapes how Americans understand them, especially those individuals who participate unintentionally.*

Because there are few data sources that examine market-based activism and none that look specifically at cause marketing, I conducted a nationally representative telephone survey of 1,500 American adults (1,200 landlines and 300 cell phones) in September and October 2010. The 2010 Citizen Consumer Survey (CCS) probed respondents' political participation, asking about their activities such as volunteering for a campaign or donating money, as well as their market activities, whether they used their purchasing power for social or political ends. It also asked about a number of factors that may play into participation, such as knowledge about politics and knowledge about consumer choices. The survey was intentionally fielded across two months: September (control) and October (National Breast Cancer Awareness Month). During October, many companies roll out pink versions of their products, a portion of the sale of which purportedly benefits breast cancer research (for more information on the survey, see Appendices C and D). The data that follow establish what cause marketing is, who participates in it, and for what reasons.

CAUSE MARKETING IS AN EVERYDAY PRACTICE

Cause marketing is a common part of American culture; it is woven into Americans' everyday practices. Consumers see products that benefit causes daily on their trips to the supermarket or the shopping mall. As illustrated by Figure 3.1, *nearly 80 percent of survey respondents report having seen cause marketing in the past month.*

Furthermore, not only do Americans see cause marketing, they also actively participate in it. As shown in Figure 3.2, almost 80 percent of

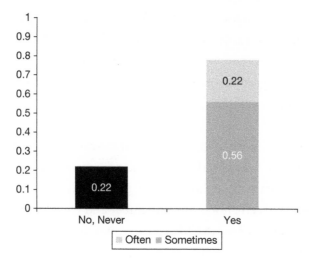

Figure 3.1 **Americans see cause marketing.**
$N = 1,500$.
QUESTION WORDING: *In the past month, how often have you seen products that advertise some portion of the purchase price supports a particular cause? Never; Sometimes; Often.*
SOURCE: CCS data, weighted proportions. May not sum to 1 due to rounding. See Appendices C and D for more information.

those who reported seeing cause marketing (63 percent overall) have bought products that support a particular cause.

Most often these products are small-ticket items, like groceries (48 percent). Data collected from media stories show that cause marketing is regularly used for food and beverages, from soup to cereal and alcohol to lemonade. Survey respondents, however, mentioned yogurt in particular and often. Yoplait yogurt partnered with Komen in a Save Lids to Save Lives campaign. For every lid that consumers mailed in, the General Mills company donated ten cents to Komen. Between 1997 and 2013, Yoplait donated more than $34 million.[5] The success of cause-marketing campaigns, such as Save Lids to Save Lives, has motivated *other* companies to do the same thing. In 2010 and 2011, for example, Dannon yogurt partnered with the National Breast Cancer Foundation to "Give Hope with Every Cup" by donating ten cents for each container to the foundation.

5. Yoplait: http://www.yoplait.com/yoplait-in-action/save-lids-to-save-lives, accessed December 20, 2013.

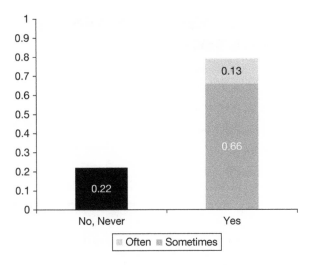

Figure 3.2 **If they see cause marketing, Americans participate in it.**
$N = 1,213$.

QUESTION WORDING: *How often have you purchased a product that advertises some portion of the purchase price supports a particular cause? Never; Sometimes; Often.*
SOURCE: CCS data, weighted proportions. May not sum to 1 due to rounding. See Appendices C and D for more information.

Consumer purchases often include wearable items like T-shirts, clothing, and shoes (15 percent) that show *others* the purchaser supports a cause. For example, Hanes and Macy's teamed up to offer red shirts for a Go Red campaign for heart health, while Gap and Converse created red clothing for AIDS awareness.[6]

In short, cause-marketing products span the gamut of items Americans use every day: food and beverages, clothes and shoes, personal care items like soap, household cleaners, office supplies, and scores of other items. Figure 3.3 indicates the prevalence of various cause-marketing products.

Because cause marketing is used most often for consumer packaged goods—groceries, personal care, and cleaning supplies—it becomes a part of Americans' everyday lives. When consumers purchase these products,

---

6. Respondents were equally likely to report having seen cause marketing and participating in it in September and October, although the goods they purchased and the causes they supported were slightly different.

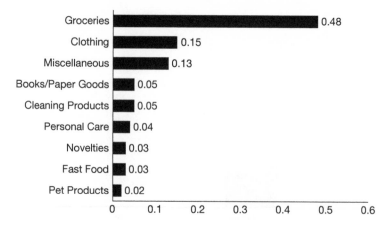

Figure 3.3 **Cause marketing messages appear on the packaging of everyday items.**
$N = 531$.
QUESTION WORDING: *To the best of your knowledge, what was the last product you*
bought where a portion of the purchase price supports a particular cause?
SOURCE: CCS data, weighted proportions. May not sum to 1 due to rounding.
See Appendices C and D for more information.

they bring cause marketing into their homes and incorporate it into their
daily routines.

In contrast to the way Americans seek information from articles or stories or even receive information passively from advertising on television
or in magazines, they do not have to *try* to learn from cause marketing,
they do not have to tune in to any particular medium, and the message
they get is not a one-shot deal that takes place during a television show
or even at the point of sale.[7] It is in their home and on the items they use
most often: the cereal box at breakfast, their detergent while doing dishes,
and their clothes while getting dressed.

Americans learn lessons from these items about issues. Most often,
the issues are middle-class social welfare concerns, especially ones that
are disease-related.[8] Figure 3.4 shows the distribution of causes that

7. Not dissimilar to discussions of effortful thinking; see, e.g., Cindy Kam's "Who Toes the
Party Line? Cues, Values, and Individual Differences," *Political Behavior* 27, no. 2 (2005):
163–82.

8. John K. Ross III, Mary Ann Stutts, and Larry Patterson, "Tactical Considerations for the
Effective Use of Cause-Related Marketing," *Journal of Applied Business Research* 7, no. 2

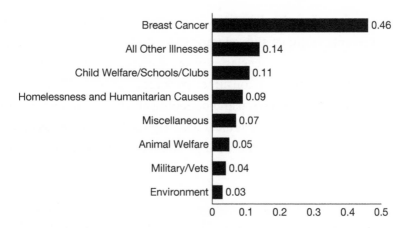

Figure 3.4 Breast cancer is the most common issue addressed by cause marketing.
$N = 668$.
QUESTION WORDING: *Can you tell me what cause the product supported?*
SOURCE: CCS data, weighted proportions. May not sum to 1 due to rounding.
See Appendices C and D for more information.

Americans supported through their purchases in September and October 2010. The lion's share of purchases benefited breast cancer (46 percent). Even in September, which is not Breast Cancer Awareness Month, 43 percent of survey respondents participated in cause marketing that supports breast cancer.

Breast cancer dominates cause marketing. However, what makes it the crucial case for this book is that it did not always enjoy this privileged position. Indeed, in the 1980s when Komen's founder, Nancy Brinker, first approached corporations to create the kinds of partnerships that I talk about here, she was told in no uncertain terms that it was bad for business to be associated with death and dying. Today, however, breast cancer advocates have become what many other issue advocates (especially around disease) seek to be.

Other diseases, especially AIDS, heart disease, and cancer (14 percent), child well-being, such as education and opportunities for low-income children (11 percent), humanitarian causes like disaster relief and clean

(2011): 58–65; Sarah Lorge, "Is Cause-Related Marketing Worth It? Altruism Shouldn't Be the Only Reason to Support Charities," *Sales & Marketing Management* 150, no. 6 (1998): 72.

water (9 percent), animal welfare, especially saving endangered species (5 percent), military and veterans (4 percent), and the environment (3 percent) are also big beneficiaries of cause marketing (see Figure 3.4).

Because they appear on consumer packages, cause-marketing issues are framed as noncontroversial and nonpolitical. They are often short and symbolic.[9] For example, consumers are helping children in need, supporting military veterans, and saving endangered species.[10] As Till and Nowak explain:

> Certainly cause-related marketing activity is not right for every brand in every situation. Associating with potentially polarizing causes such as the NRA, Planned Parenthood, or even a "radical" environmental group like Greenpeace can do as much to alienate potential customers as to enhance the value of the brand. Additionally, marketers face an increasingly cynical public suspicious of companies exploiting associations with causes as simply another way to fatten their bottom line.[11]

Unsurprisingly, cause marketing does not address complex issues (such as banking regulation) or issues already framed as controversial (such as prisoner rehabilitation or abortion). Indeed, as I show in Chapter 4, it does not address complexities inherent in the issues that companies do market.

WHO PARTICIPATES AND WHY?

Cause marketing is a big umbrella, and who participates and why varies based on the motivation and meaning it holds for individuals. However,

9. See also Fung, Graham, and Weil, *Full Disclosure.*

10. See also Linda I. Nowak and Judith H. Washburn, "Marketing Alliances between Non-Profits and Businesses: Changing the Public's Attitudes and Intentions Towards the Cause," *Journal of Nonprofit & Public Sector Marketing* 7, no. 4 (2000): 33–44.

11. Till and Nowak, "Toward Effective Use of Cause-Related Marketing Alliances," 481.

most scholarly attention is focused on one small slice: individuals who use consumer purchasing to further their broader social and political commitments, such as Americans who buy cereal that gives back to endangered animals or products in which employees share in the proceeds. According to the CCS, only 21 percent of Americans say they actually participate in this way. A more common motivation for participation is individuals' belief in a specific cause, such as the environment or breast cancer. Thirty-six percent of respondents said that we should be doing more for the cause (for which they purchased a product), however possible. But the most common motivation was not at all about making a difference—generally through consumption or specifically for a particular cause—or acting with any mindfulness about the issues that products support. *Thirty-nine percent of respondents participate in cause marketing unintentionally, saying they would purchase the item regardless of whether a portion of the purchase price supports a cause.*

Figure 3.5, then, tells two important stories. The first is that a minority of cause-marketing purchases is about politically motivated consumption

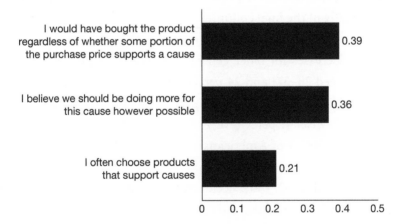

Figure 3.5 People often participate in cause marketing unintentionally.
N = 930; 2 percent responded "Don't know" and 1 percent refused to answer; not shown in figure.
QUESTION WORDING: *Which of the following statements comes closest to explaining your motivation for purchasing this product?*
SOURCE: CCS data, weighted proportions. See Appendices C and D for more information.

and the plurality is about consumption—not making a social or political difference. The second is that participation in cause marketing is not a singular phenomenon, but rather three different, but related, actions. In the analysis that follows, I refer to cause marketing generally when I provide the picture from afar, but I also break it down along these three categories: *lifestyle buyers*, who choose products that support a particular cause because they believe in cause marketing; *cause followers*, who believe in a particular cause like the environment or breast cancer; and *accidental activists*, who participate unintentionally.

Who Participates?

Lifestyle buyers and cause followers are different from accidental activists in important ways. Table 3.1 shows the characteristics of individuals who participate in cause marketing by their motivation for participation. Key demographic characteristics—like age, race, gender, and ideology—show one pattern for those who participate in cause marketing intentionally in the first two columns and the reverse pattern for those who participate unintentionally in the final column.

The proportion of Americans who participate in cause marketing intentionally decreases for older generations. While 28 percent of young Americans (aged 26–37) and 24 percent of middle-age Americans (aged 38–56) are lifestyle buyers, only 16 percent of Americans aged 57 and above are. Likewise, 41 percent of young Americans are cause followers, while only 30 percent of Americans aged 57 and above are. But the pattern is reversed for the unintentional participators: 31 percent of young Americans (aged 26–37) are accidental activists, while 54 percent of Americans aged 57 and above are.

Likewise, the pattern for race is similar for the intentional participators in the first two columns, but it differs from that for the unintentional participators in the final column. Twenty-one percent of whites and 26 percent of nonwhites are lifestyle buyers, while 36 percent of whites and 41 percent of nonwhites are cause followers. However, that

Table 3.1 LIFESTYLE BUYERS AND CAUSE FOLLOWERS LOOK DIFFERENT
FROM ACCIDENTAL ACTIVISTS

	Lifestyle Buyers (0.21)	Cause Followers (0.36)	Accidental Activists (0.39)
Age			
26–37	0.28	0.41	0.31
38–56	0.24	0.39	0.37
57 and up	0.16	0.30	0.54
Race			
White	0.21	0.36	0.43
Nonwhite	0.26	0.41	0.33
Gender			
Female	0.24	0.42	0.34
Male	0.20	0.32	0.48
Education			
Up to High School	0.22	0.37	0.41
College or Postgraduate	0.21	0.40	0.40
Income			
$20,000 or less	0.27	0.26	0.46
$75,000 and above	0.26	0.32	0.42
Ideology			
Conservative	0.19	0.32	0.48
Liberal	0.28	0.41	0.30
Nonideological	0.24	0.39	0.38
	N = 174	*N* = 327	*N* = 391

SOURCE: CCS data, weighted proportions. For more information, see Appendices C and D.

pattern is reversed for accidental activists, with a larger difference between whites and nonwhites (ten points) and more participation by whites: 43 percent of whites are accidental activists compared with 33 percent of nonwhites.

Turning to gender, women more often participate in cause marketing intentionally. Twenty-four percent of women and 20 percent of men are lifestyle buyers. Forty-two percent of women and 32 percent of men are cause followers. However, while only one-third of women are accidental activists, nearly half of the men are.

Finally, looking at ideology shows that liberals most often participate with intent and conservatives most often participate unintentionally. Twenty-eight percent of liberals and 19 percent of conservatives are lifestyle buyers, while 41 percent of liberals and 32 percent of conservatives are cause followers. But, once again, that pattern changes in the final column, where only 30 percent of liberals are accidental activists compared with nearly half of conservatives.

Somewhat surprisingly, education stays remarkably constant across the three categories. Americans who have up to a high school degree and those who have completed some college or more participate in cause marketing in roughly equal proportions across the three motivations. And even though people participate in cause marketing by shopping, income plays little role: the biggest gap between low-income Americans (who make $20,000 or less) and high-income Americans (who make $75,000 or more) is found among cause followers, but even this is only a six-point difference.

What Drives Their Participation?

In their classic study of political behavior, Verba, Schlozman, and Brady pointed to three key factors driving Americans' political participation: resources (they can), motivation (they want to), and mobilization (they've been asked).[12] Ten years later, Zukin et al. reevaluated how Americans participate in political and civic life and, more specifically, how participation trends differ by generation.[13] Zukin et al. demonstrate that older generations are more politically active, while younger generations engage in more civic actions—including participation in market activism.

12. Sidney Verba, Kay Lehman Schlozman, and Henry E. Brady, *Voice and Equality: Civic Volunteerism in American Politics* (Cambridge, MA: Harvard University Press, 1995).

13. Zukin et al., *A New Engagement*.

Are the predictors of activism the same regardless of what kind of activity is involved? Or do different forms require different resources, different motivations, or different forms of mobilization? Is generation, with its shared experiences and views of government and approaches to politics, a key factor in determining what kinds of activities Americans engage in?

To better understand why individuals engage in market activity, I examine the CCS data using regression analysis, which has the benefit of disentangling many moving parts that go into complex human behavior. Regression analysis allows researchers to evaluate particular factors (e.g., does efficacy play a role?) while holding other variables that may also play a part (e.g., age, income) constant. Because I want to examine *whether* an individual participates in market activities and not *how much* he or she participates, I rely on logistic regression to evaluate the predictors for lifestyle buyers, cause followers, and accidental activists.

Using what we know about why people participate in political activities more broadly, I constructed models to examine why Americans might participate in cause marketing. I took into account those factors that influence political participation, such as knowledge and efficacy, as well as those factors that are likely to be important for cause marketing, such as responsibility for household purchases. Because some characteristics—such as being an active participant generally—may influence *whether* one participates, and other characteristics—such as having a close family member with breast cancer—may influence *how* one participates, the models include measures of participation in charitable activities, confidence in business, personal connection to breast cancer, as well as standard sociodemographic characteristics like age, race, gender, education, and income (more information and full results are provided in Appendix A).

The more nuanced models confirm the basic descriptive data provided in this chapter: because cause marketing means different things, the predictors vary by motivation. Lifestyle buyers are young, liberal, and active in their communities. Their participation is a reflection of their broader ideological beliefs: individuals can make a difference through their lifestyle choices.

Cause followers are also young and active in their communities. Cause followers tend to be women. These individuals have a strong sense of local efficacy, or the belief that they can make a difference in their communities. Unlike lifestyle buyers, cause followers are not making a broad ideological statement about the way they live their lives. Instead, they are expressing interest and support for a particular issue through their purchases.

Accidental activists look different from both lifestyle buyers and cause followers. Accidental activists are less often liberal and more often white. They express confidence that business can offer solutions to problems, even though they are not buying products from companies for that reason.

BREAST CANCER

Breast cancer is the focus of the largest and most successful cause-marketing campaign. More than 40 percent of all cause-marketing participation is related to breast cancer (see Figure 3.4). Still, the breast cancer case is similar in important ways to cause marketing more generally. Americans participate in the breast cancer campaign along the same three dimensions that they do for any other cause-marketing campaign: they are lifestyle buyers, cause followers, and accidental activists. They fall into these three groups in roughly equal proportion to individuals who participate in cause-marketing campaigns for all other products, as illustrated in Figure 3.6.

To learn more about breast cancer cause marketing, I relied on a battery of survey questions that asked individuals specifically about the breast cancer campaign, including whether they had purchased an item that benefits breast cancer in the past week. The 451 individuals who participated in the campaign fell into the three categories of lifestyle buyers, cause followers, and accidental activists. I ran the same model described earlier (in What Drives Their Participation?) for the individuals who purchased products that benefit breast cancer (full model results are available in Appendix A).

I found that Americans who bought products that benefit breast cancer research, *pink purchasers*, look a little different from the picture I painted

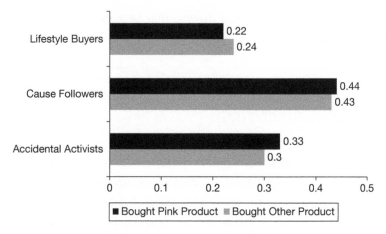

Figure 3.6 Americans' motivation for participating in breast cancer cause marketing looks like their motivation for engaging in other issues.
$N = 668$.
QUESTION WORDING: *Which of the following statements comes closest to explaining your motivation for purchasing this product?*
SOURCE: CCS data, weighted proportions. See Appendices C and D for more information.

earlier of who participates and why.[14] Pink purchasers are less politically knowledgeable than Americans who participate in cause marketing for all products. They have primary responsibility for the household shopping. They are also more active in their communities, both volunteering for charitable organizations and donating money to them. They are *less* often white. Like cause followers, pink purchasers are more often women and they are not ideological (either liberal or conservative). Instead, they have a personal connection to breast cancer.

In short, when they buy breast cancer cause-marketing products, pink purchasers are not expressing their ideological beliefs about the role of government or industry in society. They are not making overtly political statements. Instead, their purchases are deeply personal: they or someone they know has been diagnosed with breast cancer. Buying these products

14. Products benefit research to a greater or lesser degree. This wording is taken from the survey question. For a critical perspective see Reuters: http://www.reuters.com/article/2012/ 02/08/us-usa-healthcare-komen-research-idUSTRE8171KW20120208, accessed November 23, 2015.

makes them feel better about a disease that is painful, disfiguring, and sometimes fatal.

UNDERSTANDING CAUSE MARKETING
IN BROADER PERSPECTIVE

As I explained in Chapter 2, scholars have examined politically motivated consumerism, but they have not found many results. I show that cause marketing looks different from purchasing with intent, especially buycotting, or choosing to buy a product because one supports the social or political values of the company that produces it (the opposite of boycotting). The survey asked respondents about typical forms of political behavior, like signing a petition. It asked about charitable behavior, like volunteering.[15] It asked about political consumerism, buycotting, and boycotting. It also asked about cause marketing. Figure 3.7 ranks these different forms of political, charitable, and market-based behavior.

Consistent with existing research on political consumerism, 16 percent of the survey respondents reported buycotting in the past month, while one-quarter reported boycotting (not buying something from a company because they disagree with the social or political values of the company that produced it) during that same time frame.[16] Buycotting is as common as contacting government and more common than the traditional forms of political participation: displaying a sign, signing a petition, giving to a political campaign, attending a political meeting, working for a political party. But buycotting, like all of the other political and civic activities I asked about, is far less common than participating in cause marketing.

15. Analysis conducted by the author (but not shown here) does not show that cause marketing has an impact on participation in other types of activities (e.g., volunteering or giving to charitable organizations).

16. Dhavan V. Shah et al., "The Politics of Consumption/The Consumption of Politics," *Annals of the American Academy of Political and Social Science* 611, no. 1 (2007): 6–15; Stolle, Hooghe, and Micheletti, "Politics in the Supermarket"; Zukin et al., *A New Engagement*.

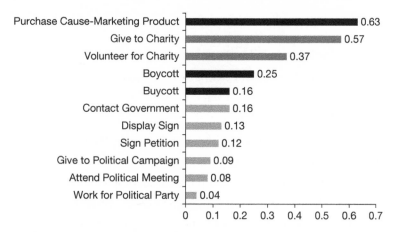

Figure 3.7 Participation in cause-marketing campaigns is more common than other charitable, political, or market activities.

$N = 1,500$.

QUESTION WORDING: *For each of the following, please tell me whether you have done an activity or not in the past month.*

SOURCE: CCS data, weighted proportions. See Appendices C and D for more information.

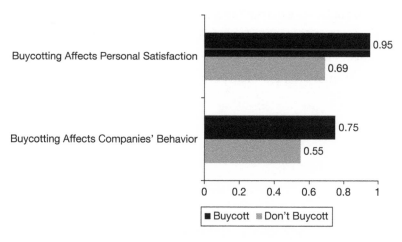

Figure 3.8 People who buycott believe it affects personal satisfaction and corporate behavior.

QUESTION WORDING: *Please tell me if you agree or disagree with the following statements: When an individual buys something because he or she agrees with the political or social values of the company that produces it has an effect on companies' behavior; When an individual buys something because he or she agrees with the political or social values of the company that produces it has an effect on an individual's personal satisfaction.*

SOURCE: CCS data, weighted proportions of people who agree. See Appendices C and D for more information.

Cause marketing pervades American culture, but it means very different things to different Americans who engage in it. Americans who buycott—like lifestyle buyers—treat consumer purchases as an extension of their broader ideological beliefs. They want to make a difference, and buycotting is a way of doing so. These individuals are not disconnected and not checked out of their communities. They volunteer for and donate money to charities. They have strong liberal ideological beliefs. As Figure 3.8 shows, they believe that their purchases make a difference both in personal satisfaction (95 percent) and in how companies behave (75 percent).

But buycotting is just one narrow way that Americans engage issues. All of the attention on those people who participate in market activities with the intention of making social or political change neglects what market mechanisms look like and the impact they have. Far more common, cause marketing reaches a mass audience and has an effect on *how Americans think and feel about issues.* Cause marketing frames issues as simple, positive, and consensual. In the following chapter, I show how issues are framed through cause marketing and how that differs from what we know about framing in the policy process. In Chapter 5, I show how cause marketing affects the way Americans think about issues and, in Chapter 6, how these frames are then incorporated into the policy process.

Telling Stories

Americans see cause marketing in consumer advertising, read about it in traditional and social media, buy products that support it, and bring it home with them on consumer packaged goods. But cause marketing is not just a slogan or a picture on a product; it tells a story about social problems and ways to address them. Problems are portrayed as tractable and solutions as easy and convenient; they do not require more than buying a product or clipping a box top. Every American can get involved, make a difference, and feel good about doing so.

What issues does cause marketing address and how does it address them? In this chapter I analyze cause-marketing campaigns, and I use the federal policy process—specifically, congressional hearings—as a benchmark for understanding and comparing cause marketing and policymaking. Although cause marketing shares many features with political advertising and public speeches more generally—such as a focus on symbols and short messages offering easy solutions—the analysis here provides snapshots of what happens in cause marketing and the policymaking process. This analysis is useful for understanding typical cause-marketing issues and how market actors address them; it is useful for understanding typical policy process issues and how policy actors address them; and it is useful for understanding how they differ. By looking across issues, the analysis here also lays the groundwork for understanding breast cancer cause marketing, which shares many of the same features as cause marketing more generally, and the effect of cause marketing on breast cancer policymaking. Compared with policymaking for other issues generally, and other cancers specifically, breast cancer policymaking invokes a disproportionate use of cause-marketing symbols and features.

I produced the analysis inductively by first selecting the most common issue areas for cause marketing, the policy process, and both together, examining cause-marketing campaigns and congressional hearings chosen at random.[1] The analysis, then, provides a picture of typical kinds of issues that are addressed and in what ways. It describes the key features of stories in each process and illustrates them with examples across issue areas. For example, what kinds of health issues does cause marketing address and how does it address them? How might the policy process address health issues? And in what ways does breast cancer policymaking look similar to and different from typical issues in cause marketing and the policy process?

I find that cause-marketing stories differ in focus and substance from stories generated in the federal policy process. While cause marketing takes difficult problems and tells simple stories with easy solutions, the policy process often justifies governmental intervention by telling complex stories with difficult solutions that need the full force of the federal government. While cause marketing tells individuals they can do something to make a difference, the policy process often paints individuals as the problem that government must fix. And while cause marketing feels good, the policy process can appear overwhelming. Yet, even though there are fairly systematic differences between cause marketing and policymaking processes, federal breast cancer policymaking shares many of the features and symbols of cause marketing.

Cause-marketing stories are more than just a feel-good way to shop: they affect how Americans think and feel about issues (Chapter 5) and how policymakers address them (Chapter 6). In fact, stories generated through market processes do not stay in market arenas but become integrated into the policy process. Congressional policymakers adopt the

---

1. See Appendix C for more information on methodology.

symbolic action and language of market mechanisms and even create public policies that reflect them.

Much of what we know about how ideas make it to the policy agenda comes from studies of the federal policy process.[2] Ideas germinate in specialized policy communities; entrepreneurs introduce them to the policy process at strategic points in time, when they are taken up and addressed more widely or returned to policy communities where they may lie dormant or even fade away.[3] In the federal policy process, experts and media play a key role in framing issues.[4] But this is only one way that ideas make it to the policy process. They also arrive through market channels, which have a different structure, logic, and story.[5] If framing determines *how* issues are addressed, problems that are framed through market channels may have a different trajectory in policymaking.[6]

Cause marketing makes an end run around the "issue-attention cycle," whereby Americans lose interest in a problem when it becomes clear that solutions will be long, complicated, and require sacrifice.[7] Cause marketing generates, promotes, and sustains the initial sense of optimism by the way it defines issues: simple, positive, and easily solved. In doing so, it removes the conflict at the center of American politics, essentially depoliticizing the issues it addresses. As the case of breast cancer illustrates, these simplified understandings can be imported into the policy process, shaping the way that policymakers talk about an issue and the public policies they create to address it.

2. Kingdon, *Agendas, Alternatives, and Public Policies*; Baumgartner and Jones, *Agendas and Instability in American Politics.*

3. Kingdon, *Agendas, Alternatives, and Public Policies.*

4. Baumgartner and Jones, *Agendas and Instability in American Politics.*

5. Stone, *Policy Paradox*, ch. 6. Stone explains that policy problems are defined through stories, complete with a narrative structure and heroes and villains. These stories shape how people think about problems and what the proper response to them should be.

6. Ibid.; Anne Schneider and Helen Ingram, "Social Construction of Target Populations: Implications for Politics and Policy," *American Political Science Review* 87, no. 2 (1993): 334–47; Nelson, *Making an Issue of Child Abuse.*

7. Anthony Downs, "Up and Down with Ecology: The "Issue-Attention" Cycle," *Public Interest* 28 (1972): 38–50.

PROCESSES THAT GENERATE STORIES

The processes that generate stories for cause marketing are different from the processes scholars have described for public policy. Cause-marketing stories are created by businesses and nonprofits that wish to gain attention for their organization or issue. Cause marketing requires action by consumers, such as buying a product or sending in a box top; it needs relationships with nonprofits; and it relies on advertising. Cause marketing is handled most often by a company's marketing department and, unsurprisingly, the benefits are marketing-related: attracting new customers, reaching niche markets, increasing sales, and building "positive brand identity."[8] According to a recent study by Cone Communications, consumers around the globe respond to cause marketing: 96 percent say they have a more positive image of a company that engages in cause marketing; 94 percent would be more likely to trust that company; 93 percent would be more loyal to that company; and 91 percent would switch to a brand associated with a good cause.[9] Spending on cause marketing reached $1.85 billion in 2014.[10]

Although research shows that long-term commitments and a greater percentage of proceeds donated build consumer confidence in a company, cause-marketing campaigns vary greatly in the length they run as well as the amount of money they raise or distribute.[11] For example, for three hours one day a year, Cold Stone Creamery gives out ice cream in exchange for a donation to the Make-A-Wish Foundation. In 2005, this campaign raised $750,000, enough to grant 123 wishes of children

8. Kotler and Lee, *Corporate Social Responsibility*, ch. 4.

9. 2013 Cone Communications/Echo Global CSR Study: http://www.conecomm.com/global-csr-study, accessed June 25, 2013.

10. IEG Sponsorship Report: http://www.sponsorship.com/IEG/files/4e/4e525456-b2b1-4049-bd51-03d9c35ac507.pdf, accessed March 22, 2016.

11. Barone, Miyazaki, and Taylor, "The Influence of Cause-Related Marketing on Consumer Choice"; Bloom et al., "How Social-Cause Marketing Affects Consumer Perceptions"; Dahl and Lavach, "Cause-Related Markets"; but see Holmes and Kilbane, "Cause-Related Marketing."

with life-threatening illnesses. By contrast, General Mills's Box Tops for Education has raised more than $500 million continuously over twelve years (discussed later). The donations that companies make vary in size, from a few thousand dollars for small start-ups like Color Me Co.'s partnerships with children's charities to multimillion-dollar endeavors like Nike's partnership with the Lance Armstrong Foundation (cancer) or Macy's partnership with the American Heart Association to raise money for heart disease. Not all companies are equally likely to get involved. As mentioned earlier, companies most involved with this form of activism produce and sell consumer packaged goods (in contrast to, say, a petroleum company or plastics manufacturer)—for example, Proctor & Gamble, Macy's, Target, and Nike. Similarly, the nonprofits with which they partner are mainstream organizations that work to improve individual and community health and well-being, such as Komen (breast cancer), the American Heart Association (heart disease), Share Our Strength (hunger), Children's Miracle Network (children's health), Feeding America (hunger), and UNICEF (children's health and well-being).

General Mills offers an instructive example of how cause marketing works. The company has used coupons on the tops of products to build a group of loyal customers since the 1930s. However, while these earlier efforts used reward points toward the purchase of goods for home use, the program that General Mills created in 1996, Box Tops for Education, makes use of box tops that consumers clip from General Mills products: for every box top clipped and given to a school coordinator, the company donates ten cents to that school. In 2006, General Mills decided to shift its resources entirely from reward programs for home use to the "newer and more popular" Box Tops program.[12]

General Mills, like many companies involved in cause marketing, does not sell an abstract issue based on principle, but concrete stories told in local communities like Selma, Alabama. Selma middle-school band director Ivan Jones got involved with Box Tops to raise money for

12. See Samantha Beerman, "Bye-Bye Betty," *Incentive* 180, no. 9 (2006): 11.

the purchase of musical instruments. Only a fraction of Selma Middle CHAT Academy's sixty-five instruments were in good condition, forcing students to rent instruments that many parents could not afford.[13] Jones decided to raise money partly through General Mills's Box Tops program. He tells a story about how students learn what corporate relationships can do for them and their community by participating in the program:

> What inspires me in being the coordinator is I am presenting something to my kids that they can participate in, too. They see that if they bring Box Tops coupons, more money will come to the school and they see that their efforts helped. They know the routine: eat a box of cereal, cut the Box Top off, and bring it to Mr. Jones. They're good kids. They want to make sure that if they don't have instruments, someone who comes after them will.[14]

To promote his plan, Jones contacted a local newspaper, which subsequently ran a story about the school and the Box Tops program. He placed yard signs around town. And he created a competition in the school. General Mills promotes Box Tops campaigns and individual stories, like Jones's, through regional events, posting success stories on its website, and sponsoring blogs, including that of Ronnie Tyler, who writes about cause-marketing campaigns. Tyler and her husband, Lamar, are bloggers for *Black and Married with Kids* and—along with President Barack Obama, athlete LeBron James, and entertainer Rihanna—were among those featured in *Ebony* magazine's "Power 100" in 2012.[15] Tyler writes:

> Over the last two weeks, we have been discussing many disheartening things about our education system and our children: from finding out that nationally, African American kids are being given

13. Desiree Taylor, "CHAT Band Seeks Help," *Selma Times Journal*, September 27, 2011.

14. Box Tops for Education: http://www.boxtops4education.com/share/StoryDetail.aspx?Id=1725, accessed July 8, 2013.

15. *Ebony*: http://www.ebony.com/entertainment-culture/ebony-reveals-its-2012-power-100-list-100#axzz2XoMAgjcK, accessed July 8, 2013.

out-of-school suspensions at a much higher rate than all other ethnic groups to discovering that some Mississippi schools have a "school to prison pipeline" where they are arresting kids for minor infractions. It's enough to make you think all is lost.

But there is always something or someone that reminds me that there is hope. As long as we have people that are willing to work on behalf of our children by being involved parents, by being volunteers, and by being community activists, then we have hope.

And this is why I am so happy to share the story of Ivan Jones with you.[16]

Though Tyler talks about serious structural problems—disproportionate penalties for African Americans in the education and criminal justice systems—she turns attention away from these overwhelming, intractable "bad news" stories and toward "good news" stories about solving problems with individual actions. In doing so, she does not frame Selma CHAT's problem as one of structural inequality in American urban schools, which would require restructuring resources; instead, she sees it as a tractable problem (buying new instruments) with an easy solution (sending in box tops) in which everyone can participate. Actions like this make Americans feel good: the people who are directly involved with the program, such as students, parents, and teachers, and the people who identify with well-behaved children in a band without proper instruments.

General Mills, Jones, and Tyler also tell a deeply apolitical story. There is no conflict and no question about the allocation of resources. Instead, individual action and nonprofit–corporate partnerships can make a positive difference. Contrast this story with the Women's International League for Peace and Freedom's iconic phrase, "It will be a great day when our schools get all the money they need and the air force has to hold a bake

16. Black and Married with Kids. August 22, 2012: http://www.blackandmarriedwithkids. com/2012/08/one-teacher-decides-to-take-matters-into-his-own-hands/, accessed June 27, 2013.

sale to buy another bomber." For the league, lack of funding is a political problem with a political solution: policy actors ought to reallocate defense dollars to domestic funding. This story is inherently conflictual, pitting issues and actors against one another.

The federal policy process—or how government determines what it will address, how it will do so, and how it will implement its decisions—looks strikingly different from cause marketing. In the policy process, ideas bounce around in policy communities in a long process John Kingdon calls "softening up."[17] When the political opportunity arises to join particular solutions to policy problems, policy entrepreneurs take action: they testify at hearings, make speeches, and suggest legislation. Congress takes up these issues in committees and floor debates where new policies are made or existing ones amended. Once policies are enacted, they must be implemented by federal, state, and local administrators. Details left out of the authorizing legislation can stymie reform on the ground. Controversy and dissent are common at each step: declaring an issue important, creating and passing legislation, and implementing policy.

Education initiatives in the federal policy process provide an instructive comparison with education cause marketing. After being elected president in 2000, George W. Bush outlined an agenda to improve education that focused on testing, flexibility, assisting low-performing schools, and choice.[18] Members of Congress worked on translating the president's ideas into policy that would pass Congress, be signed by the president, and result in successful implementation by the states. They worried about the fallout of potentially nationalizing education. They tried to set standards for meeting adequate yearly progress targets, but the formulas led to poor results for some of the nation's strongest state education programs. Education policy experts criticized the government for being unable to find an adequate measure of success or failure. State representatives lobbied congressional conference and appropriations committees working

---

17. Kingdon, *Agendas, Alternatives, and Public Policies.*

18. Paul Manna, *School's In: Federalism and the National Education Agenda* (Washington, DC: Georgetown University Press, 2006).

on the education bill to fix the adequate yearly progress formula and to give states greater flexibility.

In the final legislation, members of Congress defined the problem they sought to address broadly as closing "the achievement gap with account-ability, flexibility, and choice, *so that no child is left behind.*"[19] Reducing discrepancies between rich and poor schools, majority and minority pop-ulations, and high- and low-performing students is a massive undertak-ing. Congress set desirable but unrealistic goals, including high-quality assessments and accountability systems, closing the achievement gap, in-creased teacher training, and holding schools accountable.

In 2001, the 670-page No Child Left Behind Act passed Congress. In 2002 President Bush signed it into law, declaring post-9/11, "We're going to win the war overseas and we're going to win the war against illiteracy at home as well."[20] Policymakers claimed that this was a major education reform, but implementation proved to be difficult.[21] Although the states wanted additional federal funds, they worried about the new require-ments and sanctions that might take place. Virginia's House of Delegates challenged the law as a "sweeping intrusion" that would overwhelm its finances and displace the progress it had already made. Despite tough language, the authorizing legislation let states set their own tests. After enactment, the federal government made further concessions, granting waiver requests to individual states and issuing blanket revisions. While these modifications eroded standards necessary to achieve No Child Left Behind's lofty goals, they made it easier for states to comply.[22]

In 2008, as they considered reauthorizing No Child Left Behind, policymakers debated whether the program really did what they in-tended: Did it improve education? Did it reduce the gap in student

19. PL 107-110, No Child Left Behind Act of 2001. Emphasis mine.

20. Elisabeth Bumiller, "Focusing on the Home Front, Bush Signs Education Bill," *New York Times*, January 9, 2002.

21. David K. Cohen and Susan L. Moffitt, *The Ordeal of Equality: Did Federal Regulation Fix the Schools?* (Cambridge, MA: Harvard University Press, 2009).

22. Manna, *School's In.*

achievement? Did it prepare teachers? Were schools held accountable? And was it adequately funded? The policy had major problems: 28 percent of schools were failing to meet adequate yearly progress, and appropriations slumped to roughly half of authorizations, leaving schools to figure out how to pay for these expensive measures.[23] No Child Left Behind remained a contentious policy and it was replaced by the Every Student Succeeds Act in December 2015.

Although General Mills's Box Tops program is a major initiative for cause marketing and No Child Left Behind was a major initiative for the policy process, these programs obviously have striking differences that reflect the types of problems and solutions that cause marketing and the federal policy process address. The Box Tops program is much smaller than No Child Left Behind was. It is less ambitious, it is less controversial, and it will have a smaller impact than No Child Left Behind did. Yet, because it is more lim-ited, Box Tops is far more likely to achieve its stated goals and, therefore, be successful than No Child Left Behind. Americans are potentially more likely to know about and participate in it.[24] Therefore, it is important to under-stand how cause marketing works and the effect it has on the policy process.

The processes that generate stories also generate the data used for this analysis, making comparison challenging. Unlike the federal policy pro-cess, where government records are thorough, there are no centralized databases on cause-marketing issues. Unlike the overabundance of data on the federal policy process, information on cause marketing is brief, spotty, and incomplete. These challenges, while frustrating to social sci-entists, reveal how each process functions. To address them, I employ a two-pronged strategy.

In the first part, I systematically analyze stories generated through market processes and benchmark them against stories generated through policy processes. Because there are no cause-marketing databases,

23. Wayne C. Riddle, "The No Child Left Behind Act: An Overview of Reauthorization Issues for the 110th Congress," in CRS Report for Congress (Washington, DC: Congressional Research Service, 2008).

24. After passage, nearly half of the parents in urban districts had not heard of No Child Left Behind. Diana Jean Schemo, "New Law Is News to Many," New York Times, October 15, 2002.

I created one by searching business publications and wires for stories about cause marketing. The resulting database includes 381 cause-marketing campaigns. The federal policy process has the opposite problem: it is multifaceted, complicated, and generates too much data. Here, I chose to look at congressional hearings, which have the distinct advantage of providing a window into what Congress pays attention to and how key policy actors—both officials within government and experts outside of it—talk about issues (i.e., part function, part performance). I used the Agendas Project coding of hearings and replicated the coding in the cause-marketing database.[25]

The second part of my strategy is interpretative. Policy and cause-marketing processes are different in many ways: they generate different quantitative and qualitative data. I use this fact to interpret my results. What does it mean that there are far more hearings than cause-marketing campaigns? Part of the answer is that there really are more hearings, but part is that I do not have comprehensive data on cause marketing as I do for hearings, because nobody bothers to keep records. The implications are that we do not have a full picture of what cause marketing does, how it works, and what its effects are.

Together, these two prongs tell me about the knowledge and ideas generated by each. At the end of the day, Americans can find out what Congress is talking about; journalists and academics can write stories about what is happening and why. But Americans are left with superficial impressions about cause marketing—what it is, what it does, and what effect it has—that are an accurate reflection of the available information. In short, what Americans know reflects the data that are available.

In the following sections, I analyze the database of cause-marketing campaigns and congressional hearings to better understand what cause marketing is and how it works. I find that cause marketing (a) focuses on a different set of issues than the federal policy process and (b) addresses them in a different way. Yet, even though there are many differences, I use

25. See Chapter 1, this volume, and the Policy Agendas Project: http://www.policyagendas. org/, accessed June 10, 2011.

the case study on breast cancer to show that (c) cause marketing bleeds into the federal policy process, shaping how policymakers talk about and act on issues. In the next two sections I discuss the issues that cause marketing addresses and the federal policy process addresses, as well as how each address them. In addition, I show how cause marketing is similar to and different from the policy process.[26]

THE ISSUES LANDSCAPE

Cause-marketing campaigns and congressional hearings focus largely on different issues. The Agendas Project assigns congressional hearings one of nineteen major codes.[27] Figure 4.1 displays all nineteen issues by the number of cause-marketing campaigns and congressional hearings (1988–2008), providing a broad overview of what cause-marketing campaigns and policy hearings devoted their attention to. Cause-marketing campaigns focused most on domestic policy concerns: health, social welfare, education, the environment, and international affairs. By contrast, Congress exerted itself most often according to the powers granted it in the Constitution: the business of government (Government Operations), international affairs, commerce, health, and defense.

It is not surprising that marketers and policy actors talk about different issues. There are no prescribed rules on the issues that cause marketers may address; the only limitation is what will sell to the consumers they wish to target and the vehicle (marketing) available to them. Kotler and Lee suggest a number of ways that companies can select an issue: choose one that the company and target audience are passionate about; choose a nonprofit partner with existing and potential relationships (because campaigns need high volume); and choose the intersection of customer base, product, and people who care about the cause.[28] Campaigns tend

26. See Appendix C for more information on methodology.

27. See Appendix C.

28. Kotler and Lee, *Corporate Social Responsibility*, 102.

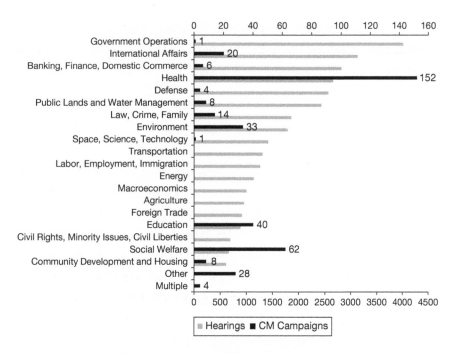

Figure 4.1 **Cause marketing emphasizes different issues.**

N = 381 cause-marketing campaigns, 32,086 hearings.

NOTE: Cause-marketing campaigns read on the top axis, hearings on the bottom axis.
SOURCE: Cause-marketing campaigns from a database of business publications
and congressional hearings from the Agendas Project. See Appendix C for more
information.

to focus on issues that appear easily marketable and that are tangible to
most Americans—that is, we can see or feel them without much effort.[29]
Companies communicate their message about an issue on the product or
package label, according to Cone the most effective way to do so.[30]

Clearly, the federal policy process is more highly regulated and prescribed by institutional structures: the committee system, the appropriations process, and the electoral cycle. The Constitution lays out powers
for the federal government in general (e.g., common defense) and for
Congress in particular (e.g., power of the purse, oversight of government

29. See also Till and Nowak, "Toward Effective Use of Cause-Related Marketing Alliances."

30. 2013 Cone Communications/Echo Global CSR Study: http://www.conecomm.com/
global-csr-study, accessed June 25, 2013.

affairs). State actors have more leeway, and, one might argue, the need, in areas prescribed for them. But not only do the two processes tend to emphasize different issues, they talk about issues in very different ways.

THE STORIES THEY TELL

As I discuss in this section, cause marketing tells distinctive stories of problems that can be solved by generating awareness or purchasing products. Marketers often frame issues as positive and consensual. They enable and empower their beneficiaries to do things they otherwise would not be able to do. They give Americans an opportunity to participate in a solution. The policy process, by contrast, tells stories of problems that are complex, potentially unsolvable. Policy actors often frame issues as difficult and controversial, they constrain what individuals and organizations can do through bureaucratic rules, and they see Americans as part of the problem they must fix.

Cause marketing emphasizes awareness; by contrast, the policy process emphasizes information. Awareness is a key word in cause-marketing campaigns. It means being familiar with a particular issue, knowing *of* it, not necessarily *about* it. Awareness does not require one to know the causes of a problem or the consequences of it, merely that an issue exists. Contrast awareness with information, which is often the goal of the policy process. Information is used to understand the root causes and consequences of complex problems, though often in politically motivated ways.

Cause marketers do not shy away from serious issues.[31] For example, they devote disproportionate attention to social welfare, especially hunger relief. While hunger is a big problem that is not easily solved, cause marketers get around this by setting modest goals, such as raising awareness. Since 2000, Tyson has paired with Share Our Strength (a hunger organization) and, in 2011, Tyson began the KNOW Hunger campaign: "In an effort to help raise awareness of hunger in the United States ... [t]he

31. Nowak and Washburn, "Marketing Alliances between Non-Profits and Businesses."

project is designed to encourage people to KNOW the scope of hunger in their own communities and get involved in relief efforts, so someday there will be NO hunger in our country."[32] Tyson also has a website "designed to raise hunger awareness" and "uses social media tools to create hunger awareness." Tyson is not alone. Weight Watchers runs a Lose for Good campaign "to raise awareness about ... obesity and hunger";[33] Walmart used a Facebook page "to help spread awareness of this serious issue and encourage everyone to do something to help";[34] and Kraft sponsors events as part of "Hunger Awareness Day."[35] Awareness is an important goal of many cause-marketing campaigns: ribbons raise awareness, symbols on packages raise awareness, products raise awareness. Cause marketing sets awareness as a goal and raises awareness simply by bringing attention to an issue.

When cause marketing does offer *information*, it is cursory and intended to inform a broad range of consumers. The information it provides is usually surface-level. Though cause marketers shy away from commerce issues, they do get involved in one particular way—domestic disaster relief.[36] The database showed six cases where companies worked to aid disaster victims. For example, in 2009, Tide (a Proctor & Gamble company) ran a Loads of Hope campaign in which a "laundromat fleet" washed, dried, and folded clothes in disaster-stricken areas. The company website explains how this works: "A disaster occurs making relief necessary for the families affected. We send our mobile laundromat fleet to the location. We spend multiple days at the disaster site washing, drying and

---

32. Tyson: http://www.tysonhungerrelief.com/our-commitment/, accessed March 3, 2014.

33. Weight Watchers: https://www.weightwatchers.com/about/prs/wwi_template.aspx?GCMSID=1165381, accessed March 3, 2014.

34. The *Examiner*: http://www.examiner.com/article/walmart-creates-facebook-campaign-to-help-fight-hunger, accessed March 3, 2014.

35. *CSR Wire*: http://www.csrwire.com/press_releases/13889-Kraft-Foods-and-America-s-Second-Harvest-to-Fight-Hunger-in-10-Cities-on-Hunger-Awareness-Day, accessed March 3, 2014.

36. See also Ross, Stutts, and Patterson, "Tactical Considerations for the Effective Use of Cause-Related Marketing."

folding clothes for the families affected." Tide does this because "sometimes even the littlest things can make a big, big difference."[37] The Loads
of Hope website provides information about the disasters and communities in which Tide has gotten involved—the floods in Waterloo, Iowa,
Fargo, North Dakota, and Austell, Georgia; the wildfires in San Diego;
and the hurricanes in New Orleans and Baton Rouge—as well as ways
that consumers can support Tide's efforts by purchasing specially marked
bottles of detergent ($1 dollar toward disaster relief) or a Tide T-shirt ($4
toward disaster relief).

Congressional action on well-being and commerce issues has an entirely different narrative, one with complicated stories that need a great
deal of information. Congress deals with big issues by addressing the
most difficult pieces. On June 10, 2002, the Senate Committee on Health,
Education, Labor, and Pensions met to discuss the impact of 9/11 on the
psychological and emotional well-being of children in New York City. In
the US Custom House in New York, Senator Hillary Clinton (D-NY) explained the three themes to be discussed: "experiences of children, parents, schools, and professionals who suffered great losses and trauma on
September 11th; response of the public sector to mental health needs of
both our children and our families; and research and best practices—what
are the mental health needs that can be defined and what should we do
to meet them."[38] Witnesses included New York City education officials,
students, city, state, and federal agencies associated with mental health, as
well as researchers and nonprofit organizations. They testified about children's increased fear, aggression, and sleeplessness. The relentless attention to the tragedy and its violence replayed events for young Americans
over and over again. For children, coming to grips with a violent death
that even adults had difficulty understanding presented grave challenges.
A 9/11 widow and mother explained, "My son came home from school one
day in tears, saying that . . . one of the students in his class had come up to

37. Tide: http://www.tide.com/en-US/loads-of-hope/about.jspx, accessed June 22, 2011.

38. See US Congress, Senate, Committee on Health, Education, Labor, and Pensions,
Children of September 11: The Need for Mental Health Services, Second Session, 1992.

him and said, 'They are only finding body parts at the World Trade Center and they are putting them in garbage bags. Do you think that that is where your daddy is?'" Though the federal government addresses difficult issues, it is unclear how it can ameliorate the indelible effect of seeing bodies fall from the World Trade Tower (as one young student mistakenly thought, "The birds are on fire") or the sudden and inexplicable loss of a parent. Nonprofits, individual schools, and government agencies offered counseling, educational, and afterschool programs. Administrators looked to Oklahoma City officials, who dealt with their own terrorist attack in 1995, but the nature and magnitude of 9/11 were unprecedented.

Sometimes all that actors in the policy process do is generate data and float ideas. Congress has authority over interstate commerce and gave the most hearings in this issue area to small business. In October 1995, the Small Business Committee's Subcommittee on Procurement, Exports, and Business Opportunities met to review the export information available to small businesses. In 1995, exports reached $512 billion, accounting for 11 million jobs. But the vast majority of exports (80 percent) come from large companies.[39] Subcommittee chairman Donald Manzullo (R-IL) explained, "Many small businesses are intimidated to enter the export market. Yet, we need more small businesses to enter the export arena if we are to advance our nation's competitiveness."[40] The committee heard testimony from public agencies, public-private partnerships, and private companies about available resources and saw firsthand demonstrations about how to access them. In this case, the hearing was not about solving a particular problem or determining a specific amount of resources, but providing general information that legislators and small businesses would need to make these determinations.

Though cause marketing and the policy process both address well-being, the objective of the former is to bring attention to an issue, like

39. See US Congress, House of Representatives, Committee on Small Business, Subcommittee on Small Business Procurement, Exports, and Business Opportunities, *Private Sector Resources for Exports*, First Session, 1995.

40. Ibid.

fighting hunger. When it does provide information, as Tide does for national disasters, it is cursory and symbolic. The federal policy process, by contrast, seeks not merely to raise attention but also to generate information, as the Small Business Committee did in 1995, and to grapple with it, as Senator Clinton did for the long-term mental health effects of 9/11. But it is not clear that policy officials know the answers. While the policy process is designed to provide information, such as data about specific problems and programs, cause marketing is designed to do just the opposite: provide little information and few specifics.[41]

Cause marketing emphasizes enabling and empowering individuals; by contrast, the policy process explicitly addresses limitations. Cause-marketing campaigns appear to create opportunities for individuals and communities that might otherwise not be there. The campaigns raise money that is spent with few restrictions. Because education touches communities across the country, it is a good issue for cause marketing and a frequent beneficiary of campaigns. General Mills's Box Tops for Education is the largest education cause-marketing campaign.[42] As mentioned earlier, General Mills donates ten cents for every tag consumers (most often parents) clip from box tops of specially marked products and bring to school. Currently, 284 products benefit the Box Tops programs. Local parents coordinate the efforts and collect the tags. They are responsible for motivating students and parents to get involved. Figure 4.2 shows a standard ad run for the program on the Monroe, Michigan Public Schools' website.

In black and white, the ad makes clear that Box Tops "makes it easy" to help American schools. To "make a difference," Americans need only purchase participating products and send the box top to local schools.

---

41. Government often requires entities to provide information to the public, ostensibly so they can make informed decisions. Fung, Graham, and Weil, *Full Disclosure*; Janet A. Weiss, "Public Information," in *Tools of Government: A Guide to the New Governance*, ed. Lester Salamon (New York: Oxford University Press, 2002), 217–54. But market campaigns do not make use of information as much as they do awareness. They pair a cause with an often-unrelated product (e.g., endangered animals and breakfast cereal) rather than pair information about a product with the product (nutritional information on boxes of cereal).

42. Box Tops for Education: http://www.boxtops4education.com/, accessed June 24, 2011.

Earn cash for our school with Box Tops

Box Tops for Education makes it easy to help our school earn the extra cash it needs.
Make a difference every time you go to the grocery store!

How to earn cash for our school

Clip Box Tops	**Send Box Tops to School**	**Our School Earns Cash**
Find Box Tops on hundreds of your favorite products. Each Box Top is worth 10¢ to our school.	Turn in your Box Tops. Our school will collect the Box Tops and send them to Box Tops for Education.	Twice each year, Box Tops will send our school a check worth 10¢ for each Box Top redeemed, up to $20,000.

Our school can earn up to $20,000 per year from the Box Tops you clip!

These are just a few of the great brands you can find Box Tops on.
See boxtops4education.com for a current complete list of **participating products.**

Visit **boxtops4education.com** for more great ideas to **earn cash for our school!**

Figure 4.2 **General Mills's Box Tops for Education campaign makes solutions easy.**
SOURCE: Monroe Public Schools: http://www.monroe.k12.mi.us/view/737.pdf.

Box Tops does not have strict rules about what to spend its money on or how to spend it. Schools that raise money consider it a bonus to do things they otherwise would not have the opportunity to do. The boxtops4education website keeps track of local schools' progress. The top money earner overall, Shepherd Elementary School, Mooresville, North Carolina, raised $52,194. In total, schools have earned more than $375 million since 1996. Of course, these numbers pale in comparison with local, state, and federal outlays (approximately $650 billion for K–12 in 2009–2010).[43]

Cause marketing is direct-to-communities. Corporations and non-profits work together to provide opportunities, but they engage local communities in their efforts. The objective is not only to make a difference, but to get people to participate. Cause marketers are involved in general environmental concerns like water pollution, trees, and parks as well as protecting specific endangered animals. In 2010, Nestlé Pure Life bottled water partnered with Keep America Beautiful for the "Great American Cleanup." An estimated 4 million volunteers were involved in 33,700 communities across the United States. These groups cleaned up 76 million pounds of litter over 124,000 miles of streets, 71,000 acres of public lands, 3,100 playgrounds, 6,800 miles of shore, and 10,500 acres of wetlands.[44] At the same time, they planted trees and flowers, removed graffiti, and raised awareness for millions of Americans. Nestlé's primary focus was on recycling, and it created a new recycling program for Keep America Beautiful. Nestlé awarded $25,000 for distribution to the communities collecting the most plastic bottles during the 2010 cleanup event.[45]

The federal government's attention to the same two policy areas—education and the environment—reflects a different approach. Although the federal government actually does more (provides more funding, has more policy proposals), it also must address real bureaucratic constraints and cost-benefit analyses. The federal government's interest in a policy

43. See National Center for Education Statistics, Digest of Education Statistics, Table 28: "Expenditures of educational institutions related to the gross domestic product, by level of institution: Selected years, 1929–30 through 2009–10": http://nces.ed.gov/programs/digest/d10/tables/dt10_028.asp?referrer=report, accessed June 24, 2011.

44. Keep America Beautiful: http://www.kab.org/site/PageServer?pagename=GAC_2010Results, accessed June 24, 2011.

45. "Nation's Leading Bottled Water Brand Announces Four-Year Partnership and Is Official Bottled Water of 2010 Great American Cleanup Campaign," PR Newswire, March 24, 2010.

area, like education, lies not only in funding schools' needs or devising new education standards, but also in the nitty-gritty issues of managing federal agencies: topics that, short of a severe scandal (like a $640 toilet seat), go without any notice whatsoever.[46] On July 24, 2001, the House Committee on Education and the Workforce Subcommittee on Select Education brought representatives of the Department of Education to a hearing to discuss the department's efforts to institute better financial management practices. Previously, in October 2000, the Government Accounting Office (GAO) issued a report describing the Department of Education's shortcomings, and in this hearing the Inspector General's Office responded with regard to financial management for purchasing cards, erroneous grant disbursements, misuse of cellular phones, contractor compliance with record keeping, reporting, and inventory, information technology security, and the creation of a system to estimate improper payments. The amount of bureaucratic detail provided to the committee is stunning. For example, the Inspector General's Office set out to review the Department of Education's progress in two areas: "requiring that all approving officials review and sign monthly purchase card statements" and reconciling department-wide statements to those approved in the department's accounting system. They evaluated 184 purchase card transactions for February 2001 and found that "six statements lacked required signatures" and "68 statements were not submitted timely."[47]

When Congress devotes attention to the environment, the focus is national and the language is sterile. It is a financial cost-benefit analysis. On May 10, 1994, the Senate's Committee on Energy and Natural Resources held hearings to review President Clinton's Climate Change Action Plan. Witnesses testified about both the international and state-level impact

---

46. In 1985, Lockheed Martin charged the Navy $640 for a custom toilet seat cover, which made headlines nationally. See, e.g., Wayne Biddle, "Price of Toilet Seat Is Cut for Navy," *New York Times*, February 6, 1985.

47. See statement of Lorraine Lewis, US Congress, House of Representatives, Committee on Education and the Workforce, Subcommittee on Select Education, *Status of Financial Management at the U.S. Department of Education*, First Session, 2002.

of the proposed plan. The secretary of energy, Hazel O'Leary, however, was concerned about her ability to meet the targets with cutbacks to her agency. She talked in the language of "public-private partnerships" that would be used to meet their goals, explaining:

> If fully funded, the Climate Change Action Plan would cost the Federal government $1.9 billion between now and the year 2000. But our partners would leverage this spending by investing over $60 billion in environmental technologies. These investments offer competitive rates of return, and would save over $260 billion in energy costs between now and the year 2010. This new private investment will occur—with some government encouragement— because it makes good economic sense.[48]

Corporations provide money to schools to spend on initiatives of their choosing: new band instruments or a playground, for example. Even though not much money is provided, it is framed as enabling schools— the administrators, teachers, staff, parents, and students—to do things they otherwise would not have the resources to do. Cause marketing provides opportunities for Americans to get involved and to make a difference. But the policy process actually creates large-scale mandatory public programs and it appears bureaucratic: providing rules and regulations to run large organizational systems. The effect is to set parameters, constrain, and appear to say no.

In cause marketing, individuals are part of easy solutions; by contrast, in the policy process, individuals are often part of difficult problems. In effect, by enabling and empowering local communities and consumers to get involved and make a difference, cause marketing tells people that through their actions they are contributing to a solution. But the opposite often occurs in the policymaking process. Public officials look at individual

---

48. See statement of Hazel O'Leary, US Congress, Senate, Committee on Energy and Natural Resources, *Energy Policy Act of 1992 and the President's Climate Change Action Plan*, Second Session, 1994.

behavior as something that must be shaped or changed through education or inducements.

Disease advocacy through cause marketing is common, especially for diseases that affect women and diseases without cures, like breast cancer (fifty-three mentions in the database described earlier in this chapter), heart disease (seventeen mentions), cancer generally (fourteen mentions), and AIDS (eight mentions).[49] But cause marketing provides a way for individuals to make a difference, to be part of the solution. These solutions are *easy*, often entailing actions that individuals take as part of their daily routines.[50]

Yoplait's Save Lids to Save Lives illustrates these types of campaigns (see Figure 4.3). In 2010, Yoplait sponsored its successful campaign on behalf of breast cancer for the thirteenth year. For every specially marked lid that consumers mailed to the company, Yoplait donated ten cents to Komen (up to $1.6 million). The Komen Greater Nashville website explains that "the fight against breast cancer starts right next door. . .. Komen Nashville supporters can impact efforts to help women in our community fighting breast cancer because General Mills is tracking the zip codes from lids redeemed to make sure donations that start here come back to local breast cancer programs in our community."[51] For the Save Lids to Save Lives campaign, consumers need only wash a lid and mail it in. With these small actions, consumers can "help women in our community."

Congress, however, is focused on solving problems by changing individual behavior, asking Americans to do things they may not want to do

49. The remaining diseases (mentioned once in the database described earlier in the chapter unless otherwise indicated) are ovarian cancer (two mentions), obesity/weight loss (two mentions), smoking cessation, stem-cell research, women's health, cystic fibrosis, lung disease, colorectal cancer, pancreatic cancer, prostate cancer, skin cancer, arthritis.

50. See also Varadarajan and Menon, "Cause-Related Marketing"; Angela M. Eikenberry, "The Hidden Costs of Cause Marketing," *Stanford Social Innovation Review*, Summer (2009): 51–55; Patricia Mooney Nickel and Angela M. Eikenberry, "A Critique of the Discourse of Marketized Philanthropy," *American Behavioral Scientist* 52, no. 7 (2009): 974–89.

51. Susan G. Komen, Nashville: http://www.komennashville.org/make-a-donation/yoplait-save-lids-to-save.html, accessed February 16, 2014.

Figure 4.3 **Yoplait's Save Lids to Save Lives.**
SOURCE: Ecouterre: http://www.ecouterre.com.

or may not prioritize doing. It spends the majority of its efforts when it comes to health on the vexing problem of the rising cost of healthcare. On September 26, 2006, the Senate Subcommittee on Healthcare met to examine the benefits of and experience with health savings accounts (HSAs). Witnesses noted that HSAs make patients better consumers of medical services because they share the cost of healthcare services. John Goodman, of the National Center for Policy Analysis, noted: "HSA accounts have the potential to revolutionize the health care system. Yet they will succeed in doing so only if they free patients to perform consumer functions that they have not been hitherto performing: (1) make tradeoffs between health care and other goods and services; (2) become savvy shoppers in the medical marketplace; and (3) become managers of their own care."[52]

When Congress did take up the issue of disease, it focused on stopping the spread of contagious diseases, one of the core functions of government. On January 24, 2007, the Senate Appropriations Subcommittee on Labor, HHS, Education, and Related Agencies examined federal plans for a potential influenza outbreak in light of infected birds and outbreaks abroad. In preparing for the worst-case scenario, the Department of Health and Human Services set goals to stockpile vaccines (for 20 million people) and to provide the vaccine within six months of an outbreak to all US citizens.[53] The federal government's efforts involved investment in research and development of a vaccine, international aid to fight the disease abroad, and coordination (through the Centers for Disease Control) with state and local governments.

Dr. Julie Gerberding, director of the Centers for Disease Control and Prevention, Department of Health and Human Services, described the avian flu as "a very virulent flu. . ... We're talking here about a virus when it does affect people, has a mortality rate of greater than 50 percent . . . people do not have any immunity to the H5 virus, so we have to assume that basically everyone in the world is susceptible."[54] The problem with the vaccine lies not just in its development but in its implementation. For government agencies and government programs, the mass public is often portrayed as the biggest obstacle. Senator Tom Harkin (D-IA) responded to Dr. Gerberding by asking, "Now, I hear you on the radio advising people to get their flu shots . . . but there seems to be some reticence

52. See statement of John C. Goodman, US Congress, Senate, Committee on Finance, Subcommittee on Health Care, *Health Savings Accounts: The Experience So Far*, Second Session, 2006.

53. See US Congress, Senate, Committee on Appropriations Subcommittee on Labor, HHS, Education, and Related Agencies Appropriations, *Pandemic Influenza: Progress Made and Challenges Ahead*, First Session, 2007.

54. Ibid.

among a lot of people in this country at getting their flu shots. . ... I just wonder . . . what we can do besides your urging everyone."[55]

Cause marketing takes diseases for which there are no cures, like breast cancer, and suggests that small individual actions that are often part of routines anyway can make a difference. Americans can help find the cure or spread awareness by buying yogurt and sending in the lid. There are no sanctions or penalties for individuals who do not participate. The policy process, however, tells a story that often points to individual behavior as the problem and asks, like Senator Harkin, how government can fix it.

Cause marketing frames how Americans ought to feel about issues; by contrast, the policy process often addresses how Americans ought to think about them. Scholars who study media and public policy show that how issues are framed affects how individuals think about them, including how changes in issue framing affect support. But cause marketing relies on emotional frames, like hope and gratitude, to foster understanding about issues. Though companies and nonprofits may create an emotional message, Americans participate in and often reinforce that theme.

In the case of defense, proponents of increased spending in the policy process argue that military matters are complex, expensive, and a high priority. They worry that budget cuts will lead to declining quality in the nation's defense. But in cause marketing, a lack of resources is met by telling individuals to be grateful for anything they receive, even an opportunity to participate in initiatives.

A core governmental feature is providing for the common defense of the nation. Over five days in the spring of 1994, the Senate Committee on Armed Services Subcommittee on Military Readiness and Defense Infrastructure met to consider Department of Defense authorization requests. The subcommittee heard testimony from dozens of individuals: various members of the military went on record testifying about the impact of shrinking budgets and proposed base closures on equipment

---

55. Ibid.

and personnel, while the army, navy, and Department of Defense also testified about the military's environmental programs. Senators heard a familiar story in both cases: cutting back the military could endanger America's readiness to defend itself. Lieutenant General Thad A. Wolfe of the air force told the senators:

> [I]n drawing down we must strike the most effective balance between fighting strength and infrastructure. We've worked hard to trim the fat from our organization. If more reductions become necessary, we must continue to look critically at trimming overhead and infrastructure across the Air Force in order to preserve our combat forces.

The effects of such cuts are apparent in systems and equipment where "day-to-day availability is good, but . . . sustaining this level of readiness is not easy and may become increasingly difficult."[56]

Although some of the testimony was about the positive steps the military had taken and would continue to take, most of it focused on the challenges of doing more with fewer resources. Senators heard again and again the difficulties President Clinton's reductions would create and the need to protect (and in some cases expand) resources.

Cause marketing, on the other hand, has focused very little attention (only four campaigns overall) on defense matters, mostly related to soldiers who have returned stateside. These campaigns generate feelings of gratitude among the people who receive the benefits, and they generate norms of gratitude that individuals *ought* to show. Perceived shortcomings are attributed to individuals who do not appreciate what cause-marketing programs attempt to do, *not* to program failure. For example, in 2010 Sears ran a Heroes at Home program in which it partnered

---

56. See statement of Lieutenant General Thad A. Wolfe, US Congress, Senate, Committee on Armed Services, Subcommittee on Military Readiness and Defense Infrastructure, *Department of Defense Authorization for Appropriations for FY95 and the Future Years Defense Program Part 3: Military Readiness and Defense Infrastructure*, Second Session, 1994.

with Rebuilding Together to fix homes of returning soldiers and created a registry for others. During the holiday season, soldiers and veterans received gift cards for purchases at Sears. According to the Heroes at Home Facebook page, more than five hundred homes have been repaired and more than fifty thousand military families have been helped.[57] Companies like Sears get a lot of positive feedback from people who are helped by such programs. One grateful recipient posted this comment on the Heroes at Home Facebook wall:

> Today I was honored and over whelmed by all the people who made a hero at home today. Medic Johnny felt like he won the lottery with everyone pitching in to help him. His expressions when he saw the Sears new appliances are memories I will hold forever. He is an outstanding military vet who truly felt tears of joy today. It was an honor to be part of Sears and the Heroes at Home program.[58]

Unlike Congress, those who talk about the program's shortcomings—sometimes in harsh terms but often with routine complaints—are met with personal attacks. Other recipients and potential recipients police public forums to counter negative comments. On Facebook there are entire discussions about the proper level of appreciation: "I am sorry that there are people out there that have the nerve to be so ungrateful. Honestly they're lucky they were accepted and should be grateful they're getting anything." Even eligible individuals who had not yet received anything talked about being grateful for the opportunity:

> I too am sorry for any negative reactions people seem to be having I have yet to recieve my email but i am not worried. I am not entitled to ANYTHING and appreciate the oppurtunity to even be involved.

57. Sears Heroes at Home Facebook page: http://www.facebook.com/SearsHeroes AtHome? sk= info, accessed June 23, 2011.

58. Sears Heroes at Home Facebook page: http://www.facebook.com/SearsHeroes AtHome? sk= info, accessed June 23, 2011.

If I never get my email i will assume it went to someone that needed it more than i did .... to those that feel the need to complain ... get over yourselves, it is a GIFT, you were entitled to NOTHING from this program and you really need to learn to be thankful for anything and everything you get in life.

One can hardly imagine recipients of federal programs and the beneficiaries of federal regulations using language like the following: "Its embarrassing how some of these people are acting. This is a fantastic and generous program and its not an entitlement."[59] Such comments are routinely answered with "Amen!" or "couldn't have said it better myself!" In the policy process, shortcomings are framed as potentially harmful to the military's mission: defense of the nation. But in cause marketing, shortcomings are framed not as problems with the program or with Sears, but with individuals who do not appreciate what they get. Gratitude is enforced by other members of the community.

Cause marketing focuses on consensus; by contrast, the policy process is often steeped in controversy. Cause marketing defines issues around consensus. Even though issues have many sides and stakeholders have perspectives at odds with one another, cause-marketing stories are usually presented as only good. In promoting this narrative, cause marketing stifles disagreement in ways that the policymaking process does not.

Cause marketers pay close attention to developing countries, where the primary focus is on health, especially that of mothers and babies. Cause marketers ran campaigns for clean water as well as AIDS/tuberculosis/malaria, and tetanus vaccines. To illustrate, in 2008, Pampers ran the 1 Pack = 1 Vaccine marketing campaign. Pampers explained:

For each pack of specially marked Pampers diapers and wipes that you buy during the promotion period, Pampers donates the cost of

59. These comments run throughout the Facebook discussion board. These quotes are taken from a single thread, "im so sorry to all of Sears and the Donors alike," http://www.facebook.com/topic.php?uid=95180737704&topic=14703, accessed June 23, 2011.

one [tetanus] vaccine to UNICEF. It's a small step but it can and does lead to big change. Thanks to parents like you in Western Europe and the United States, the Pampers/UNICEF 1 Pack = 1 Vaccine program has helped provide more than 100 million vaccines [total] that protect moms and babies from maternal and neonatal tetanus.[60]

To promote its efforts, in 2008 the New York advertising giant Saatchi and Saatchi created a commercial for Pampers narrated by actor Selma Hayek. Pampers also flew a number of "mommy bloggers" to New York to introduce them to the campaign. Pampers raised enough money to fund 28 million vaccines. Caryl Stern, president and CEO of the US Fund for UNICEF, explained that "[p]artnerships with organizations such as Pampers have helped us see the number of tetanus-related deaths drop significantly."[61] At roughly seven cents a vaccine, Proctor & Gamble gave an estimated $2 million.[62]

Cause marketing frames issues as having one side, being overwhelmingly positive, and noncontroversial. While it may seem as though only a heartless person would be opposed to childhood vaccinations that save babies' lives, the issue is far more complicated: Are vaccinations effective? If so, why doesn't Pampers give more? Why aren't individual nations or international organizations paying for them? In short, cause marketing makes issues apolitical. But the policy process thrives on controversy—winning or losing is as much about telling a compelling story as it is about implementing institutional changes that favor a particular side.

Policymakers generate controversy and publicly attack one another. On September 6, 2007, the Committee on Foreign Affairs and the Committee on Armed Services held a joint hearing about developments in US policy toward Iraq. Witnesses that day included the former vice chief of staff and

60. Pampers: http://www.pampers.com/en_US/childrens-charities-around-the-world, accessed June 27, 2011.

61. UNICEF, USA: http://www.unicefusa.org/news/releases/pampers-together-with-actress.html, accessed June 27, 2011.

62. UNICEF: http://www.unicef.org/childsurvival/index_45847.html, accessed June 27, 2011.

former commander as well as former defense secretary William Perry. Before a crowded chamber, chairman Tom Lantos (D-CA) did little to hide his own position:

> I expect ... that the September report written ... by administration political operatives, will be a regurgitation of the same failed Iraq strategy. ... The administration won't listen, not to Congress, not to the American people and not to the military and foreign policy experts who have repeatedly told both our committees that the current course in Iraq is failing and failing miserably.[63]

But Republicans on the committee had a different viewpoint about the information in the report (that it should be read before being discredited) and the testimony of military officials. Representative Duncan Hunter (R-CA) noted, "When people come and sit in that witness chair, as our witnesses do today—two distinguished retired generals and one distinguished former Secretary of Defense—their candor and their integrity is their trademark, and that's what makes us effective, being able to elicit testimony from people that have a lot of experience and a lot of insights and know that we're getting their testimony."[64]

In sum, cause marketing generates stories about problems that are very different in general from stories in the policy process. Market stories seek to raise awareness, they enable and empower individuals to be part of the solution, they frame issues in terms of feeling, and they are positive, noncontroversial, and ostensibly apolitical. But these stories do not just encourage particular kinds of consumer behavior (e.g., choosing Tide over All); they also affect elite political behavior and public policy. For all of the general differences between typical cause marketing and

63. See US Congress, House of Representatives, House Foreign Affairs Committee and the House Armed Service Committee, *Beyond the September Report: What's Next for Iraq?*, First Session, 2007.

64. Ibid.

typical policy stories, breast cancer policymaking incorporates many cause-marketing features and symbols.

BREAST CANCER

My analysis, based on a random sample of all cause-marketing issues, shows that cause marketing has distinct features: it emphasizes awareness, enables and empowers individual action, encourages individual solutions, promotes marketable emotions, and focuses on consensus. In this section, I show how the same features characterize the specific case of the breast cancer campaign. It is important to note that many (not all) cause-marketing features are also apparent in breast cancer policymaking. In this case, cause marketing has not been contained in the consumer realm but has bled into the policy process affecting how policymakers talk about issues and the kinds of policies they promote. Breast cancer cause marketing has defined the language around a significant segment of breast cancer policymaking as well as policymaking for other diseases.

As I explained in Chapters 1 and 2, breast cancer was one of the first cause-marketing issues and has become the most successful. Though Komen's founder, Nancy Brinker, had to knock on a lot of doors before corporations would partner with her organization, today directors of breast cancer organizations across the country explain that "business comes to us."[65] Companies partner with nonprofits to create products a portion of the sale of which benefits breast cancer. Though cause-marketing partnerships can be for a single item, often they are part of broader campaigns: Belk department stores runs "Pink Is Our Passion"; Ford motor company has "Pink Warriors"; New Balance "Lace[s] Up for the Cure"; and Sun Chips reminds consumers that "Hope Shines On." Breast cancer cause-marketing campaigns portray the disease with the same core features as other cause-marketing campaigns.

---

65. Interview with representative of a large breast cancer organization, 2009 (no. 091113).

Awareness, not information, is the goal of most breast cancer cause-marketing campaigns. For example, pen and pencil manufacturer Pentel supports awareness through its Pinky Promise products. Pentel, like most breast cancer cause marketers, imbues cause-marketing products with special significance: "These are not just ordinary pens and pencils ... they are pens with meaning and pencils with a purpose." But Pentel provides little concrete information about the amount of the donation, what it will be used for, or anything about breast cancer. Instead, it says that for each Pinky Promise product sold, Pentel donates a portion of the proceeds to the Breast Cancer Research Foundation, because "striving to make the world a healthier, cancer-free place continues to be an important priority for us."[66]

Individuals who buy these products are framed as part of the solution. They can make a difference with a pen or a Brillo pad. According to Jeremy Bakken, a spokesperson for Brillo (maker of steel wool pads): "We're honored to partner with BCRF [Breast Cancer Research Foundation] once again this year to promote breast cancer awareness. ... Brillo offers inexpensive products that many consumers purchase regularly anyway, so this partnership provides consumers with an opportunity to support BCRF by simply purchasing a product they already know and trust."[67] Brillo tells consumers that they can be part of the solution by just doing what they would do anyway. By telling individuals that solving big problems is easy, it decontextualizes, depoliticizes, and makes simple what is otherwise complicated and difficult.

Not only is breast cancer easy to address in the marketplace, taking these actions offers hope. There is little deviation from this emotion. Bra manufacturer Wacoal has worked with Komen since 1999, when it created an "Awareness Bra." In 2001, it created the Fit for the Cure campaign. For every woman who gets fit for a bra, Wacoal will donate $2 to Komen and

66. Pentel: https://www.pentel.com/pink, accessed February 17, 2014.

67. *PR Newswire*: http://www.prnewswire.com/news-releases/brillo-partnership-with-bcrf-enters-into-third-year-174217931.html, accessed March 5, 2014.

an additional $2 for every item purchased. Like most breast cancer cause marketers, Wacoal does not provide information about breast cancer as much as it promotes awareness and sets the stage for how Americans ought to feel about the disease. Although women with breast cancer cannot control the disease, they can master their reaction to it. As part of its Fit for the Cure campaign, for example, participants have the opportunity to have lunch with Hollye Jacobs, author of *The Silver Lining: A Supportive and Insightful Guide to Breast Cancer*. Wacoal frames cancer in a positive way and gives others the opportunity to likewise reflect this positive framing by allowing women to "share [their] silver lining."

Breast cancer cause marketing promotes an understanding of breast cancer as overwhelmingly positive, even as campaigns acknowledge some of the disease's darker statistics. Kohl's, a Wisconsin-based department store, has been a longtime partner of the local Wisconsin Komen affiliate. In 2014, Kohl's launched a national campaign with Komen Dallas. For five days in February, every consumer who spent $50 would receive a $10 pink-cash coupon. For every coupon redeemed between February 18 and March 8, Kohl's donated $1 to Komen. Kohl's goes beyond most corporate cause marketers. It has a website devoted to the "pink elephant" in the room, breast cancer, telling Americans, "Let's not ignore it. Together we can start the conversation about breast cancer." But that conversation conveys little information, and what it does tell is overwhelmingly positive: next to a statistic indicating that the lifetime risk for breast cancer is 1 in 8, Kohl's posts an upbeat quote from a survivor: "Cancer has in some ways been a gift and I am grateful for the journey." Next to the statement that "all women are at risk of breast cancer" it posts another survivor quote: "I was taught by cancer that the people in your life are most important—not your looks or what you have."[68]

Having breast cancer may not feel like a gift, and the complications of the disease may not be a silver lining. Yet breast cancer cause marketing does not address the different ways that Americans may experience

---

68. See also *Psychology Today*: https://www.psychologytoday.com/blog/pink-ribbon-blues/ 201403/kohl-s-cash-the-cure-pretties-breast-cancer, accessed December 8, 2015.

the disease, let alone the controversy associated with broader questions about the marginal benefits of funding more breast cancer research (as opposed to research on AIDS, lung cancer, or other fatal diseases), or suggest equal access to treatment. Instead, breast cancer campaigns take a dreaded disease with no known cure and give Americans the opportunity to do something "by simply purchasing a product they already know and trust." These actions allow them to feel hopeful: to "share their silver lining," to experience "the journey," and to learn lessons about what is important in life.

Breast cancer campaigns extend beyond supermarkets and shopping malls and are integrated into Americans' daily experiences by companies like American Airlines and organizations like Major League Baseball. They permeate American culture, and affect the policy process too.

Looking across issues, the analysis in this chapter shows that cause marketing and the policy process address distinct issues and tell distinct stories about those issues. *Yet breast cancer policymaking disproportionately reflects the features and symbols of breast cancer cause marketing.* To get a sense of what breast cancer policymaking looks like, I searched Proquest Congressional for breast cancer mentions in bills, hearings, and speeches from 1789 to 2014. From the 1,377 items the search returned, I selected the top 100 (sorted by relevance) and coded these items as symbolic, substantive, or both.[69]

In accord with the snapshot of the policymaking process presented earlier in this chapter, Congress spends most (51 percent) of its time on substantive issues related to breast cancer: breast cancer research and treatment, links to the environment, and the impact of the Affordable Care Act. In 1991, the House Committee on Government Operations, Subcommittee on Human Resources and Intergovernmental Relations, held a particularly notable hearing on breast cancer research and treatment. It brought together representatives of emerging breast cancer organizations, as well as government officials from the National Institutes of

69. See Appendix C for more information on methodology.

Health, the National Cancer Institute, and the Government Accounting Office.[70] In 2009, the House Energy and Commerce Committee, Subcommittee on Health, held hearings about a controversial US Task Force Recommendation to eliminate blanket mammograms for women in their 40s. Frank Pallone (D-NJ), chairman of the Subcommittee on Health, opened the hearing by recognizing that "there are a lot of questions, frustration, and confusion around these new recommendations. The controversy that was ignited by the report" pitted evidence-based advocacy groups, like the National Breast Cancer Coalition, against Komen's Advocacy Alliance. Women and medical providers across the country expressed strong opinions about the value of mammograms, doctor recommendations, and the process by which the Task Force came to its recommendations and even the role of the government in making decisions about women's health.

Although the content of congressional hearings is often technical—the number of women with breast cancer, the ability of technology to detect breast cancer and of doctors to use it successfully to decrease breast cancer—a significant portion (one-third) of congressional attention was largely symbolic. For these symbolic actions, Congress appropriated much of the market-based breast cancer language—urging "awareness," not knowledge, and "recognition," not concrete spending initiatives. In these symbolic measures, policymakers often followed the same logic as cause marketers, acknowledging a structural problem but connecting it to individual solutions. Unlike breast cancer cause marketing, however, congressional policymaking did not use emotion to frame the issue, urging cancer survivors to think about the bright side of breast cancer or its positive effects on their lives.

The origins of National Breast Cancer Awareness Month illustrate how Congress addresses breast cancer as a symbolic issue and the role of market mechanisms in shaping congressional discussion. Breast Cancer Awareness

70. US Congress, House Committee on Government Operations, Human Resources and Intergovernmental Relations Subcommittee, *Breast Cancer Research and Treatment: Progress and Failures in the 20-Year War on Breast Cancer*, First Session, 1992.

Month began as a partnership between nonprofits and industry. National Breast Cancer Awareness Week was sponsored by Stuart Pharmaceuticals as early as 1985 and became National Breast Cancer Awareness Month sponsored by the National Alliance of Breast Cancer Organizations, Komen, the American Academy of Family Physicians, ICI Pharmaceuticals, the National Cancer Care Foundation, the American Cancer Society, the American College of Radiology, and the National Cancer Institute by 1989.[71]

At the same time, Congress had been recognizing issues, especially disease, by designating awareness months. Between 1982 and 1994, Congress created roughly three awareness months per year. In October 1990, Congress first added October as National Breast Cancer Awareness Month. The measure that the Senate considered and passed starts with a discussion of a very significant problem (deaths from breast cancer). It even acknowledges that socioeconomic status plays a role in whether women get mammograms. But like cause-marketing stories it moves away from structural solutions to promote individual action:

> Whereas breast cancer will strike an estimated 150,000 women and 900 men in the United States in 1990;
>
> Whereas one out of every ten women will develop breast cancer at some point in her life;
>
> Whereas the risk of developing breast cancer increases as a woman grows older;
>
> Whereas breast cancer is the second leading cause of cancer death in women, killing an estimated 43,000 women and 300 men in 1989;
>
> Whereas the 5-year survival rate for localized breast cancer has risen from 78 percent in the 1940s to over 90 percent today;
>
> Whereas most breast cancers are detected by the woman herself;
>
> Whereas educating both the public and physicians about the importance of early detection will result in reducing breast cancer mortality;

71. *NABCO News*, April 1989, RKP, box 12, file 197.

Whereas appropriate use of screening mammography, in conjunc-
tion with clinical examination and breast self-examination, can
result in the detection of many breast cancers early in their development and increase the survival rate to nearly 100 percent;

Whereas data from controlled trials clearly demonstrate that
deaths from breast cancer are significantly reduced in women
over the age of 40 by using mammography as a screening tool;

Whereas women do not have mammograms for a variety of reasons, such as the cost of testing, lack of information, and fear;

Whereas access to screening mammography is directly related to
socioeconomic status;

Whereas increased awareness about the importance of screening
mammography will result in the procedure being regularly requested by the patient and recommended by the health care
provider; and

Whereas it is projected that more women will use this lifesaving test
as it becomes increasingly available and affordable: Now, therefore, be it Resolved by the Senate and House of Representatives
of the United States of America in Congress assembled, That
October 1990 is designated as "National Breast Cancer Awareness
Month," and the President is authorized and requested to issue
a proclamation calling upon the people of the United States to
observe the month with appropriate programs and activities.[72]

With awareness, mammography will be "regularly requested by the patient and recommended by the health care provider." Congress empowers
the president to "issue a proclamation . . . to observe the month with appropriate programs and activities." Observing Breast Cancer Awareness
Month is the most common way that policymakers address breast cancer
symbolically. Nearly 40 percent of symbolic attention was directed at
Breast Cancer Awareness Month and 20 percent of all breast cancer attention (symbolic and substantive) included awareness. Although breast

72. To designate October 1993 as "National Breast Cancer Awareness Month," S.J. Res.95,
103th Cong., First Session (1993).

cancer was not the first awareness month, it is one of the most highly recognized (five times) and the last disease for which Congress approved an awareness month (October 1994).

Congress engages other symbolic features of cause marketing too. In 1998, it allowed the use of the Capitol grounds for a breast cancer survivors' event sponsored by the National Race for the Cure (Komen). In 2004 it authorized "the Gateway Arch in St. Louis, Missouri, to be illuminated by pink lights in honor of breast cancer awareness month."[73] It recognized the organizations, researchers, and individuals who worked on behalf of breast cancer; for example, a Senate resolution of November 2009 acknowledged "the outstanding achievements and profound impact of Stefanie Spielman in the fight against breast cancer" and celebrated "her life as a wife, mother, and advocate for breast cancer awareness, research, and treatment."[74] In 2013, Congress introduced a bill for a "breast cancer awareness commemorative coin" to be produced by the Treasury.[75] Like the breast cancer stamp created in 1997, the coin would essentially create cause-marketing programs with government products. But while proceeds of the stamp benefit federal agencies (National Institutes of Health and the Department of Defense), the coin would benefit the organizations that created breast cancer cause marketing: the Breast Cancer Research Foundation and Komen.[76]

By way of contrast, a similar search for lung cancer—the most deadly cancer—showed less attention overall (only 211 mentions) and later attention to symbolic aspects. Congressional attention to lung cancer was mostly substantive (60 percent). Only 16 percent of congressional interest

73. A bill to authorize the Gateway Arch in St. Louis, Missouri, to be illuminated by pink lights in honor of breast cancer awareness month, Pub. L. No. 108–348, 118 Stat. 1388 (2004).

74. Honoring the Life and Service of Breast Cancer Advocate, Stefanie Spielman, S. Res. 363, 111th Cong., First Session (2009).

75. Breast Cancer Awareness Commemorative Coin Act, H.R. Res. 3680, 113th Cong., First Session (2013).

76. "Since the modern commemorative coin program began in 1982, the United States Mint has raised more than $418,000,000 in surcharges to help build new museums, maintain national monuments like the Vietnam War Memorial, preserve historical sites like George Washington's home, support various Olympic programs, and much more." US Mint: https://www.usmint.gov/mint_programs/?action=commemoratives, accessed November 22, 2015.

was focused solely on symbolic aspects of lung cancer, and this occurred overwhelmingly *after* 2003. Early hearings on lung cancer, unlike those on breast cancer, focused exclusively on controversial public health measures: the relationship between radiation, mining, smoking, radon, and lung cancer and the government's responsibility for populations with the disease, such as veterans. Unlike early "awareness" breast cancer programs, early "awareness" lung cancer programs were directed not at awareness of lung cancer but at illuminating its causes. The federal government sought to increase awareness about the harms of radon in homes and schools (mid-1980s to early 1990s) and imposed mandatory cigarette labeling/advertising restrictions on tobacco (1970s). However, lung cancer activists started to sound a lot more like breast cancer activists in the early to middle 2000s. They pushed for greater symbolic measures for lung cancer, including recognizing individuals and organizations that worked on behalf of the disease (two of sixteen symbolic mentions) and creating Lung Cancer Awareness Month (thirteen of sixteen mentions).

In November 2003, the Senate introduced a bill to recognize November as Lung Cancer Awareness Month. Like the 1990 bill to recognize October as Breast Cancer Awareness Month, the bill for lung cancer also began with statistics about the incidence and mortality of this form of cancer:

> Whereas lung cancer is the leading cancer killer of both men and women;
> Whereas the National Institutes of Health predict that there will be 171,900 new lung cancer cases in 2003, an estimated 157,200 deaths due to lung cancer in 2003;[77]

The bill starts by implicitly comparing lung cancer, "the leading cancer killer of *both* men and women," with breast cancer (disproportionately affecting women) and prostate cancer (affecting men). Unlike the bill on behalf of breast cancer, however, the lung cancer bill continues by explicitly comparing it with *other* forms of cancer. It stresses that lung cancer

---

77. Recognizing November as National Lung Cancer Awareness Month and expressing the sense of Congress that Federal efforts need to increase in the areas of lung cancer screening and research, H.Con.Res. 322, 108th Cong., First Session (2003).

is more deadly than other cancers while at the same time it is funded at lower levels:

> Whereas lung cancer kills more people annually than breast, prostate and colorectal cancer combined;
>
> Whereas per person, Federal research funding for breast cancer ($11,500) is almost 10 times more than research funding for lung cancer; research funding for prostate cancer ($8,000) is almost 7 times more than research funding for lung cancer; and research funding for colorectal cancer ($3,300) is almost twice as much as research funding for lung cancer;

The language of the bill reflects lung cancer activists' late arrival to the symbolic politics of disease that breast cancer created. In addition to Breast Cancer Awareness Month in 1990, Congress considered bills to recognize March as Colorectal Cancer Awareness Month in 1999 and September as Prostate Cancer Awareness Month in 2001.

Congress has long engaged in symbolic action around issues. What is important in the study of breast cancer is not only that Congress takes a lot of symbolic action, but that the words and symbols map neatly onto existing market-based frames: like breast cancer cause marketing (and unlike lung cancer), one-half of congressional symbolic attention to breast cancer was focused on "awareness"; like breast cancer cause marketing, which promotes October as National Breast Cancer Awareness Month, 31 percent of congressional attention took place in October; and like breast cancer cause marketing that brands the disease as pink (even though the original breast cancer ribbon color was peach—Komen, Estée Lauder, and *Self* magazine promoted pink when they could not get the rights to the peach ribbon), Congress authorized symbolic attention specifying the color pink. Congress even created a cause-marketing program within the federal government (US Postal Service) and considered another that would benefit the nonprofits that pioneered breast cancer cause marketing.

Congress uses symbolic language more often to talk about breast cancer than lung cancer, and it used symbolic language for breast cancer much earlier than for lung cancer, prostate cancer, or colorectal cancer. Eventually, however, it adopted the same awareness language to talk about these forms of cancer too.

CONCLUSION

Corporations and individuals with corporate backgrounds exercise enormous influence, shaping how Americans think and feel about issues (Chapter 5) and how the policy process addresses them (Chapter 6). They exercise influence not by lobbying Congress or federal agencies, but by telling stories about issues. These stories are a reflection of the process that creates them. Cause marketing does not seek to convey information, to mediate between competing sides, or to invest significant and sustained resources to address problems. Instead, industry uses cause marketing to sell products and boost brand loyalty.[78] As a result, market processes tell stories about tractable problems that can be easily solved. They give Americans the opportunity to make a difference and feel good when they do.

But these stories do not stay contained in supermarkets and shopping malls. Cause-marketing framing bleeds into congressional action, increasing the number of symbolic initiatives and changing the language and symbols that policymakers use. In the case of breast cancer, the emphasis on awareness, October, and the color pink became a part of congressional attention and even public policy. These frames and symbols were then adopted by *other* disease advocates, multiplying the effect they have on how policymakers address or fail to address problems and policy solutions.

---

78. Wymer and Sargeant, "Insights from a Review of the Literature on Cause Marketing."

5

Effects

Cause-marketing stories differ from stories generated and told in the policymaking process: they emphasize awareness over information, they promote individual over collective solutions, they enable and empower individuals, they frame issues around marketable emotions (like hope), and they are consensual, positive, and seemingly apolitical. Americans' understanding of breast cancer reflects the stories that cause marketing tells. Americans demonstrate awareness of the symbolic aspects of breast cancer, such as October is National Breast Cancer Awareness Month and pink ribbons are its symbol. Yet greater awareness leads neither to greater knowledge about the specifics of the disease nor to a desire for collective solutions from government or industry officials. Instead, cause marketing enables individual solutions and makes people who participate feel good about what they do.

Cause marketing frames how Americans understand breast cancer, but the stories it tells and the effects it has are different from framing through more traditional avenues, like the media. Media attention shapes what issues Americans see as important.[1] Media coverage of issues, even

---

1. Roy L. Behr and Shanto Iyengar, "Television News, Real-World Cues, and Changes in the Public Agenda," *Public Opinion Quarterly* 49, no. 1 (1985): 38–57; Shanto Iyengar and Donald R. Kinder, *News That Matters* (Chicago: University of Chicago Press, 1987); Shanto Iyengar, Mark D. Peters, and Donald R. Kinder, "Experimental Demonstrations of the 'Not-So-Minimal' Consequences of Television News Programs," *American Political Science*

when not connected to politics, can prime citizens to use their evaluations of those issues in assessing government and government officials.[2]
Depending on how issues are framed, media attention can also change
how citizens understand them.[3] Though scholarly studies look at formal
media sources (especially newspapers), citizens receive messages about
issues from a far broader range of sources,[4] including cause marketing.
But cause-marketing stories are fundamentally different from media stories: they present complex issues in a cursory, symbolic way that is devoid
of controversy to a greater degree even than political campaigns do. Thus,
even though cause marketing is prevalent and Americans see it and remember it, unlike exposure to media stories it does not lead to greater
issue salience.

Understanding the effect of cause marketing is complicated, and
I employ three strategies to figure it out. First, I look at the effect of a
real-world campaign. I compared the differences between the answers
survey respondents gave in September with those respondents gave in

Review 76, no. 4 (1982): 848–58; Maxwell McCombs and Donald Shaw, "The Agenda-Setting
Function of the Mass Media," *Public Opinion Quarterly* 36, no. 2 (1972): 176–87.

2. Iyengar and Kinder, *News That Matters*; Nicholas Valentino, "Crime News and the
Priming of Racial Attitudes During Evaluations of the President," *Public Opinion Quarterly*
63, no. 3 (1999): 293–320; Jon A. Krosnick and Donald R. Kinder, "Altering the Foundations
of Support for the President Through Priming," *American Political Science Review* 84, no. 2
(1990): 497–512. Gabriel Lenz shows that Americans' policy opinions often *follow* rather than
lead politicians. See his *Follow the Leader? How Voters Respond to Politicians' Policies and
Performance* (Chicago: University of Chicago Press, 2012).

3. William A. Gamson and Andre Modigliani, "Media Discourse and Public Opinion on
Nuclear Power: A Constructionist Approach," *American Journal of Sociology* 95, no. 1
(1989): 1–37; Franklin D. Gilliam, Jr., and Shanto Iyengar, "Prime Suspects: The Influence
of Local Television News on the Viewing Public," *American Journal of Political Science* 44,
no. 3 (2000): 560–73; Daron R. Shaw and Bartholomew H. Sparrow, "From the Inner Ring
Out: News Congruence, Cue-Taking, and Campaign Coverage," *Political Research Quarterly*
52 (1999): 323–51.

4. Katherine Cramer Walsh, *Talking about Politics: Informal Groups and Social Identity
in American Life* (Chicago: University of Chicago Press, 2003); Samuel Lewis Popkin, *The
Reasoning Voter* (Chicago: University of Chicago Press, 1991); Matthew A. Baum, "Sex, Lies,
and War: How Soft News Brings Foreign Policy to the Inattentive Public," *American Political
Science Review* 96, no. 1 (2002): 91–109.

October. October is National Breast Cancer Awareness Month, when companies roll out pink versions of their products, when nonprofits put on sponsored fundraising walks or runs, and when the media report about breast cancer. For the campaign to have an effect, people have to be aware of it—see it, remember it, or participate in it. If cause marketing has an effect, there ought to be differences between answers given in September and in October. Looking at blunt differences between months, however, fails to capture the effect of cause marketing (in contrast to walks or races or news stories) and fails to control for all of the confounding factors that might play a role, like age, race, and socioeconomic status. The CCS asked the sample of 1,500 adults (750 in September and 750 in October) if, in the past week, they had seen products that benefit breast cancer research, walks or races or runs in support of breast cancer research, or stories about breast cancer. In addition to comparing September and October responses, I use more nuanced models across both months that include explanatory variables about exposure to cause marketing, walks or races, and news stories about breast cancer. I compare the results for cause marketing with the results for walks or races and news stories. Finally, I compare the effect of cause marketing by motivation. In Chapter 3, I introduced three types of cause-marketing participators: *lifestyle buyers*, who are committed to making a difference through consumption; *cause followers*, who believe in the cause the product supports; and *accidental activists*, who purchase a product regardless of the cause it supports. While it is difficult to untangle causality for lifestyle buyers and cause followers—do their ideological beliefs and practical commitments come from participation in cause marketing or precede it?—the accidental activists have no prior commitments. They participate unintentionally. Comparing this group with the two others (plus nonparticipators) suggests the impact that campaigns have.

In all three of these strategies, the conclusion remains the same: cause marketing leads Americans to think about breast cancer in ways consistent with the stories that it tells. It increases awareness but not information or collective demands for government or industry officials to do more. Instead, breast cancer cause marketing enables and empowers individuals to make a difference and feel good when they do.

AWARENESS OVER INFORMATION

Cause marketing is ubiquitous, and breast cancer is the most common issue addressed through this mechanism (Chapter 3). But cause marketing tells a particular type of story, which emphasizes awareness over information (Chapter 4). Because cause marketing takes place in advertising and is often visible on consumer packaged goods, messages are short and symbolic. For example, during the month of October, Campbell Soup Company creates pink versions of its iconic soup can and places them in supermarkets across the country. The back of the can reads: "Your purchase of this can will help Campbell make a donation in support of breast cancer awareness. *Together we can make a difference.*" Campbell raises awareness of the disease but does not provide information about it.

Breast Cancer Awareness Month in October showers attention on this particular issue. Consistent with the extent of marketing, Americans take notice. Compared with individuals in September, those in October reported seeing significantly more (18 points) cause marketing for breast cancer, more (17 points) breast cancer walks and runs, and more (20 points) media stories about breast cancer. Not only did Americans see and register the increased attention to breast cancer, they also reported buying more breast cancer cause-marketing products. Compared with those in September, October respondents reported more (14 points) pink purchases.

The effect of this overwhelming attention to breast cancer in October is to raise awareness of the disease. Americans in October more often (37 points) knew that October is National Breast Cancer Awareness Month than did those in September. Americans did not, however, identify pink ribbons as the symbol of breast cancer more often in October than they did in September, but there is extraordinarily high familiarity with this fact to begin with. Shockingly, 82 percent of Americans know that pink

ribbons are the symbol of breast cancer—more than know standard political facts like Joe Biden is vice president (66 percent), consumer culture
facts like Yoplait produces yogurt (77 percent), or even cause-marketing
campaigns that are not promoted to the same degree, such as yellow ribbons indicate support for American troops (57 percent).

Though Breast Cancer Awareness Month raises attention overall, the
effect is greatest for Americans who are not ideologically committed to
either market mechanisms or breast cancer (see Table 5.1). The overwhelming attention to breast cancer has the greatest impact on accidental activists, who were introduced to a cause (breast cancer) and a means (cause
marketing) to which they were not already committed. Accidental activists were more aware of breast cancer in October than September: they saw
more pink products (22 points), more pink walks (19 points), and more
pink stories (27 points). Conversely, Breast Cancer Awareness Month has
the least impact on lifestyle buyers, who are often already aware of the
issue and opportunities to be involved with it. Lifestyle buyers did not see
more pink products or pink stories in October than in September, though
they did see more pink walks (17 points).

Although Breast Cancer Awareness Month had the greatest impact on
the *awareness* of accidental activists, it had the largest effect on the *behavior* of cause followers, who reported purchasing significantly more pink
products in October than September (16 points).

Yet, while these high-visibility campaigns raise awareness, they do
not inform. Consistent with the cursory nature of information provided,
the heightened awareness generated by Breast Cancer Awareness Month
translates into awareness of the cause rather than knowledge of the disease
or solutions to it. Compared with those in September, people in October
did not more often correctly identify a woman's lifetime risk of breast
cancer or the sources of funding for breast cancer research. Figure 5.1
shows that nearly equal proportions of individuals in September (gray)
and October (black) know a woman's risk of being diagnosed with breast
cancer and nearly equal proportions in September and October know who
funds breast cancer research. Regardless of whether a respondent was a lifestyle buyer, cause follower, accidental activist, or opted out of participating

Table 5.1 AMERICANS ARE MORE AWARE OF BREAST CANCER DURING BREAST CANCER AWARENESS MONTH (OCTOBER)

	See Pink Products			See Pink Walks			See Pink Stories			Buy Pink Products			Know Breast Cancer Awareness Month			Know Pink Ribbons		
	Sep	Oct	Diff	Sep	Oct	Diff	Sep	Oct	Diff	Sep	Oct	Diff	Sep	Oct	Diff	Sep	Oct	Diff
All Respondents	0.54	0.72	0.18***	0.38	0.55	0.17***	0.51	0.71	0.20***	0.23	0.37	0.14***	0.18	0.54	0.37***	0.82	0.83	0.01
Lifestyle Buyers	0.63	0.68	0.04	0.43	0.60	0.17+	0.61	0.74	0.12	0.30	0.35	0.06	0.35	0.62	0.27**	0.88	0.90	0.01
Cause Followers	0.69	0.87	0.18**	0.47	0.62	0.15*	0.57	0.77	0.20**	0.31	0.47	0.16*	0.24	0.63	0.39***	0.93	0.91	−0.02
Accidental Activists	0.57	0.79	0.22***	0.41	0.60	0.19**	0.47	0.74	0.27***	0.28	0.40	0.12+	0.14	0.56	0.42***	0.90	0.87	−0.02
Nonparticipators	0.39	0.61	0.22***	0.29	0.46	0.17**	0.46	0.64	0.20***	—	—	—	0.09	0.46	0.36***	0.68	0.73	0.04

+ $p < .10$, * $p < .05$, ** $p < .01$, *** $p < .001$.

QUESTION WORDING: Now, focusing on just the last week have you seen: Pink products, a portion of the sale of which supports breast cancer research; Walks, races, or runs in support of breast cancer research; Stories about breast cancer. In the past week, have you purchased a product in the supermarket, shopping mall, large general retail stores or on the internet where a portion of the proceeds benefits breast cancer research? When is "National Breast Cancer Awareness Month"? (Correct answer: October) Many people put ribbons on their cars or wear them on their clothes in order to show their support for a social or political issue. Can you tell me what causes the following ribbons stand for . . . Pink ribbon? (Correct answer: Breast cancer).

SOURCE: CCS data. See Appendices C and D for more information. Difference of means for independently weighted samples for September (control) and October (Breast Cancer Awareness Month).

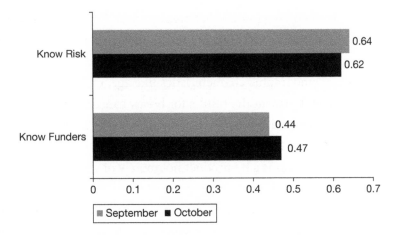

Figure 5.1 Americans do not have more information about breast cancer in October.
Difference of means for independently weighted samples September (control) and October (National Breast Cancer Awareness Month).
QUESTION WORDING: *Which of the following best describes a woman's risk of breast cancer? 1 in 2 women will be diagnosed with breast cancer, 1 in 8 women will be diagnosed with breast cancer, 1 in 25 women will be diagnosed with breast cancer (Correct answer: 1 in 8). Which of the following organizations does NOT fund breast cancer research? National Institutes of Health, Susan G. Komen for the Cure, Health Resources and Services Administration (Correct answer: Health Resources and Services Administration).*
SOURCE: CCS data, weighted proportions. For more information, see Appendices C and D.

altogether, individuals did not have more information in October than in September.

Although comparing September with October (Breast Cancer Awareness Month) provides an opportunity to see the effect of a real-world campaign, a simple comparison between months cannot isolate the effect of cause marketing. To do that, I employed more developed logistic regression models that compare those individuals who report exposure to breast cancer campaigns (across both months) with those who do not. The survey asked respondents if they had seen products, walks or runs, or media stories about breast cancer. I use responses to these questions to examine the independent effect of different kinds of attention to breast cancer. For example, does cause marketing have a different effect than media? Because other characteristics—such as being the primary shopper in a household or having a close family member with breast cancer—might also account for knowing more about breast cancer, I created models that control for the month of October, political knowledge, responsibility for household purchases, personal connection to breast cancer, as well as standard sociodemographic characteristics like age, race, gender, education, and income. I present the results for breast cancer cause marketing here and note when the results are different for walks or runs or media stories. Full results of this model can be found in Appendix B.

I find that awareness is a by-product not merely of greater attention to breast cancer across all sources during Breast Cancer Awareness Month, but of cause marketing specifically. Figure 5.2 shows the predicted probabilities generated from logistic regression models evaluating the effect

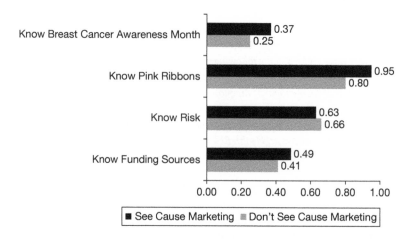

Figure 5.2 Cause-marketing campaigns lead to more breast cancer awareness than to substantive issue information.
Predicted probabilities generated from logistic regression models in Appendix B, Tables B5.1 and B5.2.

QUESTION WORDING: *When is "National Breast Cancer Awareness Month"? (Correct answer: October). Many people put ribbons on their cars or wear them on their clothes in order to show their support for a social or political issue. Can you tell me what causes the following ribbons stand for . . . Pink ribbon? (Correct answer: Breast cancer). Which of the following best describes a woman's risk of breast cancer? 1 in 2 women will be diagnosed with breast cancer, 1 in 8 women will be diagnosed with breast cancer, 1 in 25 women will be diagnosed with breast cancer (Correct answer: 1 in 8). Which of the following organizations does NOT fund breast cancer research? National Institutes of Health, Susan G. Komen for the Cure, Health Resources and Services Administration (Correct answer: Health Resources and Services Administration).*

SOURCE: CCS data weighted. For more information, see Appendices B, C, and D.

of cause marketing on awareness, specifically October as National Breast Cancer Awareness Month and pink ribbons as the symbol of breast cancer (full results in Appendix B, Table B5.1). The black bars represent individuals who report seeing cause marketing and the gray bars individuals who do not. Americans who see cause marketing are both more likely to know that October is Breast Cancer Awareness Month and more likely to know that pink ribbons are the symbol of breast cancer.

Thirty-seven percent of individuals who have seen pink products will likely know that October is Breast Cancer Awareness Month, compared with 25 percent of individuals who have not. Even though the comparison between months does not indicate any difference in knowledge about the pink ribbon, the predicted probabilities show that there is an effect for exposure to breast cancer cause marketing. An astounding 95 percent of individuals exposed to cause marketing will likely identify the pink ribbon as the symbol of breast cancer, compared with 80 percent (still a large number) of Americans who will not. *Only cause marketing has an impact on awareness of pink ribbons.* I did not find similar significant results for the effect of exposure to walks or races or media stories.

Though Americans exposed to cause marketing are more likely to be aware of breast cancer, they are no more likely to know a woman's lifetime risk of breast cancer. Sixty-three percent of Americans who have seen cause marketing are likely to know a woman's risk of breast cancer, compared with (statistically insignificant) 66 percent who have not.

Americans who see pink products, however, are more likely to correctly identify funding sources; 49 percent of individuals who have seen pink products are likely to identify correctly breast cancer research funders, compared with 41 percent who have not (full results in Appendix B, Table B5.2). Once again, *these results are only for Americans exposed to cause marketing and do not hold for those who saw walks or runs or who read media stories for which there was no statistical difference.*

The educational effect of cause marketing on Americans' knowledge about breast cancer funding, however, makes it more likely that individuals will know that Komen is a source of funding than will know that the National Institutes of Health is a funding source; in fact, NIH is the single largest funder of breast cancer research in the United States. The CCS asked Americans, Which of the following organizations does NOT fund breast cancer research? It then gave three possible answers: 45 percent of respondents correctly identified the Health Resources and Services Administration as the organization that does not fund breast cancer research, 41 percent volunteered they did not know or refused to answer, 10 percent misidentified the National Institutes of Health, while only 4 percent misidentified Komen (Figure 5.3). Americans who saw breast cancer cause marketing misidentified the NIH as an organization that does not fund research as often as those who did not see cause marketing. But they misidentified Komen less often than those who did not.

In short, cause marketing educates people in ways consistent with the stories it tells. It generates awareness but not information. Americans exposed to cause marketing were no more likely to know a woman's lifetime risk of breast cancer than those who were not exposed. And though Americans exposed to cause marketing more often correctly identified funding sources, this was due to increased familiarity with cause-marketing giant Komen, not the federal government.

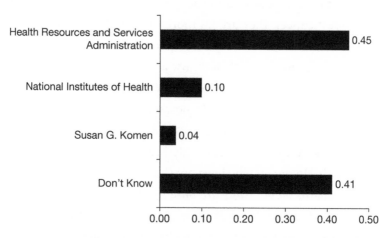

Figure 5.3 **Which organization does not fund breast cancer research? Americans incorrectly identified the National Institutes of Health more often than Komen. Correct answer: Health Resources and Services Administration.**
QUESTION WORDING: *Which of the following organizations does **NOT** fund breast cancer research? 1. National Institutes of Health; 2. Susan G. Komen for the Cure; 3. Health Resources and Services Administration.*
SOURCE: CCS data, weighted proportions. See Appendices C and D for more information.

INDIVIDUAL OVER COLLECTIVE SOLUTIONS

If the Breast Cancer Awareness campaign generally, and cause marketing specifically, do not lead to greater knowledge about the disease,
they also do not lead Americans to think breast cancer is a more important problem than other diseases. They do not lead to collective
grievances and demands for change from either government or industry officials.

Awareness does not translate into greater political importance. The CCS
asked about the relative importance of breast cancer and whether government ought to be doing more for research and treatment. But, as Table
5.2 shows, there are no significant differences between responses given
in September and in October. Greater awareness did not spur people in
October to change their views about breast cancer's place on the national

Table 5.2 BREAST CANCER AWARENESS DOES NOT PROMOTE COLLECTIVE
GOVERNMENTAL SOLUTIONS

	September	October	Difference	*p*-value
Breast Cancer Top Disease Priority	0.21	0.23	0.03	0.337
Government Should Do More Research	0.43	0.40	−0.03	0.362
Government Should Do More Treatment	0.41	0.43	0.03	0.395
Business Should Do More Research	0.23	0.28	0.05	0.058
Business Should Do More Treatment	0.30	0.27	0.03	0.353

QUESTION WORDING: *The federal government spends money every year on research
and education for a variety of diseases. Knowing that there are limited funds available,
which of the following should be the federal government's top priority? Breast cancer,
Diabetes, Heart disease; Many different organizations spend time working on the
problems associated with breast cancer. In your opinion, which of the following should
spend the most on scientific research? The Federal government, Private corporations,
Charitable Organizations; And in your opinion which of the following should spend
the most time and money on breast cancer treatment and support? The Federal
government, Private corporations, Charitable Organizations.*

SOURCE: 2010 CCS data. See Appendices C and D for more information. Difference of
means for independently weighted samples September (control) and October (Breast
Cancer Awareness Month). Values rounded.

agenda or the government's role in ameliorating problems associated with the disease. Roughly 20 percent of Americans in both September and October thought breast cancer should be a top disease priority. Roughly 40 percent in both September and October thought government should do more research and more for treatment.

When they did indicate that an actor ought to do more, individuals suggested business should play a bigger role in research. While 23 percent of Americans in September thought that business should do more for research, 28 percent in October thought that business should do more for research. But these results are only marginally significant and disappear in regression models (as discussed later). Roughly 30 percent thought that business ought to do more for treatment in both months.

A comparison between September and October shows that greater awareness in October did not lead Americans to demand collective solutions to the problems associated with breast cancer from officials in either government or industry. But the information people acquire during Breast Cancer Awareness Month has many different sources: Does cause marketing, in particular, have an effect? Using logistic regression once again, I asked whether exposure to cause marketing led respondents to change their ranking of breast cancer relative to heart disease and diabetes (full results in Appendix B, Table B5.3). Figure 5.4 graphs the predicted probabilities and shows statistically similar results.

Cause marketing does not influence how individuals prioritize breast cancer relative to other diseases, but media stories do. Nearly equal proportions of Americans who saw cause marketing (0.20) and those who did not (0.19) are likely to identify breast cancer as a top priority. But Americans who read or watched media stories about breast cancer are more likely to rank the disease as a top priority. Twenty-two percent of Americans who reported watching or reading media stories are likely to rank breast cancer as the top disease priority, in contrast to 16 percent who did not.

Scholars have shown that media stories influence what issues Americans think are important, and I replicate these results for breast

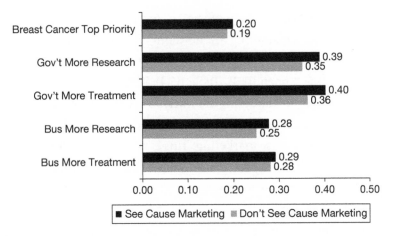

Figure 5.4 **Cause marketing does not motivate Americans to push for additional solutions.**
Predicted probabilities generated from logistic regression models in Appendix B, Tables B5.3, B5.4, B5.5.
QUESTION WORDING: *The federal government spends money every year on research and education for a variety of diseases. Knowing that there are limited funds available, which of the following should be the federal government's top priority? Breast cancer; Diabetes; Heart disease. Many different organizations spend time working on the problems associated with breast cancer. In your opinion, which of the following should spend the most on scientific research? The Federal government; Private corporations; Charitable Organizations. And in your opinion which of the following should spend the most time and money on breast cancer treatment and support? The Federal government; Private corporations; Charitable Organizations.*
SOURCE: CCS data weighted. For more information, see Appendices B, C, and D.

cancer stories.[5] But cause marketing does not have the same effect, suggesting that the mechanism that drives agenda status is not merely attention in any form, but a particular type of attention that media sources give issues. The agenda-setting function that scholars have discussed is specific to media and the way these sources tell stories.

If cause marketing did not enhance the salience of breast cancer relative to other diseases, it also did not spur Americans to demand collective

---

5. Iyengar, Peters, and Kinder, "Experimental Demonstrations"; McCombs and Shaw, "The Agenda-Setting Function of the Mass Media"; Behr and Iyengar, "Television News, Real-World Cues, and Changes in the Public Agenda"; Iyengar and Kinder, *News That Matters*.

solutions for breast cancer from officials. Americans who were exposed to breast cancer cause marketing are no more likely to report that government should do more for research or treatment on this disease than those who were not (see Appendix B, Table B5.4). Thirty-nine percent of individuals who see cause marketing are likely to say that government should do more for research, compared with (statistically insignificant) 35 percent who do not see cause marketing. This is not an artifact of the type of action that individuals expect government to take, because there are no differences when it comes to treatment either. Forty percent of individuals exposed to cause marketing are likely to think government should do more for treatment, compared with (statistically insignificant) 36 percent who did not see cause marketing. Taken together, these numbers suggest that the marketing does not inspire any significant call for greater governmental action or investment, either for research or for treatment.

If awareness does not lead to a higher spot for breast cancer on the national agenda or a desire for government to take action, it also does not lead to greater demands on industry (see Appendix B, Table B5.5). Twenty-eight percent of Americans exposed to cause marketing are likely to think business should do more for research compared with (statistically insignificant) 25 percent who are not. Twenty-nine percent of Americans exposed to cause marketing are likely to think business should do more for treatment compared with 28 percent who are not. Instead, the important predictor of whether or not individuals report that government or business should do more for breast cancer research and treatment is a respondent's faith in government or business.

In sum, Breast Cancer Awareness Month and cause marketing generate awareness, but that awareness does not translate into collective solutions. Cause marketing does not encourage Americans to place greater importance on breast cancer (as news stories do) or to consider it a problem that government or business ought to do more about.

ENABLING AND EMPOWERING INDIVIDUALS

Instead, cause marketing enables and empowers individual action. Americans believe that socially responsible purchasing can make a difference. In fact, more Americans think that purchasing has an effect than think that getting involved in the policy process does. While 58 percent of Americans report that buying products can have an effect on companies' behavior, only 44 percent of Americans believe that contacting a government official has an effect on policy.[6]

Not only do Americans think that cause marketing has an impact, it actually does have individual-level effects. Using logistic regression, I created a model to examine the perceived impact of socially responsible purchasing. If cause marketing has an effect, there ought to be a difference between what people who participate in it think it does and what people who do not participate in it think. Clearly, motivation to participate is tied up with perceived effect: usually, people do not engage in action if they do not believe something will come of it, whether the impact is political, social, or personal. But accidental activists do. They engage in an action without intent to participate. If participating in cause marketing has an effect (rather than some other preexisting characteristic), we ought to see it in this key group. My model uses motivation for cause-marketing purchases (lifestyle buyer, cause follower, or accidental activist) as the key explanatory variable but also controls for other characteristics that might be related to views about impact such as knowledge, responsibility for household purchases, efficacy, charitable activities, confidence in business and government, and personal connection to breast cancer, as well as standard sociodemographic characteristics like age, race, gender, education, and income (full results in Appendix B, Table B5.6).

I find that people who participate in cause marketing are more likely to say that purchasing makes a difference than those who do not. Figure 5.5 graphs the predicted probabilities from the logistic regression models. More than two-thirds of lifestyle buyers and cause followers are likely to believe that individual consumer action has an impact on what corporate

6. Question wording: *Please tell me if you agree or disagree with the following statements.* (a)   *When an individual contacts an elected official it has an effect on government policy; . . . (e) When an individual buys something because he or she agrees with the political or social values of the company that produces it, it has an effect on companies' behavior.*

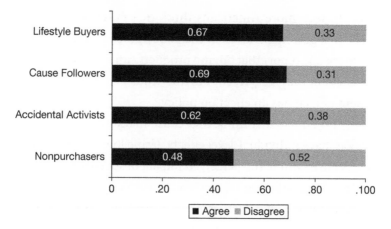

Figure 5.5 People who participate in cause marketing are more likely to believe socially responsible purchasing changes companies' behavior.
Predicted probabilities generated from logistic regression models in Appendix B, Table B5.6.
QUESTION WORDING: *Please tell me if you agree or disagree with the following statements ... When an individual buys something because he or she agrees with the political or social values of the company that produces it, it has an effect on companies' behavior.*
SOURCE: CCS data weighted. See Appendices B, C, and D for more information.

actors do. More important, more than 60 percent of accidental activists are also likely to believe that individual consumer action has an impact on what corporate actors do, compared with just half of the nonpurchasers. These results are statistically significant.

Not only do Americans think that socially responsible purchasing changes corporate behavior, they also believe that it has individual psychological benefits. Nearly three-quarters of the survey respondents said that when individuals purchase something because of their social or political values, it has an effect on their personal satisfaction. Creating a logistic regression model similar to the one described earlier, I evaluated the effect of socially responsible purchases on perceptions of individual satisfaction (full results in Appendix B, Table B5.6). I found that cause followers and accidental activists (though not lifestyle buyers) are more likely than nonpurchasers to say purchasing feels good. Figure 5.6 graphs the predicted probabilities. Eighty-two percent of cause followers

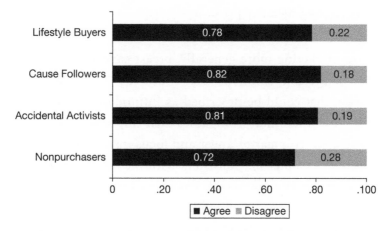

Figure 5.6 **Americans are likely to believe socially responsible purchasing benefits personal satisfaction.**
Predicted probabilities generated from logistic regression models in Appendix B, Table B5.6.
QUESTION WORDING: *Please tell me if you agree or disagree with the following statement. When an individual buys something because he or she agrees with the political or social values of the company that produces it, it has an effect on an individual's personal satisfaction.*
SOURCE: CCS data weighted. See Appendices B, C and D for more information.

and 81 percent of accidental activists were likely to agree that purchasing a product has an effect on an individual's satisfaction, compared with 72 percent of nonpurchasers. Lifestyle buyers—who act ideologically—are statistically no more likely than nonpurchasers to say these purchases feel good.

Cause marketing raises awareness but leads Americans neither to place greater importance on breast cancer nor to think that government or industry ought to be doing more for it. Instead, it enables and empowers individual action: Americans believe that consumer purchases have an effect on companies' behavior, and they think it has an effect on personal satisfaction. *But people who purchase products are more likely to think they make a difference, even accidental activists, who are not participating with intent.* In short, cause marketing has an impact on how Americans think and feel about breast cancer—but that effect is built around breast cancer largely as a consensual social issue, not a conflictual political one.

PROMOTING MARKETABLE EMOTIONS

Like cause marketing more generally, breast cancer cause marketing promotes marketable emotions. While breast cancer is a potentially fatal disease that could be described as intimidating, overwhelming, scary, harmful, and unfair, companies turn emphasis away from emotions associated with fear or anger and focus instead on hope and the "silver lining" (Chapter 4). Consistent with the messages of indidividual empowerment and marketable emotions, breast cancer cause marketing makes Americans feel good. The CCS asked individuals who purchased breast cancer cause-marketing products specifically about how it makes them feel. Two-thirds said that buying products that benefit breast cancer makes them feel good, one-third said it made no difference, and only 2 percent said it made them feel uncomfortable (Figure 5.7).

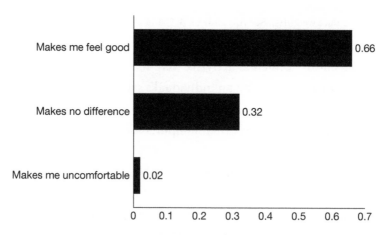

Figure 5.7 **Purchasing a product that benefits breast cancer research makes Americans feel good.**
$N = 451$.
QUESTION WORDING: *In the past week, have you purchased a product in the supermarket, shopping mall, large general retail stores or on the internet where a portion of the proceeds benefits breast cancer research? If yes, Did purchasing this product, Make you feel good, Make you feel uncomfortable, Make no difference?*
SOURCE: CCS data, weighted proportions. See Appendices C and D for more information.

The overwhelming positive emotional response is striking. Breaking it down by motivation, I find that cause followers feel the greatest effect: nearly 80 percent say it makes them feel good. And two-thirds of lifestyle buyers say buying pink products makes them feel good too. But, remarkably, buying pink products *has an effect even for accidental activists*. Figure 5.8 graphs these results.

Although we might expect lifestyle buyers to feel good about what they do because they are committed to making a difference through consumption or cause followers to feel good about what they do because they are committed to supporting breast cancer, I would expect accidental activists—who are not committed to cause marketing or to the breast cancer campaign—to say it makes no difference or even claim that it makes them uncomfortable. Yet nearly two-thirds of accidental activists said it makes them feel good too.

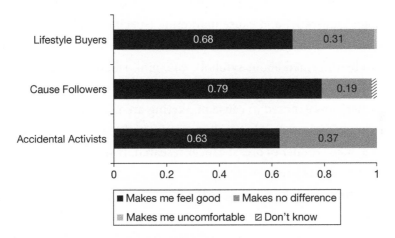

Figure 5.8 Even accidental activists feel good.
N = 162.
QUESTION WORDING: *Which of the following statements comes closest to explaining your motivation for purchasing this product? 1. I often choose products that support causes, 2. I believe we should be doing more for this cause however possible, 3. I would have bought the product regardless of whether or not some portion of the purchase price supports a cause; AND Did purchasing this product, Make you feel good, Make you feel uncomfortable, Make no difference?*
SOURCE: CCS data, weighted proportions. May not add to 1 due to rounding. See Appendices C and D for more information.

Even though I demonstrated that those individuals who participate in cause marketing unintentionally look different from those who participate with intent (Chapter 3), breast cancer cause marketing has an effect on the vast majority of Americans who purchase the ubiquitous products on store shelves *regardless* of motivation to purchase. *In short, cause marketing affects how Americans feel about breast cancer—even when they do not intend it to.* The overwhelming emotional response mirrors cause-marketing frames.

CONCLUSION: CONSENSUAL, POSITIVE, AND APOLITICAL?

Cause marketing shapes the way Americans think and feel about breast cancer. Like cause-marketing stories that focus on awareness over information, so too, Americans demonstrate that exposure to the breast cancer campaign (generally) and cause marketing (specifically) leads to greater awareness. In fact, Americans exposed to cause marketing are more likely to be informed about symbols, e.g., pink ribbons represent breast cancer. But awareness does not lead to greater information about the disease. Americans exposed to cause marketing are no more likely to know a woman's lifetime risk of being diagnosed with breast cancer or that the NIH is a major funder of breast cancer research. Instead, they more often identify Komen as a funder of research.

Cause marketing does not make breast cancer a more important priority in the way that media stories do. And it does not spur Americans to demand collective solutions from officials in either government or industry. Instead, cause marketing empowers and enables individual action. It makes individuals feel good. The effects are striking: even accidental activists say overwhelmingly that buying products that benefit a cause makes them feel good. Breast cancer has become a feel-good social issue, not a contentious political one.

Skeptics might claim that cause marketing does not drive the way Americans think about breast cancer, but rather reflects it. The politics and history of the disease suggest just the opposite. Though today more than 80 percent of Americans say that pink ribbons are the symbol of breast cancer, for most of the nation's history pink was the color of socialism (not breast cancer) and the topic of breast cancer was taboo. In the 1970s and 1980s, breast cancer organizations rarely used *breast* in their organization's name and local reporters tiptoed around it in newspaper stories. Breast cancer was not widely agreed upon, and it was not discussed openly.

Though portrayed as apolitical—who could possibly be in favor of more breast cancer?—framing breast cancer as pink is controversial within the breast cancer community and within the politics of disease and women's health more generally. Chapter 6 tells the story of breast cancer cause marketing and the rise of consensus politics around the disease.

6

Defining Issues

Breast Cancer and the Creation of Consensus Politics

For most of the nation's history, a breast cancer diagnosis was stigmatiz-ing and not publicly discussed. But corporate-connected breast cancer organizations have worked hard to change its image through market mechanisms, partnering with industry to raise awareness and funding through walks or runs and cause marketing. Susan G. Komen (Komen), the pioneer of breast cancer cause marketing, alone has 130 corporate partners, an annual income of more than $340 million, and a $1.5 billion investment in breast cancer health.

In raising awareness about breast cancer, however, organizations have reframed what breast cancer is and redefined what it means to be a woman with breast cancer.[1] Their actions have taken away the stigma associated with breast cancer and have given it a public face. Breast cancer is a dis-ease that is marketed to Americans daily, on breakfast cereal boxes, for example, and through an extraordinary number of sporting events, from walks and runs to adventure expeditions.

1. King, *Pink Ribbons, Inc.*; Sulik, *Pink Ribbon Blues*; Ehrenreich, "Welcome to Cancerland"; Ehrenreich, "The Pink Ribbon Breast Cancer Cult"; Elliott, "Pink!"; Patricia Strach, "Gender Practice as Political Practice: Cancer, Culture, and Identity," *Politics, Groups, and Identity* 1, no. 2 (2013): 250–52.

This type of activism has portrayed breast cancer as pink—positive, hopeful, and nice—and it has created a new sort of identity for those diagnosed with breast cancer as survivor, not victim.[2] At the same time, it has portrayed breast cancer as a consensus issue—one that all sides agree on. Yet that is not the case. Although nobody is in favor of *more* breast cancer, there are many sides to breast cancer debates: environmentalists believe industry is partly responsible for rising cancer rates, while groups that focus on low-income and minority cancer rates note the disparity in diagnosis and treatment.[3] Those outside breast cancer advocacy—and disease advocacy more generally—resent the disproportionate attention given to this one disease. Breast cancer is not the largest killer of women (heart disease is). It is not the most deadly cancer for women (lung cancer is). And it is not the fastest-growing killer (HIV/AIDS is).

Framing breast cancer as a consensus issue has both helped and hindered it in the policy realm. On the one hand, policymakers have devoted disproportionate resources to this one disease, increasing funding and creating new programs in the Department of Defense and US Post Office. On the other hand, breast cancer groups that push a broader agenda—more generous healthcare funding for men and women with breast cancer or an investigation of environmental links to breast cancer—march to Washington only to find policy officials already wearing pink ribbons offering symbolic support rather than new policy solutions.

MAKING A GOOD CAUSE

Today, many people view breast cancer as a cause du jour.[4] Breast cancer affects women—a key consumer base and political constituency—and yet

2. King, *Pink Ribbons, Inc.*; Sulik, *Pink Ribbon Blues*; Ehrenreich, "Welcome to Cancerland."

3. McCormick, *No Family History*; Ley, *From Pink to Green*; Ulrike Boehner, *The Personal and the Political: Women's Activism in Response to the Breast Cancer and AIDS Epidemics* (Albany, NY: SUNY Press, 2000); Sulik, "#Rethinkpink"; Sulik and Zierkiewicz, "Gender, Power, and Feminisms in Breast Cancer Advocacy"; King, "Pink Ribbons Inc."

4. King, *Pink Ribbons, Inc.*

it is not politically divisive (like abortion) or stigmatizing (like poverty). Views of breast cancer as a positive, bipartisan, women's issue do not reflect innate features of the disease.[5] Instead, they are the by-product of organizational activity to reshape social understandings of cancer.

Cancer was long considered the "dread disease," striking individuals and destroying them "without mercy and without pity."[6] Cancer was painful, disfiguring, and fatal. In this regard, breast cancer was no different. In the late-nineteenth through mid-twentieth centuries, women dreaded breast cancer diagnoses. Those who discovered painful lumps in their breast were treated with radical mastectomy: removal of the breast, lymph nodes, and chest wall muscles. The most extreme surgeons would take out ribs, limbs, and internal organs as well.[7] Nineteenth-century survival rates were abysmal. But even when surgical techniques improved, breast cancer diagnosis and treatment were still frightening because biopsy and mastectomy were performed in one step. When a surgeon doing a biopsy found a malignant tumor he would perform a mastectomy at the same time—without waking the patient up to consult her. Unsurprisingly, many women waited months or years to see a physician, and others chose to ignore the cancer and forgo treatment altogether.[8] Beyond the stigma of cancer generally, breast cancer was particularly taboo because it was tied to topics of reproduction unfit for public discussion.[9] When First Lady Betty Ford underwent radical mastectomy in the fall of 1974, for example, *Newsweek*'s banner ominously read, "The Operation," failing to mention breast cancer explicitly.[10]

5. King, "Pink Ribbons Inc."

6. Dr. Charles Childe in James T. Patterson, *The Dread Disease: Cancer and Modern American Culture* (Cambridge, MA: Harvard University Press, 1987), 46.

7. Lerner, *The Breast Cancer Wars*, ch. 4.

8. Ibid., 42.

9. Leopold, *A Darker Ribbon*.

10. Ibid., 232.

To challenge cancer's stigma, a group of physicians and laypeople created the American Society for the Control of Cancer (ASCC) in 1913. While the federal government devoted the lion's share of its efforts to promoting research on causes and effective treatment of cancer, the ASCC decided that addressing cancer meant targeting the public and changing attitudes. It spread the message that cancer was not fatal if discovered early and treated promptly. But ignorance and delay led to death.[11] The ASCC encouraged women to be "foot soldiers" in the "war on cancer." Beginning in 1936, the Women's Field Army—an ASCC campaign—"enlisted" mostly middle-class women to inform their local communities about cancer.[12] As the guardians of home and family, women played a pivotal role by disseminating information to other women and to their own families.

By the early 1940s, the ASCC was still run largely by physicians and raised only a few hundred thousand dollars a year, a sum inadequate for a toothpaste advertising campaign let alone the types of campaigns required to reduce the stigma of cancer and make it a household term.[13] In the mid-1940s, philanthropist Mary Lasker (wife of advertising executive Albert Lasker) convinced the ASCC to make significant changes: revamping the board of directors to include more business executives, entreating celebrities to join the cause, and renaming the organization the "American Cancer Society" (ACS). The ACS took a more active role in lobbying government for more research and in outreach campaigns.

The ACS shifted its emphasis in the 1950s from women's cancers generally to the most common cancer killer among women at the time: breast cancer. Like earlier campaigns, breast cancer campaigns during the 1950s and 1960s touted the merits of early detection as the best way to "cure" cancer, even though early detection could not catch or cure all cancers.[14]

11. Lerner, *The Breast Cancer Wars*, 30.

12. Patterson, *The Dread Disease*, 122.

13. Lerner, *The Breast Cancer Wars*, 50.

14. By the time they are detectable, some cancers have already spread, while others are vigorous even when caught early. And, for Americans with inadequate health insurance, finding out one has cancer does not mean one will have access to physicians who can treat it.

Though the campaigns attempted to remove the fatalism associated with cancer, at the same time they added a healthy dose of guilt. In the most extreme form, these messages chastised a woman who delayed treatment for having "committed suicide almost as certainly as if she had blown her brains out with a pistol."[15]

By the early 1970s, breast cancer patients began to challenge the received wisdom surrounding the disease. They criticized the conventional one-step procedure in which mastectomy automatically followed a positive biopsy because it did not give women a chance to think about, or get a second opinion on, treatment.[16] They questioned radical mastectomy, which entailed the removal of the breast as well as lymph nodes and chest wall muscles (as opposed to simple mastectomy, in which just the breast was removed, or lumpectomy, in which just the tumor was excised), the standard practice since 1915.[17] They were weary of the silence surrounding this disease. They began to talk publicly and they started to mobilize.

Women's increasingly public battles with breast cancer began to fill women's magazines and books. *Seventeen* magazine editor Babette Rosmond wrote about her experience challenging her doctors on one-step radical mastectomy in an article for *McCall's* and in her book, *The Invisible Worm* (1972), while firebrand journalist Rose Kushner challenged the established cancer orthodoxy in *Breast Cancer: A Personal History and Investigative Report* (1975).[18] High-profile political women shared their experiences in their own words and on their own terms: Shirley Temple Black in an article for *McCall's* in 1973, Happy Rockefeller in an article for *Reader's Digest* (1976), and Marvella Bayh in her book

15. Statement by the surgeon Frank G. Slaughter, 1946, in Lerner, *The Breast Cancer Wars*, 60.

16. E.g., Rose Kushner, *Breast Cancer: A Personal History and an Investigative Report* (New York: Harcourt Brace Jovanovich, 1975).

17. Lerner, *The Breast Cancer Wars*, 31.

18. Rosamond Campion, "Five Years Later: No Regrets," *McCall's*, June (1976): 113, 150; *The Invisible Worm: A Woman's Right to Choose an Alternate to Radical Surgery* (New York: Macmillan, 1972); Kushner, *Breast Cancer*.

Marvella: A Personal Journey (1979).[19] Most notably, in 1974, the nation followed First Lady Betty Ford's breast cancer diagnosis and treatment, which she insisted be made public.

Although some women, like Audre Lorde, thought about the feminist implications of breast cancer, and others, like Babette Rosmond, challenged the male medical establishment, breast cancer remained largely disconnected from the women's movement and women's health movements.[20] Breast cancer skirted controversies concerning women's health, women's bodies, and control over decision making that were central to the abortion debates.

Rather than taking part in feminist organizing, women—who had been active in raising awareness about cancer and in support groups for decades—mobilized around their personal experience with the disease. They found the American Cancer Society out of touch with their needs and experiences. They created new organizations, which started small and were composed of individuals directly affected by breast cancer. Some, like the Chicago-based Y-Me (later known as the Breast Cancer Network of Strength) and the Adelphi NY Statewide Breast Cancer Support Hotline, were support organizations designed to listen and offer advice to women with breast cancer. Other organizations like the Long Island Women's Outreach Network, Philadelphia's Linda Creed Breast Cancer Foundation, and Houston-based The Rose provided increased access to low-cost or free mammography screening for women in need. Other organizations were

---

19. Shirley Temple Black, "Don't Sit Home and Be Afraid," *McCall's*, February (1973): 82–83, 114–16; Margaretta Rockefeller with Eleanor Harris, "If It Should Happen to You," *Reader's Digest*, May (1976): 131–34; Marvella Bayh, with Mary Lynn Kotz, *Marvella: A Personal Journey* (New York: Harcourt Brace Jovanovich, 1979). Congress followed suit, holding its first hearing on breast cancer in 1976 (US Congress, Senate, Committee on Labor and Human Resources, *Breast Cancer*, Second Session, May 4, 1976). The Appropriations Committee of the House of Representatives did recommend the creation of a Breast Cancer Task Force in the National Cancer Institute as early as 1966 (Breast Cancer Task Force of the National Cancer Institute, "Report to the Profession: Breast Cancer," 1974, RKP, box 15, file 230. Schlesinger Library Archives, Radcliffe Institute for Advanced Studies, Harvard University).

20. *The Cancer Journals* (Argyle, NY: Spinsters Inc., 1980); Leopold, *A Darker Ribbon: Breast Cancer, Women and Their Doctors in the Twentieth Century.*

decidedly political. The Cambridge-based Women's Community Cancer Center and Oakland (California) Women's Cancer Resource Center were feminist in their orientation, though not particularly interested in traditional interest-group politics. At the same time, others had an explicit focus on raising money for research; among these were the Baton Rouge Breast Foundation (now the Sallie Astor Burdine Breast Foundation) and what would become the biggest breast cancer organization, Dallas-based Susan G. Komen Foundation (now Susan G. Komen).

CREATING A COMMERCIAL SOCIAL MOVEMENT

Even though there was some attention to breast cancer and a sprinkling of groups, it was still largely a silent killer in 1980 when it took the life of Susan G. Komen, a thirty-six-year-old mother of two from Peoria, Illinois. In 1982, Nancy Brinker started the Komen Foundation in her sister's memory to increase awareness about and funding for the disease. In her memoir, she notes that when Komen began,

> [t]he subject [breast cancer] made people extremely squeamish, especially men . . . they can talk about war with no problem. Murder is interesting. Bankruptcy is fascinating. But breast cancer? Next subject! . . . Yes, I had my work cut out for me. It was clear that I also had to raise the awareness of women and get their support.[21]

The taboo surrounding breast cancer made it difficult to reach men and women. As one Komen executive recalled:

> I was working for a newspaper when Nancy Brinker held her first event and I covered it. I remember I went back to the paper and had to write the story without using the words breast cancer. I know it seems so long ago, but it actually was not that long ago.

21. Brinker, *Winning the Race*, 41.

Now when I go into the grocery store, I get tears seeing all the pink. Young people today don't remember it all. But back then, you were stigmatized with the diagnosis.[22]

In the fifty-five years prior to Komen's founding, there were only 301 stories in the *New York Times* and *Reader's Guide to Periodic Literature* that used the term *breast cancer*. In the early 1980s, "[t]here was no cure, no 1-800 number, internet, no information for people facing a diagnosis."[23] Much of what Komen sought to do was to make sure women would have "information to make their own decisions."[24]

Because Nancy Brinker understood that the greatest obstacle to an effective response to breast cancer was silence, she looked for ways to educate Americans about cancer, to take away the fear and stigma, and to encourage women to talk about and seek treatment for breast cancer. In the midst of a fitness craze that brought Jane Fonda into American homes and leg warmers to many women's wardrobes, she decided to hold a race. "Everybody—I mean everybody—thought I was crazy. Even my own mother."[25] By the 1980s, fitness had become fashionable, but running— as a sport—was relatively new for American women. Yet eight hundred women attended the first Race for the Cure at a shopping mall in Dallas in 1983. As one early participant (who later joined Komen) noted, "It was a neat and novel thing. I had a lot of fun. They gave out goody bags that [had] makeup but also information about breast health."[26]

Komen's race was not about competition or even athletics. It was designed to make breast cancer more public. One Komen executive

22. Interview with Komen executive, 2009 (no. 90820).

23. Interview with Komen executive, 2009 (no. 90820); "Joint Statement on the Breast Cancer Education and Awareness Requires Learning Young (EARLY) Act of 2009, Addendum by Nancy Brinker, 'Why We Fight,'" www.KomenAdvocacy.org, accessed October 13, 2009.

24. "Joint Statement on the Breast Cancer Education and Awareness Requires Learning Young (EARLY) Act of 2009, Addendum by Nancy Brinker, 'Why We Fight,'" www. KomenAdvocacy.org, accessed October 13, 2009.

25. Brinker, *Winning the Race*, 74.

26. Interview with Komen executive, 2009 (no. 90821).

explained: "When Nancy first started the race, it was to educate women about breast cancer. Her vision for the Race was an all-women's event. It was [a] fun, motivating, inspirational event" helping participants "feel good and in the course it could help educate about breast cancer."[27]

Like many organizations before, Brinker was determined to overcome breast cancer's stigma through social means. But unlike the American Cancer Society, Komen was not just going to educate and publicize. It wanted to market breast cancer. Brinker explained, "We weren't creating another charity; we were creating a movement. That meant Komen needed a mechanism to carry its message to every town and city in the nation."[28] The Race for the Cure and its ensuing corporate partnerships became that very public (though nongovernmental) mechanism. Relying on industry, however, meant Brinker had to sell the idea that a stigmatized disease could reflect positively on the companies that chose to get involved, which proved to be difficult. According to one Komen affiliate:

It was a hard task and there were doors slammed in her [Brinker's] face. Her first idea was to approach the intimate apparel industry. You know, put a hang tag on bras. But they said, *why would we want to do that? Why would we want to associate a female product with death and dying?* She was thrown out of the boardroom and still points to the spot in New York where she cried.[29]

Komen's marketplace vision was very different from that of charitable actions in the past. One person familiar with Komen's strategy explained: "This is not a philanthropic donation, it is a business relationship. It needs to be approached like a business relationship."[30] Nancy Brinker knew how to do that. She had worked with Stanley Marcus in Neiman Marcus's executive training program. Her husband and lifetime

27. Interview with Komen executive, 2009 (no. 91009a).

28. Brinker, *Winning the Race*, 75.

29. Interview with Komen executive, 2009 (no. 90820).

30. Interview with Komen executive, 2009 (no. 91009a).

Komen board member, Norman Brinker, was the chairman of Pillsbury's Restaurant Group and later head of Brinker International, a multibillion-dollar restaurant group that owns and runs Chili's.[31] Nancy Brinker used her knowledge and connections to create a new form of activism around breast cancer. One Komen executive noted:

> Companies like American Airlines and Pier One Imports in Dallas were the first to sign on: Bob Crandall, the CEO of American Airlines, when he was asked, "why do something like this?" He said, "I just got tired of Nancy Brinker." That's not too far off from the truth of it. [An executive at] Pier One would say it was pressure from Nancy and she was married to a powerful businessman.[32]

Though Brinker had knocked on many doors before she could convince executives in her locale (Dallas) to support the Race for the Cure, with the benefit of positive media coverage, Komen, breast cancer, and the races caught on. According to this executive, "Leaders of other organizations would see the event was benefiting breast cancer, which was not a cool thing. They started to see how companies' business goals were being met and in sponsoring events like those at a local restaurant, a consumer would return and would support the establishment because the cause was important to them."[33] Komen was transforming breast cancer into a cause célèbre, one that American businesses would get behind.

However, breast cancer needed a symbol to brand it. Following AIDS activists' success with the red ribbon, corporate-connected breast cancer activists wanted a ribbon too. Yet breast cancer already had a ribbon (peach), and its creator was not willing to relinquish control. Sixty-eight-year-old Charlotte Haley, who had a family history of breast cancer, used peach ribbons to raise awareness of a political problem: too few federal

31. William Grimes, "Norman Brinker, Casual Dining Innovator, Dies at 78," *New York Times*, June 10, 2009.

32. Interview with Komen executive, 2009 (no. 90820).

33. Interview with Komen executive, 2009 (no. 90820).

resources were devoted to cancer prevention. Worried that the peach ribbon would become too commercial, Haley was not willing to give it up. Evelyn Lauder (of the cosmetics giant Estée Lauder), instead, distributed pink ribbons at Estée Lauder counters in New York City. Komen started promoting pink ribbons at the 1991 Race for the Cure, and *Self* magazine ran a spread featuring them in the fall of 1992.[34]

As the Race for the Cure grew, Komen set out guidelines about how to add cities and build support.[35] Komen sponsored thirty-five races in 1993, forty-six in 1994 (twenty-nine states and Washington, DC), and fifty-seven in 1995.[36] Brinker explains that companies "understood it was the right thing to do ... and good business too. ... Women were becoming an economic force to be reckoned with, and we were giving them an opportunity to reach women through their hearts and minds along with their pocketbooks.[37] Komen found itself in the enviable position of having generated more interest in sponsoring the Race for the Cure than it could accommodate.

According to one Komen insider: "What happened with the Race for the Cure is that we had national sponsors like Yoplait and Ford. Because of their commitment to the cause, we were looking for ways to expand the program to find other ways for them to get involved."[38] When the board limited the number of race sponsors, Komen developed cause-marketing programs, which expanded the options for industry. Together, industry partners developed products in which a portion of the sale would benefit breast cancer research. For example, Campbell Soup sells a pink version of its iconic soup can during Breast Cancer Awareness Month in October (see Figure 6.1). For every can sold, Campbell donates money to Komen.

34. King, *Pink Ribbons, Inc.*, xxiv.

35. Interview with Komen executive, 2009 (no. 91009a).

36. See US Congress, House of Representatives, Committee on Ways and Means, Subcommittee on Health, Statement of Ann Polk, Co-Chair, Susan G. Komen Breast Cancer Foundation, Inc., *Health Care Reform*, Second Session, 1993.

37. Brinker, *Winning the Race*, 77.

38. Interview with Komen executive, 2009 (no. 91009a).

Figure 6.1 Campbell's partnership with Komen (2006).
SOURCE: *Business Wire*: http://mms.businesswire.com/bwapps/mediaserver/
ViewMedia?mgid=109436&vid=5

As a measure of its success, Campbell *doubled* its sales of soup to Kroger grocery stores in October 2006.[39] According to one Komen representative, "Consumers were likely to switch their loyalty ... based on a cause [that] they supported. Nancy [Brinker] was doing that eight years before it became typical in the culture."[40]

Though social movement scholars often associate movements with contentious politics, Komen sees its work as a movement of a different kind: mobilizing men and women through cooperative relationships with

39. Stephanie Thompson, "Raising Awareness, Doubling Sales; Idea Spotting: Pink Campbell Cans a Hit with Kroger," *Advertising Age*, October 2, 2006.

40. Interview with Komen executive, 2009 (no. 90820).

industry. Cause marketing is more than just a way to generate revenue. It makes change through awareness. Komen's original sponsors, American Airlines and Pier One, did not just get involved because of Brinker and her connections. And Komen did not just want their financial support. As one Komen executive explained:

> [T]he truth of it is after they started the campaign, an associate with breast cancer walked up and thanked him for saving our lives. And [the executive] realized that this program really worked. They had pride beyond making a profit. . . . It was really interesting as the movement was happening, we would not just accept anybody. They had to be in it for the long term. They had to be committed to the mission. They had to have appropriate insurance for their employees. We wanted to make sure they are in it for the right reason.[41]

Komen looks to industry partnerships to provide a platform to reach consumers. Yoplait, for example, donated money based on consumer action, in this case for every specially marked lid that is sent back to the company. But that is not all that companies do. "[B]ehind that, they [Yoplait] have a campaign that includes print and broadcast media, employee engagement. The Yoplait website has a section on breast help. It is a lot deeper than the transaction to generate money."[42]

Through industry partnerships that generate awareness, Komen mobilizes men and women to change their behavior: to talk about breast cancer or to take positive actions to address it. The Komen executive continued:

> In the past there was a program with Kellogg's. They would dedicate the back of packages to breast health and Komen. That can generate a [useful] conversation. . . . With Komen, it is the first step in engaging support. Volunteering, running the Race for the Cure. We did a

---

41. Interview with Komen executive, 2009 (no. 090820).

42. Interview with Komen executive, 2009 (no. 091009a).

non-scientific survey within Komen and found that participation in the program changed behavior (they would have a mammogram, or talk to friend or family about it).[43]

While some outsiders see opportunism, Komen insiders see a way to make change. Through industry partnerships and mechanisms like the Race for the Cure and cause marketing, Komen has reframed breast cancer and mobilized individuals around a new understanding. When she testified in 1991 before the Senate Labor and Human Resources Aging Subcommittee, Brinker explained:

> [I]n Washington last week 14,000 volunteers participated in one of our Race for the Cure events, for which the corporate community raised $750,000. This kind of race, which creates awareness opportunities to be screened and to learn about prevention activities, will be sponsored by the Komen Foundation in 16 cities in America this year. Each of these races will create funding for the communities in which they are held to benefit the screening treatment programs and to offset the cost of mammograms.[44]

Social movement scholars typically see government, and to a lesser extent industry, as the target of change, and disruptive tactics as the means of change for actors who cannot gain traction in governmental venues.[45] But Komen turns this model on its head.

Brinker has a great deal of political capital, serving on President Reagan's National Cancer Advisory Board, on the President's Cancer Panel under George H. W. Bush, as the ambassador to Hungary, and as

43. Interview with Komen executive, 2009 (no. 091009a).

44. Testimony of Nancy Brinker before the Senate Labor and Human Resources Aging Subcommittee, June 20, 1991, carton 1, KDP.

45. Walker, Martin, and McCarthy, "Confronting the State, the Corporation, and the Academy"; Doug McAdam and David A. Snow, "Social Movements: Conceptual and Theoretical Issues," in *Readings on Social Movements: Origins, Dynamics, and Outcomes*, ed. Doug McAdam and David A. Snow (New York: Oxford University Press, 2010), 1–8.

the Department of State chief of protocol.[46] Her ties have garnered the support of top political figures like Betty Ford, Dan and Marilyn Quayle, Al and Tipper Gore, George and Laura Bush from the beginning.[47] She could have taken a more traditional "inside politics" approach. Instead, Brinker chose to work cooperatively with industry to make change to American society. Can this really be considered a social movement?

Komen insiders repeatedly use movement (though not social movement) language to describe what it is that they do. I have named their actions a "commercial social movement" because the goals are to change broad cultural understandings, but the means are to work with and through industry. Partnering with industry gives Komen a platform to reach American men and women, and to alter the way they think about and act on breast cancer. This is a significant change, but it is a fundamentally conservative one. It does not challenge basic social, political, or economic institutions in America. And it does not represent a break from the past. In fact, it does not even appear to be very controversial (though Komen was caught up in a scandal around defunding Planned Parenthood in 2010). Komen articulates a model whereby the Race for the Cure creates opportunities to mobilize individuals and their actions trickle up to government. In testimony before the Senate, Brinker explained: "Our thousands of volunteers have become advocates" who have helped get insurance coverage for mammography, pass informed-decision laws, assist with national breast and cervical education programs in the Centers for Disease Control, and provide mobile mammography vans in underserved areas.[48] But the activism that the Race for the Cure and cause marketing create is only the start. The federal government must step in where Komen cannot; Brinker continued, "We are doing our part, and now we have to look at our partners in the public sector *to help us finish this important job.*"[49]

46. Linda Peterson, "A Promise Kept," *Biography* 7, no. 10 (2003): 60–91. US State Department: http://www.state.gov/r/pa/ei/biog/92472.htm, accessed March 10, 2008.

47. Belkin, "Charity Begins at . . ."; Brinker, *Winning the Race.*

48. Testimony of Nancy Brinker Before the Senate Labor and Human Resources Aging Subcommittee, June 20, 1991, carton 1, KDP.

49. Ibid.; emphasis added.

Medical philanthropist and American Cancer Society activist Mary Lasker had in mind a different (government-centered) model of activism when she told Nancy Brinker in 1990: "'The federal government will always be your largest funder of research.'" To this Brinker replied, "'That's why we hope to do both—to raise money and the consciousness of both government and the private sector.'"[50] For Brinker, innovation in the private sector could be coupled with public sector resources. But government would play a secondary role. "No government is big enough, no government can serve each individual person, nothing can work as well as a true public–private partnership."[51]

Komen's status (as an inside organization) and tactics (partnering with industry) differentiate it from social movements studied by scholars, who often look at outside groups that adopt outside tactics. And its model for making change *with* institutions rather than *to* or *within* them differentiates it from health social movements, which often work with institutional actors to make change to medical and political institutions. Whereas Komen defines the key problem of breast cancer as lack of awareness and primary solutions as industry partnerships that change individual awareness and activism, other groups see a political problem: government is not doing enough. The solution was not a commercial social movement but a health social movement, using an inside-the-Beltway strategy for change.

A HEALTH SOCIAL MOVEMENT: INSIDE STRATEGIES FOR CHANGE

"What do we have to do to prevent breast cancer—march topless on Washington?" surgeon Susan Love asked a crowd in Salt Lake City in 1991. Women responded by laughing and then, turning serious, asking, "'So, when do we leave?'"[52] If marching on the capitol could get a reaction

50. Nancy G. Brinker, "When Society Meets Science," *Nature Medicine* 11, no. 10 (2005): 1040.

51. Statement of Nancy Brinker, US Congress, House of Representatives, Select Committee on Aging, Subcommittee on Health and Long-Term Care, *Winning the Battles, Losing the War*, Second Session, October 1, 1992.

52. Interview with NBCC affiliate, 2009 (no. 90806).

in Salt Lake City, it would likely gain traction in other locations around the country. Love (of the Faulkner Breast Center) initially met with Susan Hester (Mautner Project for Lesbians with Cancer), Amy Langer (National Alliance of Breast Cancer Organizations), and Nancy Brinker (Komen) to talk about organizing a national political movement. Though Komen dropped out after two meetings, the remaining three organizations, along with representatives of Y-Me, Cancer Care, and the Greater Washington Area Coalition for Cancer Survivorship, met to determine how exactly they would form a new organization with political muscle.[53]

Armed with the alliance's list of breast cancer organizations as well as a list of their own organization's supporters, they sent out a mass mailing announcing an open meeting in May 1991. The turnout surpassed any of their expectations. NBCC affiliates explained, "We went to an office in Washington and there were all women, except one man from Komen."[54] In total there were seventy-five representatives of fifty organizations, and it was standing room only.[55] Eleanor Smeal, of NOW and the Feminist Majority, "came to talk to us and we talked about the letter-writing campaign. And some people asked if they could talk about abortion. And she said, 'no.' There can only be one issue and you cannot stray from it. . ... We had to stay focused on our issues."[56]

The participants that day formed the Breast Cancer Coalition (NBCC), an organization composed wholly of member organizations to maintain an advocacy arm for breast cancer in Washington, DC.[57] As an organization composed of other organizations, the NBCC had broad-based political expertise and experience right off the bat. The original NBCC working board consisted of twenty-three member organizations of cancer

53. "Testimony before the National Cancer Advisory Board by Frances M. Visco and Susan M. Love," December 14, 1992, 2005-M119, carton 1, KDP.

54. Interview with NBCC affiliate, 2009 (no. 90826).

55. "Dear Friend Letter," May 30, 1991, carton 1, KDP.

56. Interview with NBCC affiliate, 2009 (no. 90826).

57. Originally named the Breast Cancer Coalition and later the National Breast Cancer Coalition. I use the NBCC acronym throughout.

groups (such as the American Cancer Society), breast cancer groups (such as California Breast Cancer Organizations), and feminist groups (such as the Feminist Majority Foundation). Breast cancer activists in the NBCC navigated their own path between ACT UP's radical tactics and reputation and Komen's mainstream corporate partnerships and ladylike image.

Breast cancer activists who started the NBCC took a page from successful AIDS activism. "AIDS was the first disease where people with the disease were making decisions. All the other advocacy groups (or most of the other ones like ACS or Jerry's group) were run by doctors. . . . With AIDS, you had patients doing it. Probably white men with money, but still."[58] If breast cancer activists learned from AIDS activism how to organize themselves, they took a decidedly less confrontational political stand. Officials at the National Cancer Institute explained the new relationship disease activists had with government agencies: "Advocates asked for and received a chair at the decision-making boards; more importantly, they realized the need to be expert partners rather than patrons to add intellectual weight to their opinions."[59] Breast cancer activists wanted to distinguish themselves from ACT UP AIDS activists by working cooperatively within the political system. In the words of one breast cancer activist, "We were not going to throw blood. We'd be more prepared, more scientific."[60] And another, "We've taken it beyond the streets and into the halls of Congress."[61]

Early NBCC members staked out a position they felt was missing in the breast cancer universe. The NBCC noted, "Women's health groups are not new, but what is new is we have learned to view breast cancer as not only a medical but also a political issue."[62] They were tired of the status quo and wanted to make strides forward with research that would find a cure. Many organizations at the time were not interested in taking

58. Interview with NBCC affiliate, 2009 (no. 90806).

59. Edison Liu, Eleanor Nealon, and Richard Klausner, "Perspective from the National Cancer Institute (NCI)," *Breast Disease* 10, no. 5–6 (1998): 29–31.

60. Interview with NBCC affiliate, 2009 (no. 90813).

61. Interview with NBCC affiliate, 2009 (no. 90817).

62. "The Breast Cancer Advocacy Movement: The Growth of Patient Advocacy," Draft remarks before the President's Cancer Panel, November 18, 1991, carton 1, KDP. "Dickersin's

on a national advocacy component.[63] The American Cancer Society—the home of cancer organizing for sixty years—did not strike the tone and purpose they sought.[64] The ACS had been organizing women with breast cancer for more than two decades since it took over Reach to Recovery, a program in which breast cancer survivors visit breast cancer patients in the hospital to help them adjust to life after mastectomy. The goal of the program is not to change government policy or to publicize the disease, but to help mastectomy patients look and feel "normal" again.[65] But many women found the program inadequate and the ACS out of touch. One activist explained:

> I tried to join ACS. They wouldn't let me! I had breast cancer but I never had surgery, chemotherapy. I was "no use to them" in Reach to Recovery. They wanted at least a year out of treatment to volunteer. I was nine months and had two masters and said there must be something I can do, stuff envelopes or something. It's the story of a lot of people.... They [ACS] want to make it "comfortable"—but we don't want to be comfortable, we want to find a cure. Support is good, I'm not knocking it, but we were much more demanding. We lived through Vietnam. We couldn't get excited about it.[66]

The next obvious alternative at the time, the National Alliance of Breast Cancer Organizations, was an informational resource for breast cancer organizations and did not want to take on advocacy. Individual

---

Notes from 5/16/91," carton 1, KDP; "Working Board Minutes 6/11 & 6/20," July 8, 1991, carton 1, KDP; "Meeting of the Board of Directors, September 13 and 14, 1992," n.d., carton 1, KDP; "Board of Director's Meeting of the NBCC 6/13/1992," n.d., carton 1, KDP.

63. Interview with Fran Visco, October 22, 2009.

64. The ACS was on the original NBCC Working Board and provided resources for the organization.

65. Reach to Recovery was founded by Terese Lasser in 1952. Olson estimates that three-quarters of mastectomy patients had met with Reach to Recovery volunteers by the 1980s; Olson, *Bathsheba's Breast*, 120.

66. Interview with NBCC affiliate, 2009 (no. 90813).

groups—which came together to form the NBCC—did not have the capacity for full-time Washington organizing on their own. Komen was putting its energy into market-based solutions for change.

The NBCC hit the ground running—writing letters, testifying before Congress, and holding press conferences within months of forming. In October 1991—with 130 member organizations—the NBCC held its first grassroots letter-writing campaign, "Do the Write Thing," on behalf of increased federal spending for breast cancer research. The campaign drew on the NBCC's strengths: its membership and ability to mobilize members for grassroots lobbying. It created a system of state-level captains who collected letters from mothers, children, and spouses telling their personal stories about their daughters, mothers, and wives. Their goal was 175,000 letters—the number of women who would be diagnosed that year—which they would present to President Bush. According to one early member:

> We ended up with half a million. . . . We got the state captains and marched to the steps of the Capitol. We had women read the letters. The press came to get their sound bites. [A NBCC board member] rang a cowbell every 12 minutes (to represent another woman dying from breast cancer). I looked around and realized that the press had put down their cameras and started listening to the letters and to the bell. They stayed for quite a while, even after they had completed filming. We also invited different Congressional members [two senators and eight members of Congress spoke]. [Democratic Representative] Pat Schroeder stood up and said they don't fund what they don't fear and they don't fear breast cancer.[67]

Though ringing a cowbell was very different from ACT UP's radical tactics, the NBCC still worried about the message it sent. It was controversial within the organization "because people thought it wasn't polite. . . . I'm not sure I remember right—but there was controversy over t-shirts. Some people didn't want to wear the shirts over our clothes.

67. Interview with NBCC affiliate, 2009 (no. 90814).

I guess they didn't want to look unprofessional."[68] The NBCC struggled with "impression management," or how it would shape a particular image.[69] The minutes of a September 1992 meeting illustrate the debate the organization had over strategies, image, and effectiveness (speakers are designated by initial):

> It is important that the NBCC decide on the image that it wants to project. J___ when asked about some of the activities suggest[s] that we don't need to embarrass the representatives/senators in order to get action. M___ suggests we create a collage similar to the AIDS quilt to attract attention. B___ talks about different actions in different places and the problems of getting and keeping people involved. Are we ambitious in what we can do? A___, [said] that the organization Act up [*sic*] carefully plans all of their actions. We need to be driven by effective behavior. P___ spoke of her personal experience of pulling out her prosthesis. B___ [said] we should be cautious in our behavior ... J___ suggest[s] that we confer with the press to get their opinion of what would be more likely to be covered before we make any final decisions.[70]

Over time, the NBCC established a reputation as professional, prepared, and able to work in policy circles. It "devise[d] a strategic plan of action that will be both Washington- and grassroots-based. It will include

68. Interview with NBCC affiliate, 2009 (no. 90826).

69. Erving Goffman, *The Presentation of Self in Everyday Life* (Garden City, NY: Doubleday, 1959); David A. Snow and Doug McAdam, "Identity Work Processes in the Context of Social Movements: Clarifying the Identity/Movement Nexus," in *Self, Identity, and Social Movements*, ed. Sheldon Stryker, Timothy J. Owens, and Robert W. White (Minneapolis: University of Minnesota Press, 2000), 41–67; David A. Snow and Leon Anderson, "Identity Work among the Homeless: The Verbal Construction and Avowal of Personal Identities," *American Journal of Sociology* 92, no. 6 (1987): 1336–71.

70. "Board of Directors Meeting of the National Breast Cancer Coalition, Washington D.C. 1800 M. Street, South Lobby, 2nd Floor Monday and Tuesday September 14th and 15th, 1992," carton 1, KDP.

public pressure and behind-the-scenes negotiations dealing with budget, authorizations, and appropriations."[71]

When 1992 "became the Year of the Woman ... that helped us."[72] In an election year, policymakers in Congress were "looking for a women's issue to grab onto."[73] On the heels of a much-publicized 1990 Government Accounting Office report indicating that the NIH had done little to implement recommendations to encourage research on women,[74] "our boys humiliated themselves" during the Anita Hill–Clarence Thomas hearings.[75] NBCC was there to promote breast cancer as a bipartisan women's issue: not controversial, not radical, and not politically divisive.

The NBCC set its sights high when it went after an additional $300 million (or $433 million total) for breast cancer research at the National Cancer Institute. It found an unlikely ally in the Department of Defense (DOD). After the Cold War ended and the United States pulled back from its military commitments, Defense found itself with a "peace dividend." Senator Tom Harkin (D-IA), chair of Defense Appropriations, whose two sisters had died from breast cancer, offered his support. "He came off the floor one day, and you know how this works, if you don't spend it you don't get it back the next year. He said if you want the money, it's yours."[76] The NBCC, which had no paid staff, no office space, no steady source of income, and operated functionally as a post office box and a voicemail account, saw a long-term opportunity and was making long-term plans.

71. Memo to the Working Board of the Breast Cancer Coalition from Joanne Howes of the Federal Public Policy Taskforce, February 25, 1992, carton 1, KDP.

72. Interview with NBCC affiliate, 2009 (no. 90813).

73. Interview with NBCC affiliate, 2009 (no. 90814).

74. Carol S. Weisman, *Women's Health Care: Activist Traditions and Institutional Change* (Baltimore: Johns Hopkins University Press, 1998); Casamayou, *The Politics of Breast Cancer*, 7.

75. Interview with NBCC affiliate, 2009 (no. 90814).

76. Interview with NBCC affiliate, 2009 (no. 90817).

Because of a firewall between defense and domestic spending, Senator Harkin could not simply transfer money from the Department of Defense to the National Cancer Institute. The NBCC and sympathetic policymakers were stuck. "Then," according to one early NBCC affiliate, "someone from Harkin's office called us. There was already money for breast cancer in the Department of Defense. They funded mammogram machines we would just increase [the existing appropriation] from $2 million to $300 million."[77] Senator Harkin went to the floor and "gave an incredible speech. When it looked like it had 50 votes (and would pass), Senators went down and changed their votes. They wanted to be for breast cancer."[78] Breast cancer provided political coverage to men in the Senate who had "behaved badly." In his own words, Senator Arlen Specter (R-PA) "demolished" Anita Hill's credibility when she accused Supreme Court nominee Clarence Thomas of sexual harassment during his Senate confirmation hearing. In 1992, Senator Specter became a key advocate of breast cancer initiatives as he faced a Democratic opponent who ran television advertising drawing attention to his behavior during the hearings.[79]

If the Department of Defense breast cancer program provided good coverage to men in the Senate, it was an even bigger boon to the NBCC. The organization did not just win money for breast cancer; it was in on the ground floor creating a new model of research funding. The Department of Defense was happy that "we were not trying to break the firewall between defense and domestic spending" and was willing to help.[80] NBCC leaders met with Defense. "They told us, 'we're the army, we can turn a battleship on a dime and now we're going to take on breast cancer.'"[81] Rather than turn the funds over to the National Cancer Institute after

77. Interview with NBCC affiliate, 2009 (no. 90806).

78. Interview with NBCC affiliate, 2009 (no. 90813).

79. King, *Pink Ribbons, Inc.*; Weisman, *Women's Health Care*.

80. Interview with NBCC affiliate, 2009 (no. 90806).

81. Interview with NBCC affiliate, 2009 (no. 90817).

appropriation, Defense created its own breast cancer research program. The defense program is very different from what already existed at the National Cancer Institute. Defense funds "innovative, risk-taking research with high potential gain."[82] And the NBCC was "instrumental in getting it and now instrumental in how it would be spent."[83] Unlike the National Cancer Institute, the DOD program has citizens on the review panels that determine which proposals get funded. According to one NBCC affiliate:

[NBCC] created a process to put advocates in the peer-review process (Project LEAD). The scientists were appalled. But the lay people called them on it—why are you funding this project? They found out that lay people could better lobby for research money. It became more of a partnership. The integration panel was a real model.[84]

The Department of Defense opened up channels to work with the NBCC rather than for it or on its behalf. Unlike Komen's commercial social movement, the NBCC created a health social movement that worked within institutions for change. According to one NBCC representative, "We partnered with the army—and when I say partnered, I mean partnered. We had consumers chair the peer-review, and chair the Integration Panel. They suggested pre—and post-doctoral awards. We came up with IDEA awards—that's where you don't have a hypothesis, just the germ of an idea."[85] The irony of partnering with the ultimate masculine command-and-control agency for breast cancer was not lost on NBCC representatives. As one affiliate noted: "Here we were, all of

---

82. Irene Rich et al., "Perspective from the Department of Defense Breast Cancer Research Program," *Breast Disease* 10, no. 5–6 (1998): 33–45.

83. Interview with NBCC affiliate, 2009 (no. 90813).

84. Interview with NBCC affiliate, 2009 (no. 90806).

85. Interview with NBCC affiliate, 2009 (no. 90817).

these women. We were the hippies protesting the war and we're working with the DOD. But they were really so good. They were good at taking orders!"[86]

The NBCC has a broader, more liberal policy agenda than Komen. It shies away from the emotional appeals that Komen makes in favor of evidence-based practice. It works within institutions—lobbying the federal government and providing education (Project LEAD)—to make change. For more than a decade, the NBCC has brought women to Washington to learn about how to work with and talk to legislators to shape public policy (in Washington, DC, and in states across the nation). It holds an annual Advocacy Training Conference that culminates in a "Lobby Day," when members meet with lawmakers and legislative staff.[87] The centerpiece of its legislative efforts is the Department of Defense breast cancer program, and it lobbies on behalf of continued reauthorization of the program. It also supports minimum mammography standards, breast cancer treatment by Medicaid, genetic nondiscrimination, coverage for clinical trials, patient's bill of rights, and universal healthcare. It has put pressure on executive branch agencies like the Food and Drug Administration to set mammography quality standards and regulate genetic testing, the Centers for Disease Control to fund mammograms for underserved women, the Environmental Protection Agency and the Veteran's Administration to increase research, and the Health Care Finance Administration, Department of Education, and the Department of Defense to increase outreach.

The NBCC also trains citizens to understand scientific research. Early activists created Project LEAD (Leadership, Education, Advocacy, Development), science training that prepares activists to serve on review boards and better disseminate information in their communities. Project LEAD provides basic information on the science that activists need to

---

86. Interview with NBCC affiliate, 2009 (no. 90806).

87. Various articles in *Call to Action: The Quarterly Newsletter of the National Breast Cancer Coalition*, carton 2, KDP.

understand breast cancer—biology, epidemiology, health care, research design, and advocacy. Activists that I spoke to from both the NBCC and Komen praised the quality and success of Project LEAD.

Though the NBCC's board pointed to the success and recognition of Komen, it emphasized that it wanted to be a different kind of organization, occupy a different organizational niche. In a 1994 letter from Komen's chairperson of the board to NBCC's president, the lines between the two organizations were laid out:

> The Komen Foundation appreciates the Breast Cancer Coalition's focus on advocacy only, and understands its reluctance to be involved in other areas that might deter its course. Thank you for appreciating the position of the Komen Foundation to reserve judgment on membership in the Breast Cancer Coalition at this time. We believe a great deal can be accomplished by working collaboratively on Public Policy issues in areas of mutual interest.[88]

One early activist explained, "Komen told us they were not interested in public policy and advocacy and wanted to stick to doing fundraising through the Komen Race (now the Race for the Cure). So we were fine with building a national grassroots to get more federal funding for breast cancer research and improving access to quality care for all women."[89]

But NBCC did not just want to adopt different tactics; it wanted to differentiate itself from the message that Komen was sending about what breast cancer is and what it means to be a woman with breast cancer. One notable feature of my interviews was the marked difference between Komen representatives, who did not explicitly distinguish between their organization and others, and representatives of other leading organizations who did. Characterizing the difference between organizations, one NBCC activist explained: "Komen people tend to be more 'lady's lunch'

88. Letter from Elizabeth A. Hart, Chairman of the Board, Susan G. Komen Foundation, to Fran Visco, President of the National Breast Cancer Coalition, March 3, 1994, carton 1, KDP.

89. Interview with NBCC affiliate, 2009 (no. 90814).

and a lot of the affiliates are run by wealthier women, a little Junior League. The NBCC is more hardcore advocates or activists. They have more activism in their lives. The NBCC is in your face. Komen is pink ribbons."[90] For NBCC, change comes through working hard in the dog-eat-dog world of policymaking, not through partnering with industry. Another NBCC affiliate noted, "We didn't want to be nice ladies dressed in pink. We wanted to use our knowledge and skill… to bring about change."[91]

NBCC distinguishes itself from other organizations by emphasizing its preparedness and its political stands based on evidence. Its core philosophy is reflected in two of its centerpieces—the advocacy training program, which, as mentioned earlier, culminates in "Lobby Day," when breast cancer survivors from around the country meet with their representatives, and the intensive science training program (Project LEAD) to educate activists about the science behind breast cancer. As a result, one affiliate noted, "People have respect for the NBCC because they always do their homework. We ask based on research and decision making. Before we went down to [an] advocacy conference, we know what we want."[92]

"Always doing their homework" is a theme that popped up repeatedly in my interviews with NBCC representatives as well as those outside the organization. The president of NBCC, Fran Visco, explained the effect that being prepared has had on the NBCC's success. In the beginning, "the only ones doing this kind of thing [disease advocacy] were the AIDS activists. Most people thought it was absurd and outlandish. We took a strategic approach, we did our homework about why it [$300 million] was the right amount and we got it. That opened up a lot of eyes. . … When people saw what is going on here, the field got very crowded. Many people said 'we are advocates too.' " [93]

90. Interview with NBCC affiliate, 2009 (no. 90813).

91. Interview with NBCC affiliate, 2009 (no. 90814).

92. Interview with NBCC affiliate, 2009 (no. 90814).

93. Interview with Fran Visco, 2009.

Still, even though the NBCC takes a decidedly more political stance and pushes government to do more, it, too, frames breast cancer as a consensus women's issue.[94] NBCC representatives straddle the line between pushing hard and pushing too hard. When NBCC wanted more money for breast cancer research in 1992, one activist described their approach: "[W]e told them to figure it out. If they had money for S&L [savings and loan] buddies in Texas, why not for us too? We were not fresh, but forceful. We told them what they needed to hear."[95] The NBCC does its homework and is forceful, but not impolite or unprofessional.

Though the NBCC tries to distinguish itself from (and indeed is frustrated by) Komen's framing of breast cancer as nice and pink, at the same time it has also benefited from it. For most of the nation's history, breast cancer was not a natural fit for policymaking or for public discussion more generally. Instead, breast cancer as a diagnosis was stigmatizing and as a policy issue was threatening. But by partnering with industry and framing the disease as positive and consensual, both Komen and NBCC have benefited. According to one early NBCC activist:

> At the beginning, people were lending us money and then basically forgiving the loans. But when Revlon became a sponsor, it made us legitimate. It is hard to get money when you're doing political work.
> *Because it is more controversial?*
> Yeah, like ACT UP. Pharma's not interested in being associated with it. Individuals don't want their name on that. We went to the Capitol and they're wondering, "are they going to take their shirts off? Are they going show their breasts?" [One early member] who was really funny, said "it's a good thing we don't have breasts!"[96]

94. See also Myhre, *Medical Mavens.*

95. Interview with NBCC affiliate, 2009 (no. 90814).

96. Interview with NBCC affiliate, 2009 (no. 90813).

Partnering with industry—in this case Revlon—gave the NBCC credibility in social and policy circles that countered the threat of potentially
radical tactics (like those of ACT UP) replacing professional ones.

CONSEQUENCES

As a result of its framing—as feminine, hopeful, and uncontroversial—breast cancer has been remarkably successful in both the civic
and political realms. Industry partnerships, through corporate-sponsored races and cause marketing, mean more attention to breast cancer
and to the organizations that engage in cause marketing. As a result,
US breast cancer organizations raise hundreds of millions of dollars
a year.[97] Komen receives money through corporate advertising for its
events and organization. For example, Ford Motors, a Komen corporate partner, runs ads for local and national Races for the Cure. Ford
also sells a pink version of its iconic mustang. An independent audit
by Ernst & Young showed that in a single year (ending March 2008),
Komen and its affiliates received $56.5 million in advertising contri-
butions to promote the Race for the Cure on its behalf. In addition
to promotional advertising, Komen stocked the shelves in supermarkets and shopping malls with pink-ribbon products and held the Race
for the Cure in 114 cities across the nation. In 2008, cause-marketing
revenue totaled more than $5.8 million (16 percent of total revenue)
and the Race for the Cure revenue reached $159 million (43 percent
of total).

Komen's activities give it an enormous fundraising advantage, allowing the affiliates and parent to make a series of awards to activists in
local communities who work on behalf of community health, as well as
medical researchers who apply for grant funding. In the past thirty-two
years, Komen has established 128 local affiliates and raised more than

97. Data from IRS tax filings.

$1.5 billion. Since 1982, it has made 2,200 research grants totaling more than $800 million.[98] Outside of the government, Komen is the second-largest source of funds for cancer research overall, and the largest funder of breast cancer research.[99] Brinker claims, "[T]here hasn't been an advance in breast cancer research that hasn't been touched by a Komen grant."[100] In 2012, Komen had 100,000 volunteers and mobilized more than 1.6 million Americans (through its races and other activities).

Breast cancer has made policy gains too. As disease became more widely political, and not merely the domain of science, Congress earmarked appropriation bills for breast cancer research.[101] Since the 1990s, Congress has held more than a hundred hearings on breast cancer, created the first semi-postal stamp (a portion of the price of the stamp is directed to breast cancer research), established a multibillion-dollar breast cancer program in the Department of Defense, and boosted spending on breast cancer at the National Cancer Institute by 700 percent. Figure 6.2 shows appropriations over time for breast cancer relative to lung cancer (the biggest cancer killer) and prostate cancer (a specific gendered cancer).

The National Institutes of Health (NIH) and the Department of Defense conduct their own research as well as generously fund peer-reviewed research. Since 1992, the National Cancer Institute (NCI) has spent $7.2 billion (12 percent of NCI budget) on breast cancer research, while the DOD has spent $2.2 billion (47 percent of the DOD's Congressionally Directed Medical Research Programs budget).

Political leaders have also demonstrated symbolic support: President George Bush and First Lady Barbara Bush lent their names for breast

---

98. 2013 Research Fast Facts: Overview, http://ww5.komen.org/ResearchGrants/GrantPrograms.html, accessed December 7, 2014.

99. Gina Kolata, "Grant System Leads Cancer Researchers to Play It Safe," *New York Times*, June 27, 2009.

100. Ed Finkel, "Keeping Her Word," *Modern Healthcare* 37, no. 12 (2007): H2–H8. Though more publicly recognizable, Komen funding pales in comparison to federal investments.

101. Alissa J. Rubin, "New Breast Cancer Research Funding Raises Old Questions about Priorities," *CQ Weekly Report*, May 29, 1993.

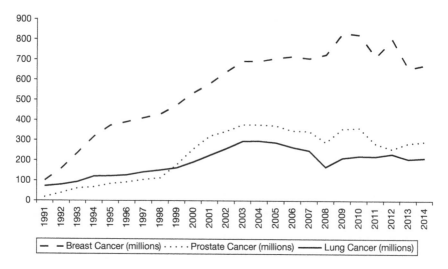

Figure 6.2 NIH spending by disease.
NOTE: 2009 figures include baseline funding supplemented by the American Recovery and Reinvestment Act.
SOURCE: Author's analysis of data from the National Institutes of Health (1991–2004), http://www.nih.gov/news/fundingresearchareas.htm (2005–2008, 2010–2014), and through Freedom of Information Act request (2008–2009).

cancer walks and runs, while the Obama administration wrapped the White House in a two-story pink ribbon.

But this success has come at the price of redefining breast cancer for all Americans. As organizations like Komen chipped away at the stigma that had long surrounded breast cancer, they relied on industry mechanisms to redefine what breast cancer is and what it means to be a woman with breast cancer (a survivor).[102] In races, runs, and product marketing, breast cancer was portrayed as feminine, hopeful, and uncontroversial. It was removed from contentious politics of the women's movement (like abortion) and from more aggressive disease advocacy tactics (like those used by AIDS activists). Organizations in the commercial social movement, like Komen, have organized women around a shared identity as breast cancer survivors or potential breast cancer survivors based on a particular understanding of what that is.

102. Strach, "Gender Practice as Political Practice."

This commercial social movement has created a monopoly around an issue understanding of breast cancer as pink, or feminine, hopeful, and uncontroversial. Rather than a group of activists, the chairs around the decision-making table are often filled by representatives of corporations and corporate-connected groups (like Komen and the Breast Cancer Research Foundation). Breast cancer was chosen by market competition and promoted through market processes rather than political controversy and the policy process. This fact has changed the nature of disease politics within the breast cancer community and among other issue activists.

The overwhelming attention to and focus on pink ribbons and consensus framing privileges one set of activists, hiding the multifaceted breast cancer community and deep divides within it.[103] The NBCC is part of a health social movement that promotes evidence-based practices. It works within policymaking channels: lobbying the federal government and educating activists on the science of breast cancer. NBCC affiliates are frustrated with symbolic attention to breast cancer and policy solutions based on emotion rather than evidence. Environmental breast cancer activists (sometimes members of the NBCC and sometimes not) believe that corporations are responsible for rising breast cancer rates, that corporations must stop carcinogens from contaminating the air, water, and commercial products.[104] But it is hard, if not impossible, to get the message across that corporations are *responsible* for breast cancer when the commercial social movement includes them as partners.

Many breast cancer activists resent Komen's success because it has defined the terms of the breast cancer debate. According to NBCC president Fran Visco: "I am sorry that breast cancer is pink. Pink is soft and sweet. And breast cancer is not soft or sweet, but it gets reduced to pink."[105] It is difficult for breast cancer groups with different perspectives to combat

103. See also Strolovitch, *Affirmative Advocacy*.

104. Ley, *From Pink to Green*; Sulik, "#Rethinkpink"; Sulik and Zierkiewicz, "Gender, Power, and Feminisms in Breast Cancer Advocacy"; King, "Pink Ribbons Inc."; McCormick, *No Family History*; Steingraber, "The Environmental Link to Breast Cancer"; Brown et al., "Embodied Health Movements."

105. Interview with Fran Visco, 2009.

Komen's success. Notes one: "It's very hard. Komen is the elephant in the room."[106] In 2002, Breast Cancer Action in San Francisco created a "Think Before You Pink" campaign, purchasing a quarter-page ad in the *New York Times* featuring a vacuum cleaner and asking, "Who is really cleaning up here?" More mutedly the NBCC launched a "Not Just Ribbons" campaign to focus attention on policy issues over pink products.

But neither Breast Cancer Action nor NBCC does without the funds that come from the sale of specially marked products (even if they do not contain a pink ribbon). The NBCC's October 2006 newsletter highlights the contradiction. At the same time that it notes Barnes and Noble is selling breast cancer merchandise, a portion of the sale of which benefits the NBCC, there is a column by Fran Visco explaining, "I discovered long ago that support comes in two kinds: the easy pink kind and the 'make a real commitment' kind. . . . Tying a ribbon is easy. Making sure breast cancer research gets funded and women have access to care is not."[107]

Groups like the NBCC and its affiliates don't seek out corporate sponsorships. Instead, they are on the receiving end. Companies *want* to get involved with causes that are important to American consumers. Komen really did create a movement, one that companies see as successful and choose to proliferate. Fran Visco explained: "We have no outreach. People call us and tell us they want to donate money from the sale of a product. . . . There are certain guidelines they have to follow. We typically say yes. We have nobody on staff that goes out and gets it."[108] The marketing director of one large nonprofit explained: "[T]his is one of the biggest viral campaigns. . . . K2 saw Wilson rackets. . . . Wilson saw a PSA [public service announcement] for somebody on a plane. It's a crazy, crazy connection."[109]

106. Interview with NBCC affiliate, 2009 (no. 90806).

107. Fran Visco, "Message from Fran Visco: Beyond Pink," *Call to Action*, October 2006, 1.

108. Interview with Fran Visco, October 2009.

109. Interview with cause-marketing expert, 2009 (no. 91009b).

Though breast cancer organizations work together to a greater or lesser extent, the relationship between large national groups is consistently described by insiders familiar with it as "competitive," because even if the *organizations* have distinguished themselves, it is unclear whether elites or the mass public make the same distinctions. The dominant way of understanding breast cancer forms an umbrella over all of the organizations involved, regardless of their own beliefs.

Komen—and other groups engaged in this commercial social movement—have branded breast cancer for everyone, whether the others agree with it or not. There is very little space for individuals or groups who think about breast cancer differently. Although men and women who care about breast cancer or are affected by it may have different problem definitions that lead to very different solutions, they are largely invisible to society. One activist summed up the sentiment from many of the individuals with whom I spoke: "They [individuals] were always mixing [us] up and coming up to me and saying 'I ran the race.' At first, I'd go into a big spiel about how that wasn't us but then I would just say 'thank you' and move on."[110]

A corporate-defined understanding of breast cancer has also influenced the politics of other health concerns. Breast cancer activists claim they did not take money away from other diseases but "expanded the pie" themselves:

[P]eople say that if breast cancer gets funded you're taking money away from kids with Leukemia. But this wasn't the case. We were not taking a bigger piece of the pie. We got new money. It was a real model of how to do it. We lobbied for it. We build grassroots organizing e-mailing and faxing. Michael Milken gets prostate cancer and picks up the phone and makes a call to Congress and gets prostate funding in the DOD. But this came from us.[111]

110. Interview with NBCC affiliate, 2009 (no. 90813).

111. Interview with NBCC affiliate, 2009 (no. 90806).

Noting that surveys of women suggested that they overestimate their risk of getting breast cancer (believing they are more likely to die of breast cancer than heart disease), however, the *New York Times* asked, "[H]as the concern about breast cancer gone too far?"[112] As a result of the commercial social movement, activists for other issues believe that it has. To gain attention—at least in the realm of disease and women's issues—one must start marketing. Disease advocates have modeled breast cancer's success. The American Heart Association now partners with Coca-Cola and Macy's in a Go Red for Women campaign to bring attention to heart disease. Peggy Orenstein explains:

> Before the pink ribbon, awareness as an end in itself was not the default goal for health-related causes. Now you'd be hard-pressed to find a major illness without a logo, a wearable ornament and a roster of consumer-product tie-ins. Heart disease has its red dress, testicular cancer its yellow bracelet. During "Movember"— a portmanteau of "mustache" and "November"—men are urged to grow their facial hair to "spark conversation and raise awareness" of prostate cancer (another illness for which early detection has led to large-scale overtreatment) and testicular cancer.[113]

Breast cancer has become a convenient symbol for women's issues more generally, allowing broad political consensus about helping women without the controversy that surrounds issues of reproduction and workplace equality.[114]

CONCLUSION

Komen wanted to make change in American society *through* market mechanisms. It has been very successful. Market mechanisms have given

---

112. Jane E. Brody, "Breast Cancer Awareness May Carry Its Own Risks," *New York Times*, October 7, 1997.

113. Orenstein, "Our Feel-Good War on Breast Cancer."

114. Mansbridge, *Why We Lost the ERA*; Kristin Luker, *Abortion and the Politics of Motherhood* (Berkeley: University of California Press, 1985).

individuals a chance to talk about problems they might otherwise be un-comfortable addressing. At the same time, these mechanisms redefine issues. Market mechanisms work only when issues have no opposition. But every issue has more than one side. Defining and redefining issues is the fundamental basis of politics, determining who wins, who loses, and how.[115] Cause marketing essentially works to redefine issues as posi-tive and uncontroversial. In the case of breast cancer, activists who find that corporations and environmental concerns are responsible for breast cancer are marginalized, activists who encourage more radical tactics (like taking off shirts to expose mastectomy scars) are quieted, and activ-ists who want to storm the halls of Congress find members of Congress already wearing a pink ribbon.

Baumgartner and Jones note that powerful motivating ideas structure policy institutions. The coalitions that have formed around breast cancer as a consensus issue certainly demonstrate this principle. But if breast cancer is understood as an issue that we can all agree on, activists out-side the mainstream have been working to publicly undermine it. During Breast Cancer Awareness Month in October, along with the scores of pink products are articles and ads critical of these market-based campaigns. Ultimately, to make change to ideas generated through market mecha-nisms, activists outside the commercial social movement will need to challenge the dominant framing.

115. Baumgartner and Jones, *Agendas and Instability in American Politics*; Stone, *Policy Paradox*; Nelson, *Making an Issue of Child Abuse*; Schattschneider, *The Semi-Sovereign People*.

7

Hiding Politics in Plain Sight

Ronald Reagan famously articulated a shift from the New Deal policies of the past when he stated in his first inaugural address, "Government is not the solution to our problem; government is the problem."[1]

The answer was to get government out of the business of providing solutions, to let the private sector take over, and to return to the free market. In the decades following this declaration there has been growing attention placed on the benefits of the private sector in American politics, with both Republicans and Democrats arguing for cutting back the size of the federal government, shifting its role to "steering rather than rowing"; in public policy with an expansion of market-based policy tools, from vouchers that allow parents to choose their child's school to tradable permits that provide incentives for companies to create cleaner emissions; and in political culture as language shifts from "clients" of an agency to "customers" or from "citizens" to "consumers."[2] Americans increasingly are asking not only whether government ought to get involved, for

1. Ronald Reagan Presidential Library and Museum: http://www.reagan.utexas.edu/archives/speeches/1981/12081a.htm, accessed October 5, 2011.

2. David Osborne and Ted Gaebler, *Reinventing Government: How the Entrepreneurial Spirit Is Transforming the Public Sector* (New York: Plume, 1992), 62; Lester M. Salamon, "The New Governance and the Tools of Public Action: An Introduction," in *The Tools of Government: A Guide to New Governance*, ed. Lester M. Salamon (New York: Oxford University Press, 2002), 1–47.

example by regulating an industry or providing a service, but also when government is involved how it ought to act: using more market-oriented principles like choice and competition or more public-oriented principles like equity, fairness, and justice. If ideas about government and public programs are changing, so, too, are expectations of industry. The rise of "corporate social responsibility" means businesses try to connect their brands or products with issues and causes that individuals are likely to support.

Breast cancer activists seized on this opportunity to make broad-based change *with* industry and *through* market mechanisms. Although the 1980s were ripe for a political strategy to address breast cancer after a number of high-profile political women made their diagnoses public and even though Komen had direct ties to elite political actors, the organization branded breast cancer as pink. It worked with industry to sponsor walks and runs and create cause-marketing events designed to take away breast cancer's stigma and encourage individuals to seek, rather than avoid, treatment.

It is hard to overstate the impact that this commercial social movement has had on public understandings of breast cancer. Breast cancer is no longer in the closet. Americans are not afraid to talk about it. Indeed, they talk about it, walk for it, purchase products that benefit it, and wear its symbol daily.

For all of the benefits that come with bringing breast cancer into public discourse, however, there are also significant costs. Breast cancer has a highly visible and broadly shared pink framing that dominates public understanding: breast cancer is feminine, hopeful, and uncontroversial. This understanding is promoted through market mechanisms, especially cause marketing and corporate-sponsored walks and runs. As a result, Americans are more familiar with breast cancer symbols than facts about the disease; more believe that buying a product will have an effect on corporate behavior than believe participating in the policy process will have an effect on public policy. In short, Americans understand breast cancer to be a feel-good *social* issue rather than a contentious *political* one; the disease requires individual social solutions more than collective political ones.

The picture that emerges from this book is that of an issue that nearly every American has been exposed to, many Americans have gotten involved on behalf of (through cause-marketing campaigns), and most feel good about. If breast cancer were truly a valence issue, if breast cancer activists believed it to be so, and if the breast cancer movement were largely united (rather than fragmented), then we could rest easy. But it is not a valence issue, a significant number of activists do not believe that it is, and the movements are sharply divided. I call a consensus frame that conceals deep divisions "hiding politics in plain sight," and I argue in this book that it is problematic.

Breast cancer is not understood to be political, because *some* individuals are able to dominate the reframing and understanding of the disease. Those individuals are not only elites (who have an advantage in American politics) but *corporate-connected* elites who have the skills and the language to succeed in market-based activities, which has implications for democratic politics.

ANATOMY OF THE PROBLEM

On their face, market mechanisms, like cause marketing and corporate-sponsored walks and runs, do not seem particularly potent or problematic. As business scholars have noted, these mechanisms bring social and ethical concerns into the marketplace. What could be wrong with corporations investing more resources (attention and money) in issues and concerns shared by their customers? How could supporting childhood vaccinations or endangered wildlife be a problem?

The answer is that not only do market mechanisms bring social and ethical concerns into the marketplace, they also bring market biases into issue framing. Political scientists study issue framing by looking at media sources and policy actors. But cause-marketing campaigns frame issues too. Unlike media or the policy process, however, individuals do not have to tune in to a particular source. Instead, these campaigns are widespread in supermarkets and shopping malls. Consumers buy cause-marketing products and bring them into their homes, integrating issue messages into their daily routines. Campaigns are highly effective, shaping how Americans think and feel about issues, *even individuals who do not intend to participate in them*. In this book, I show how cause marketing works generally and the effect it has in the case of breast cancer.

The analysis in Chapter 4 suggests that cause marketing tells a specific story, which is short, symbolic, and uncontroversial. Across the full range of issues it addresses, cause marketing has certain core features. It emphasizes awareness over information. It promotes easy solutions. It enables and empowers individuals. And it relies on marketable emotions, like hope. The same principles that work in cause marketing generally also apply to the specific case of breast cancer.

Cause-marketing stories affect how Americans think and feel about issues. Survey data in Chapter 5 suggest that individuals exposed to cause marketing have issue understandings similar to the stories that cause marketing tells. They have greater *awareness* rather than more *information*. Individuals learn from cause marketing, but they are not given concrete information with which to make decisions, as they might with information from media stories. They learn about symbolic aspects of breast cancer, for example that the pink ribbon is a symbol of the disease, rather than facts, such as the lifetime risk of being diagnosed with breast cancer. Greater awareness, however, does not translate into greater issue salience (ranking breast cancer higher than other disease concerns), and it does not lead to demands for collective solutions from either government *or* industry.

Instead, cause marketing seems to enable and empower *individual* action. Survey respondents are more optimistic that cause marketing has an effect on corporations than participating in the political process has an effect on public policy. The overwhelming majority of people who buy cause-marketing products—even unintentionally—say it makes them feel good.

Yet change brought about with industry does not stay contained within a corporation or marketplace; it becomes a part of American culture and public policy. In this model, industry exercises sizable influence not because it lobbies on issues that directly affect it, but because it shapes public understandings on issues that do not. This influence is a by-product of contemporary business practices that emphasize corporate social responsibility.

Individuals and groups with corporate connections speak the language and have the skills to create a monopoly on the way Americans understand particular kinds of issues. Because cause marketing—like other cooperative market mechanisms—works only for issues that sell products, it does not usually address issues that are abstract, complicated, or steeped in controversy. Cause marketing necessarily selects issues that are tangible, something that consumers can readily see or feel. It portrays them as issues Americans can agree on. There is no downside.

However, there is always a downside, an alternative approach, an opponent. This is what politics is all about. Politics generates controversy because "winning" in the political process means destabilizing issue understandings and realigning political coalitions. Politics is fundamentally about conflict. Scholars have shown that markets can expand the policy space and create new frontiers for action: protesting corporations or boycotting city services. Contentious activism draws political values into social spaces. But cooperative actions—like cause marketing—illustrate that the expansion into new policy spaces can promote the definition of issues by elites and reinforce this definition through corporate mechanisms that shape how Americans think about issues. When issue understandings are generated through cause marketing and then reinforced by it over and over again, Americans are exposed to the issue every day but think of it as apolitical.

If an issue is off the American agenda, there is always the possibility that it will be "discovered." There may be a focusing event, like a major disaster or bombshell research report that puts the issue on the front page. But when an issue is very public and has a consistent framing, like breast cancer, opponents of that framing are faced with an overwhelming task: destabilizing the issue understanding, dismantling the monopoly, and taking apart the market mechanisms that reinforce both.

This destabilization is challenging, especially when the issue is seen as apolitical, because we—American consumers and scholars both—assume there is nothing to fight about: breast cancer is a personal disease, not a political issue. In actuality, breast cancer is many things—potentially deadly, disfiguring, frightening, unfair, a public health problem—but it is overwhelmingly understood in American culture as "pink": hopeful, feminine, and uncontroversial.

Pink framing does not make a rational appeal to the intellect, but an emotional appeal to affect. It helps men and women with breast cancer (and their friends and family) make sense of the disease and how to respond to it. Pink framing is highly effective. As one NBCC activist explained to me, "An organization that thinks everything should be pink and is extraordinarily successful gives women and men with breast cancer a real emotional attachment—not only to the disease but with the organization and this pinkness."[3]

Deborah Gould shows how movements " 'make sense' of affective states and authorize selective feelings and actions while downplaying and even invalidating others."[4] Although Gould studies how ACT UP's AIDS activism capitalized on anger, most breast cancer organizations choose ways to address the sadness that surrounds the disease. A representative of a small breast cancer organization noted, "Cancer is a sad and depressing thing, it [sporting activity] makes it very social. . . . It takes away the sadness and the social interaction is wonderful."[5] The head of a large breast cancer organization explained, "We have [a number of sporting events]. . . . There's

3. Interview with NBCC affiliate, 2009 (no. 90817).

4. Gould, *Moving Politics*, 28.

5. Interview with representative of a small breast cancer organization, 2009 (no. 091030a).

600–700 people competing. It's a 'feel good' opportunity.... It's their chance to play. But it is more about camaraderie."[6] The activities in which the universe of breast cancer organizations engage include an extraordinary number of sporting events: walks, runs, bicycling, basketball/soccer/ tennis/golf tournaments, rock climbing, and adventure expeditions.

Far from the picture of a society that is disconnected and in which individuals "bowl alone," breast cancer organizations bring people together in communities across the country.[7] Organizations give individuals an emotional connection with the disease and with each other and the hope that we will better address breast cancer. But these are *social* opportunities more than *collective political* ones. People who come together for corporate-sponsored walks and runs are there as individuals; they are not fighting for collective goals such as more federal funding, better healthcare, or stronger corporate regulation. This can be frustrating for activists who want to engage in more traditional ways of making change. As one activist explained to me, "When you wanted to change something, you used to march. Now you do a corporate run. Breast cancer is the poster child."[8] We can and do have multiple strategies in breast cancer organizing taking place at the same time. Breast cancer activists from other movements take to the streets and show their mastectomy scars, protest large corporations that they believe contribute to cancer, and lobby Congress to give women the healthcare they need to fight the disease. But they are unable to shake breast cancer's pink brand.

Still, breast cancer's more traditional political activists have won major victories in the politics of disease funding, in part because breast cancer is seen as pink. While the National Institutes of Health has long funded disease research, in the 1990s Congress earmarked money for breast cancer. Congress—not bureaucrats or scientific researchers—determines how much

6. Interview with representative of a large breast cancer organization, 2009 (no. 091029a).

7. Robert D. Putnam, *Bowling Alone: The Collapse and Revival of American Community* (New York: Simon & Schuster, 2000).

8. Interview with national breast cancer activist, 2010 (no. 100212).

money goes to fight this problem. Understandably, activists for other issues are frustrated by the overwhelming attention to this one disease, leading some to adopt the same market-based tactics and others to abandon hope.

INTENTIONAL INFLUENCE?

My objective in choosing breast cancer cause marketing is to understand how something located so seemingly inside consumer society and outside mainstream politics shapes public opinion and public policy. In this book, I trace the mechanisms by which it happens: cause marketing's influence through everyday products, the stories these products tell about issues, the effects these issue stories have on public understanding, and the influence of public understanding on public policy.

My aim is not to attack corporations or breast cancer activists who use market mechanisms. Corporate leaders are not intentionally planning to overcome the opposition. I'm sure many of them are unaware that there *is* opposition. For many business executives cause marketing is part and parcel of their marketing departments: it is a way to build their brand. When business leaders do care, their concern is often based on a genuine desire to do good because they or someone close to them has had breast cancer. Similarly, although there are unscrupulous organizations, the original groups that turned to industry to market breast cancer had good intentions. They really were looking to make change. Breast cancer was a stigmatizing disease that needed a public image overhaul, not merely to raise money for research (an important goal, no doubt) but to save lives by encouraging men and women to seek treatment. Nobody I spoke to wanted to go back before the 1980s when the topic of breast cancer was taboo, when surgeons performed mastectomy and biopsy in "one step," and when women feared and avoided diagnosis and treatment.

But when corporations and nonprofit organizations partner, they create very public mechanisms for change. Just about every American has been exposed to cause marketing. Most Americans remember seeing cause-marketing products. A majority of Americans actually buy these products and incorporate them into their daily routines. Many of them participate *unintentionally*, learning lessons about what causes are important and how to think and feel about them without ever intending to do so.

Much of what corporations and organizations do together is described as responsible and ethical; it gives scholars optimism. In many ways it would be easier to tell a story of intentionally devious or overtly political behavior. But I found that undemocratic ends can come from the benign intentions of corporations and nonprofits as well as the unintentional participation of American consumers.

WHERE DO WE GO FROM HERE?

If corporations are not intentionally setting out to win battles, but matching their behavior with Americans' expectations of them—and still they shape understandings and outcomes in American culture, politics, and public policy—are they just more powerful than other actors? Is there anything to do about this democratic dilemma?

Industry exercises a great deal of influence in America. Political scientists study influence by looking at who wins in the political realm. But it can be difficult to tell winners and losers when there is no fight, when industry shapes the terrain on which problems are understood and addressed.[9] In this book, I look at one small way that industry gets involved in addressing public problems, through market mechanisms. In an era when government looks to market-based tools to solve many public problems, industry and individuals connected to it have a distinct advantage without even trying.

I hope this book opens up avenues for additional research, not only on cause marketing or breast cancer but building on the key results presented here. I find that there is a difference between awareness and information. Political scientists and policy scholars tend to focus on the

---

9. Bachrach and Baratz, "Two Faces of Power"; Lukes, *Power*.

latter, running experiments about whether exposure to information has an effect on behavior, suggesting public information campaigns, or writing books and articles designed to *inform*. But awareness—knowing *of* an issue, not necessarily *about* it—can be powerful too. As I show, awareness can displace knowledge, generating a different issue understanding and suggesting a different set of solutions. Who makes use of awareness? For what issues? With what effects? How does awareness compare with strategies that inform?

Additionally, I find that market mechanisms encourage *social* solutions more than *collective* ones. Market mechanisms encourage individuals to get together—for walks, runs, tournaments—and offer an important outlet to *do something* about an issue with others. But social action may differ from collective action in important ways. Social action takes place *with* others but *not to create collective solutions for others*. Although I am not an expert on the sharing economy or social media, the same kinds of analyses might be useful for understanding how individuals come together, how to define collective (even virtual) spaces, how to differentiate social, collective, and other forms of engagement, when (if ever) social action becomes collective action and vice versa, and, finally, how to think about social engagement and political engagement in the current environment.

I also hope this book opens up conversations about the real costs and benefits of market-based policies and market-based mechanisms for change. Markets are often touted as (and indeed sometimes are) more efficient than public mechanisms in accomplishing particular goals, such as providing and distributing good education or healthcare. But relying on markets comes at a cost. Markets privilege individuals with resources: education vouchers are used disproportionately by children of well-educated mothers, while the best healthcare is provided to those with the greatest willingness and ability to pay. I suggest here that market mechanisms shift power to industry and corporate-connected elites. We know that there is growing economic inequality in the United States, and we are still discovering the implications for political inequality.

Are Americans willing to make significant changes through market-based mechanisms if those changes lead to a growing concentration of wealth among a small group of people or if individuals with corporate connections are able to shape public understanding and build public policy around it? In this book I suggest that cause marketing and corporate-sponsored walks and runs change the way Americans think about breast cancer. But this has come at a high cost: *industry and individuals connected to it have a monopoly on how breast cancer is understood at the expense of activists with different causal stories and political solutions.*

We need more information on the true benefits and costs—along different vectors—of market strategies in American culture, politics, and public policy. As I show here, market mechanisms reduced the stigma of breast cancer and brought it out into the open. Yet framing breast cancer as a consensus social issue through market mechanisms gave corporate-connected actors and industry disproportionate influence in shaping public understanding, public policy, and the lives of individuals with the disease. Although I cannot say when, where, and under what circumstances (and with what protections) market mechanisms ought to be used, my research on breast cancer suggests a more tempered optimism about the ability of market mechanisms to serve as a vehicle for democratic change.

Model Details for Chapter 3

Chapter 3 asks what drives participation in cause-marketing campaigns. To answer this question, I borrowed from the broader literature in political science that examines why people participate more generally and supplemented that literature with variables specific to cause marketing. My model uses the following variables (see Table A3.1):

(1) *Knowledge*: People who are politically knowledgeable—who show interest and engagement in politics—are, unsurprisingly, more likely than others to get involved in political activity.[1] Information increases efficacy and participation in politics.[2] Thus, the models I employ include measures of how knowledgeable individuals are according to an index of political knowledge created from two open-ended CCS questions: what job Joe Biden holds (vice president) and who controls the House of Representatives (Democrats).

(2) *Responsibility for Household Purchases*: Because cause marketing takes place in supermarkets and shopping malls, the CCS asked how often the respondent was responsible for making household purchases. Individuals who are primarily responsible for purchasing will have greater exposure to cause marketing and more opportunities to engage with it.

1. Sidney Verba, Kay Lehman Schlozman, and Henry Brady, *Voice and Equality: Civic Volunteerism in American Politics* (Cambridge: Harvard University Press, 1995).

2. Stephen Bennett and William R. Klecka, "Social Status and Political Participation: A Multivariate Analysis of Predictive Power," *Midwest Journal of Political Science* 14, no. 3 (1970): 355–82.

Table A3.1 WHAT DRIVES PARTICIPATION?

	Purchase Cause Marketing Product	Lifestyle Buyers	Cause Followers	Accidental Activists	Bought Pink Products Last Week
Knowledge					
Political knowledge	−0.046 (0.121)	−0.089 (0.159)	−0.106 (0.134)	0.104 (0.128)	−0.220[+] (0.116)
Responsibility for Household Purchases	0.073 (0.083)	0.242[+] (0.137)	0.023 (0.091)	−0.023 (0.091)	0.204* (0.085)
Efficacy					
Local	0.334** (0.118)	0.157 (0.155)	0.451*** (0.122)	−0.097 (0.116)	0.057 (0.110)
National	0.042 (0.111)	0.062 (0.131)	−0.111 (0.110)	0.112 (0.102)	0.051 (0.103)
Charitable Activities					
Volunteer	0.542** (0.173)	0.449[+] (0.250)	0.330[+] (0.182)	0.021 (0.173)	0.344* (0.168)
Donate Money	0.332[+] (0.176)	−0.021 (0.260)	0.161 (0.201)	0.246 (0.179)	0.516** (0.181)
Confidence in Business	0.135 (0.108)	0.119 (0.148)	−0.124 (0.122)	0.228* (0.106)	0.009 (0.106)
Personal Connection to Breast Cancer	0.047 (0.186)	0.166 (0.248)	0.276 (0.196)	−0.208 (0.181)	0.403* (0.175)
Controls					
Age 38–56	−0.376[+] (0.217)	−0.252 (0.263)	−0.219 (0.216)	−0.151 (0.213)	0.027 (0.207)
Age 57 and up	−1.159*** (0.209)	−1.037*** (0.304)	−0.925*** (0.217)	−0.067 (0.209)	−0.142 (0.210)
Race (White)	0.712*** (0.191)	0.106 (0.273)	0.177 (0.220)	0.538* (0.210)	−0.610*** (0.183)
Gender (Female)	0.378* (0.168)	0.324 (0.242)	0.451* (0.197)	−0.215 (0.177)	0.361* (0.170)

(continued)

Table A3.1 CONTINUED

	Purchase Cause Marketing Product	Lifestyle Buyers	Cause Followers	Accidental Activists	Bought Pink Products Last Week
Education	0.069	0.003	−0.010	0.069	−0.051
	(0.056)	(0.075)	(0.062)	(0.054)	(0.054)
Income	0.058[+]	−0.028	0.065[+]	0.024	0.013
	(0.031)	(0.042)	(0.034)	(0.032)	(0.030)
Ideology	−0.443*	−0.113	−0.222	−0.163	−0.148
(Conservative)	(0.185)	(0.280)	(0.215)	(0.187)	(0.186)
Ideology	0.182	0.610*	0.279	−0.449*	−0.013
(Liberal)	(0.222)	(0.270)	(0.230)	(0.212)	(0.216)
Constant	−1.436***	−2.977***	−2.299***	−2.118***	−1.335***
	(0.401)	(0.541)	(0.461)	(0.389)	(0.403)
N	1,422	1,422	1,422	1,422	1,422

[+] $p < .10$, * $p < .05$, ** $p < .01$, *** $p < .001$ (two-tailed test).

NOTE: Logistic regression coefficients, robust standard errors in parentheses.

SOURCE: CCS data (see Appendices C and D for more information).

(3) *Efficacy*: Scholars have shown that people who get involved in politics are more likely than those who do not to feel that their participation in politics makes a difference and being on the "winning" side encourages greater efficacy, though the causal direction is unclear.[3] Because cause marketing takes place at the local level, the CCS asked respondents about the difference they could make on issues at two distinct levels: national issues (such as the economy or foreign affairs) and local community issues (like traffic or homelessness).

3. Joe Soss, "Lessons of Welfare: Policy Design, Political Learning, and Political Action," *The American Political Science Review* 93, no. 2 (1999): 363–80; Steven E. Finkel, "Reciprocal Effects of Participation and Political Efficacy: A Panel Analysis," *American Journal of Political Science* 29, no. 4 (1985): 891–913; Patrick Flavin and John D. Griffin, "Policy, Preferences, and Participation: Government's Impact on Democratic Citizenship," *Journal of Politics* 71, no. 2 (2009): 544–59.

(4) *Charitable Activities*: An individual's participation may be a function of his or her involvement in other kinds of activities. People who care deeply about their communities and choose to get involved—volunteering for charitable organizations, working for a campaign, buying products that support a particular cause—are likely to be involved in many ways because they are committed to the public good and likely to be around others who also participate.[4] In short, high participators are high participators across different participatory venues.[5] Thus, I also include measures of participation (volunteering or donating money) in charitable activities.

(5) *Confidence in Business*: One's choice to participate may be determined by the faith one places in the institutions that structure the venue. We know that people who have faith in government are more likely than others to participate in politics, and those who lack faith in government are less likely to do so.[6] The same logic applies to market activity. Those people who have faith in market mechanisms may be more likely to participate in cause marketing. The CCS asked respondents how much confidence they had in business, and I included a variable based on this measure.

(6) *Connection to Breast Cancer*: Whether one participates may be influenced by how one feels not about cause marketing generally, but about a particular cause that market activity will benefit—more pointedly, whether individuals perceive that a cause affects them directly.[7] People pay attention to—and act

4. Robert D. Putnam, *Bowling Alone: The Collapse and Revival of American Community* (New York: Simon and Schuster, 2000); James H. Fowler and Cindy D. Kam, "Beyond the Self: Social Identity, Altruism, and Political Participation," *The Journal of Politics* 69, no. 3 (2007): 813–27; James H. Fowler, "Altruism and Turnout," *Journal of Politics* 68, no. 3 (2006): 674–83.

5. Cliff Zukin, Scott Keeter, Molly Andolina, Krista Jenkins, and Michael X. Delli Carpini, *A New Engagement: Political Participation, Civic Life, and the Changing American Citizen* (New York: Oxford University Press, 2006); Verba, Schlozman, and Brady, *Voice and Equality*.

6. Suzanne Mettler, *Soldiers to Citizens: The GI Bill and the Making of the Greatest Generation* (New York: Oxford University Press, 2005); Gould, *Moving Politics*; Soss, "Lessons of Welfare."

7. Mark Baldassare and Cheryl Katz, "The Personal Threat of Environmental Problems as Predictor of Environmental Practices," *Environment and Behavior* 24, no. 5 (1992): 602–16.

on—the issues they care most about.[8] Thus, I include a variable for an individual who has breast cancer or has a close family member or friend with the disease in models that examine participation in breast cancer campaigns.

(7) *Demographic Controls*: Finally, any model must include sociodemographic controls that may influence participation. The dominant model of political participation is based on resources. More advantaged populations participate at higher rates, whether because resources reduce the costs of getting involved or because resources form the basis for other civic skills.[9] But age also plays a role in types of participation Americans choose through political learning, habitual behavior, or cohort effects.[10] Gender, race, and ideology have been demonstrated to make a difference in the ways that Americans engage in politics.[11] Thus, I control for age, race, gender, education, income, and ideology.

8. Hahrie Han, *Moved to Action: Motivation, Participation, and Inequality in American Politics* (Stanford: Stanford University Press, 2009).

9. Anthony Downs, *An Economic Theory of Democracy* (New York: Harper and Row 1957); Verba, Schlozman, and Brady, *Voice and Equality*.

10. Sidney Verba and Norman H. Nie, *Participation in America: Political Democracy and Social Equality* (New York: Harper and Row, 1972); Elizabeth Beaumont, "Promoting Political Agency, Addressing Political Inequality: A Multilevel Model of Internal Political Efficacy," *Journal of Politics* 73, no. 1 (2011): 216–31; Achim Goerres, "Why Are Older People More Likely to Vote? The Impact of Aging on Electoral Turnout in Europe," *British Journal of Politics and International Relations* 9, no. 1 (2007): 90–121; Eric Plutzer, "Becoming a Habitual Voter: Inertia, Resources, and Growth in Young Adulthood," *American Political Science Review* 96, no. 1 (2002): 41–56; Zukin et al., *A New Engagement*; Verba and Nie, *Participation in America*; Gabriel Sanchez, "The Role of Group Consciousness in Political Participation Among Latinos in the United States," *American Politics Research* 34, no. 4 (2006): 427–50.

11. Nancy Burns, Kay Lehman Schlozman, and Sidney Verba, *The Private Roots of Public Action: Gender, Equality, and Political Participation* (Cambridge, MA: Harvard University Press, 2001); Paul Mohai, "Men, Women, and the Environment: An Examination of the Gender Gap in Environmental Concern and Activism," *Society and Natural Resources: An International Journal* 5, no. 1 (1992): 1–19; Marvin E. Olsen, "Social and Political Participation of Blacks," *American Sociological Review* 35, no. 4 (1970): 682–97; Atiya Kai Stokes, "Latino Group Consciousness and Political Participation," *American Politics Research* 31, no. 4 (2003): 361–78; Robert Huckfeldt, Jeffrey Levine, William Morgan, and John Sprague, "Accessibility and the Political Unity of Partisan and Ideological Orientations," *American Journal of Political Science* 43, no. 3 (1999): 888–911; Adam Berinsky, "Silent Voices: Social Welfare Policy Opinions and Political Equality in America," *American Journal of Political Science* 46, no. 2 (2002): 276–87.

Regression Results for Chapter 5

Table B5.1 PREDICTORS OF BREAST CANCER AWARENESS

Exposure to breast cancer campaigns (products, walks, and stories) leads to greater knowledge that October is Breast Cancer Awareness Month, but only exposure to pink products increases odds of knowing that pink ribbons are the symbol of breast cancer.

	Know October Is Breast Cancer Awareness Month	Know Pink Ribbons Are the Symbol of Breast Cancer
Exposure to Breast Cancer Campaigns		
See Pink Products	0.536**	1.585***
	(0.199)	(0.236)
See Pink Fundraising	0.626***	−0.084
Walks	(0.183)	(0.242)
See Pink Stories	0.579**	−0.063
	(0.203)	(0.230)
Controls		
October	1.715***	−0.171
	(0.173)	(0.227)
Political Knowledge	0.261*	0.555***
	(0.129)	(0.154)
Responsibility for	0.086	0.070
Household Purchases	(0.087)	(0.106)
Personal Connection to	0.001	0.538⁺
Breast Cancer	(0.193)	(0.283)
Age 38–56	0.216	−0.665*
	(0.233)	(0.327)

(*continued*)

Table B5.1 CONTINUED

	Know October Is Breast Cancer Awareness Month	Know Pink Ribbons Are the Symbol of Breast Cancer
Age 57 and up	−0.439[+]	−1.518***
	(0.229)	(0.303)
Race (White)	0.068	0.900***
	(0.206)	(0.250)
Gender (Female)	0.868***	1.586***
	(0.188)	(0.271)
Education	0.021	0.222**
	(0.055)	(0.083)
Income	0.016	0.133**
	(0.033)	(0.042)
Constant	−3.748***	−1.819***
	(0.391)	(0.434)
N	1,475	1,475

[+] $p < .10$, * $p < .05$, ** $p < .01$, *** $p < .001$ (two-tailed test).

NOTE: Logistic regression coefficients, robust standard errors in parentheses.

SOURCE: CCS data (see Appendices C and D for more information).

Table B5.2 PREDICTORS OF BREAST CANCER KNOWLEDGE

Exposure to breast cancer campaigns does not increase the odds of knowing a woman's risk of breast cancer, but exposure to pink products (not walks or stories) does increase the odds of knowing about breast cancer funding.

	Know Women's Risk	Know Breast Cancer Funding
Exposure to Breast Cancer Campaigns		
See Pink Products	−0.135	0.320*
	(0.162)	(0.158)
See Pink Fundraising Walks	0.257	0.067
	(0.157)	(0.154)
See Pink Stories	0.031	0.100
	(0.159)	(0.155)

(continued)

Table B5.2 CONTINUED

	Know Women's Risk	Know Breast Cancer Funding
Controls		
October	−0.150	0.035
	(0.149)	(0.144)
Political Knowledge	0.095	0.102
	(0.104)	(0.103)
Responsibility for	−0.009	0.024
Household Purchases	(0.079)	(0.078)
Personal Connection to	−0.033	0.076
Breast Cancer	(0.167)	(0.166)
Age 38–56	0.302	−0.336+
	(0.191)	(0.188)
Age 57 and up	0.032	−0.637***
	(0.186)	(0.186)
Race (White)	0.177	0.244
	(0.174)	(0.173)
Gender (Female)	0.083	0.308*
	(0.160)	(0.156)
Education	0.038	0.191***
	(0.049)	(0.047)
Income	0.038	−0.032
	(0.027)	(0.026)
Constant	−0.204	−1.193***
	(0.318)	(0.303)
N	1,475	1,475

$^+ p < .10$, $^* p < .05$, $^{**} p < .01$, $^{***} p < .001$ (two-tailed test).

NOTE: Logistic regression coefficients, robust standard errors in parentheses.

SOURCE: CCS data (See Appendices C and D for more information).

Table B5.3 Predictors of Breast Cancer as Top Priority

Exposure to pink stories (but not products or fundraising walks) increases the odds of rating breast cancer as a top disease priority (compared with heart disease and diabetes).

	Breast Cancer Top Disease Priority
Exposure to Breast Cancer Campaigns	
See Pink Products	0.080
	(0.191)
See Pink Fundraising Walks	−0.114
	(0.194)
See Pink Stories	0.390*
	(0.194)
Controls	
October	0.072
	(0.173)
Political Knowledge	−0.342**
	(0.120)
Responsibility for Household Purchases	0.077
	(0.091)
Personal Connection to Breast Cancer	0.322+
	(0.192)
Age 38–56	−0.051
	(0.215)
Age 57 and up	−0.123
	(0.215)
Race (White)	0.162
	(0.199)
Gender (Female)	−0.326+
	(0.181)
Education	−0.062
	(0.059)
Income	0.037
	(0.032)

(continued)

Table B5.3 CONTINUED

	Breast Cancer Top Disease Priority
Faith in Government Action	0.416*
	(0.172)
Constant	−1.531***
	(0.397)
N	1,475

$^+ p < .10,$ $^* p < .05,$ $^{**} p < 0.01,$ $^{***} p < 0.001$ (two-tailed test).

NOTE: Logistic regression coefficients, robust standard errors in parentheses.

SOURCE: CCS data (see Appendices C and D for more information).

Table B5.4 PREDICTORS OF GOVERNMENT ACTION FOR RESEARCH AND TREATMENT

Exposure to breast cancer campaigns does not increase the odds that respondents say government should do more.

	Government Should Do More Research	Government Should Do More Treatment
Exposure to Breast Cancer Campaigns		
See Pink Products	0.163	0.168
	(0.169)	(0.171)
See Pink Fundraising Walks	−0.115	−0.033
	(0.161)	(0.161)
See Pink Stories	−0.045	−0.120
	(0.161)	(0.160)
Controls		
October	−0.201	0.062
	(0.152)	(0.151)
Political Knowledge	−0.109	−0.225*
	(0.108)	(0.108)
Responsibility for Household	0.000	0.061
Purchases	(0.082)	(0.087)
Personal Connection to	−0.066	0.073
Breast Cancer	(0.174)	(0.168)

(continued)

Table B5.4 Continued

	Government Should Do More Research	Government Should Do More Treatment
Age 38–56	0.187	0.122
	(0.193)	(0.198)
Age 57 and up	−0.269	−0.166
	(0.196)	(0.195)
Race (White)	0.037	0.050
	(0.184)	(0.185)
Gender (Female)	0.057	0.320[+]
	(0.169)	(0.171)
Education	−0.116*	−0.024
	(0.051)	(0.051)
Income	−0.013	−0.064*
	(0.028)	(0.028)
Faith in Government Action	0.703***	0.862***
	(0.162)	(0.164)
Confidence in Congress	0.413*	0.129
	(0.174)	(0.174)
Confidence in Agencies	−0.008	−0.040
	(0.172)	(0.176)
Constant	−0.263	−0.513
	(0.337)	(0.356)
N	1,443	1,443

[+] $p < .10$, * $p < .05$, ** $p < .01$, *** $p < .001$ (two-tailed test).

NOTE: Logistic regression coefficients, robust standard errors in parentheses.

SOURCE: CCS data (see Appendices C and D for more information).

Table B5.5 PREDICTORS OF BUSINESS ACTION FOR RESEARCH AND TREATMENT

Exposure to breast cancer campaigns does not increase the odds that respondents say business should do more.

	Business Should Do More Research	Business Should Do More Treatment
Exposure to Breast Cancer Campaigns		
See Pink Products	0.141	0.053
	(0.175)	(0.166)
See Pink Fundraising Walks	0.141	0.124
	(0.164)	(0.165)
See Pink Stories	−0.062	−0.031
	(0.173)	(0.169)
Controls		
October	0.275[+]	−0.145
	(0.157)	(0.159)
Political Knowledge	0.376**	0.363**
	(0.126)	(0.123)
Responsibility for Household Purchases	0.076	−0.075
	(0.082)	(0.090)
Personal Connection to Breast Cancer	0.150	0.017
	(0.184)	(0.173)
Age 38–56	−0.133	0.053
	(0.216)	(0.209)
Age 57 and up	−0.060	−0.021
	(0.205)	(0.201)
Race (White)	0.247	0.056
	(0.209)	(0.202)
Gender (Female)	−0.332[+]	−0.544**
	(0.170)	(0.176)
Education	0.097[+]	0.001
	(0.053)	(0.054)
Income	0.038	0.128***
	(0.031)	(0.030)
Faith in the Free Market	0.567***	0.625***
	(0.159)	(0.159)
Confidence in Business	0.084	0.270**
	(0.115)	(0.104)

(*continued*)

Table B5.5 CONTINUED

	Business Should Do More Research	Business Should Do More Treatment
Constant	−2.962***	−2.568***
	(0.436)	(0.423)
N	1,404	1,404

+ p < .10, * p < .05, ** p < .01, *** p < .001 (two-tailed test).

NOTE: Logistic regression coefficients, robust standard errors in parentheses.

SOURCE: CCS data (see Appendices C and D for more information).

Table B5.6 PREDICTORS OF THE EFFECTS OF CONSUMER ACTION

Lifestyle buyers, cause followers, and accidental activists are more likely to say that socially responsible purchasing has an impact on companies' behavior. Cause followers and accidental activists (but not lifestyle buyers) are more likely to say that socially responsible purchasing has an impact on personal satisfaction.

	Companies' Behavior	Personal Satisfaction
Motivation		
Lifestyle Buyers	0.800**	0.359
	(0.255)	(0.281)
Cause Followers	0.868***	0.580*
	(0.202)	(0.249)
Accidental Activists	0.583**	0.505*
	(0.180)	(0.220)
Political Knowledge	0.017	0.185+
	(0.085)	(0.096)
Responsibility for	−0.026	−0.165+
Household Purchases	(0.079)	(0.096)
Efficacy		
Local	0.120	0.156
	(0.103)	(0.115)
National	0.218*	0.232*
	(0.094)	(0.115)

(*continued*)

Table B5.6 CONTINUED

	Companies' Behavior	Personal Satisfaction
Charitable Activities		
Volunteer	0.030	−0.240
	(0.159)	(0.190)
Donate Money	−0.283⁺	0.011
	(0.168)	(0.190)
Confidence in Business	0.176⁺	0.050
	(0.096)	(0.109)
Personal Connection	−0.234	−0.468*
to Breast Cancer	(0.171)	(0.189)
Controls		
Age 38–56	0.125	0.141
	(0.195)	(0.237)
Age 57 and up	−0.078	−0.678***
	(0.194)	(0.232)
Race (White)	−0.098	0.556**
	(0.185)	(0.204)
Gender (Female)	−0.026	0.076
	(0.159)	(0.190)
Education	0.053	0.135*
	(0.051)	(0.060)
Income	0.005	0.054⁺
	(0.027)	(0.030)
Ideology (Conservative)	0.024	0.342⁺
	(0.167)	(0.191)
Ideology (Liberal)	0.355⁺	0.560*
	(0.209)	(0.247)
Constant	−0.870*	−0.839*
	(0.368)	(0.417)
N	1,422	1,422

⁺ $p < .10$, * $p < .05$, ** $p < .01$, *** $p < .001$ (two-tailed test).

NOTE: Logistic regression coefficients, robust standard errors in parentheses.

SOURCE: CCS data (see Appendices C and D for more information).

Notes on Methodology and Sources

CITIZEN ATTITUDES: THE 2010 CITIZEN CONSUMER SURVEY (CCS)

In October 2008, I ran four grid questions (thirty-five total items) on the October Wave of the Cooperative Campaign Analysis Project (CCAP). The CCAP is a six-wave national panel of twenty thousand adults (Simon Jackman, Stanford Vavreck, and Lynn Vavreck, UCLA Principal Investigators) and is fielded by Polimetrix online. In addition to the standard battery of questions, I asked questions about political activities in which the respondent participated in the past thirty days (including boycotting/buycotting), whether the respondent thinks about social or political concerns before purchasing particular types of goods; whether the respondent has knowledge of two particular cause-marketing campaigns; and what the respondent believes are the effects of these campaigns. The answers to these questions helped to identify useful avenues for further study.

The National Science Foundation generously granted me funds to write a survey the purpose of which was to ask about consumers' views, to probe the sources of these opinions, and to explore the consequences of the opinions. Abt SRBI pretested the survey in early September and conducted the survey in September and October 2010. The Computer Assisted Telephone Interviewing (CATI) survey consisted of a nationally representative sample of 1,500 adults (age 18 and over) with ten callbacks and one refusal conversion attempt on all soft refusals. Because previous research has shown that boycotting/buycotting is practiced disproportionately by younger individuals (who are also less likely to have or use landlines), the 1,500-person sample was broken down into 1,200 landline and 300 cell phone respondents. Cell phone users (who are harder to attract to answer questions) were given incentives to participate. The survey questions are presented in Appendix D.

ORGANIZATIONS: ARCHIVAL RESEARCH AND INTERVIEWS

To tell a complicated history in a short space, I selected two organizations for more in-depth analysis, Susan G. Komen (Komen) and the National Breast Cancer Coalition (NBCC), because these organizations exemplify inside channels to achieving change. Though both organizations do advocacy work and cause marketing, Komen is a prime force in the commercial social movement around breast cancer and the NBCC in the health social movement.

Archival Research

I collected data from publicly available sources for both organizations: newspaper stories, books, websites, IRS tax documents, and congressional hearings. In addition, early papers of several breast cancer organizations (Arm-in-Arm, Breast Cancer Advisory Center, Breast Cancer Network, National Association of Breast Cancer Organizations [NABCO], and the National Breast Cancer Coalition) are housed at the Schlesinger Library, Radcliffe Institute for Advanced Study, Harvard University. I copied approximately one thousand pages from the archives on these organizations (especially the NBCC). In writing the history of breast cancer activism in the United States and the case studies, I relied most extensively on Rose Kushner's (Breast Cancer Advisory Center, NABCO) and Kay Dickersin's

(Arm-in-Arm, Breast Cancer Network, NBCC) collections. The full cita-
tions for these papers are as follows:

> Rose Kushner's Papers, 1953–1990; item description, dates. MC
> 453, Schlesinger Library, Radcliffe Institute for Advanced Study,
> Harvard University (abbreviated RKP in the notes).
> Kay Dickersin Papers, 1991–2002; item description, dates, 2005-
> M119, carton no., Schlesinger Library, Radcliffe Institute for
> Advanced Study, Harvard University (abbreviated KDP in the
> notes).

Interviews

In addition, to learn more about these two organizations and breast cancer
activism, I conducted twenty-two interviews with individuals associated
with breast cancer organizations and/or cause marketing, including:

- eight NBCC/F affiliates (e.g., board members, executives)
- six current or former Komen executives
- three experts on cause marketing
- one national breast cancer activist
- four background interviews

Three of the interviews were conducted in person and the remainder
over the phone. The bulk of the interviews (nineteen) took place between
March and October 2009. Two interviews occurred before then, one in
2007 and one in 2008. Interviews were from one-half to two hours long—
most lasted forty-five minutes to an hour. Respondents are identified
according to one of four categories (NBCC affiliate, Komen executive,
cause-marketing expert, national breast cancer activist), except Fran
Visco, president of the NBCC, who is identified by name. I requested,
but was not granted, an interview with Nancy Brinker of Komen. Her
perspective is captured from memoirs and congressional testimony.

In addition to looking closely at these two organizations, I interviewed a random sample of organizational representatives from the broader population of breast cancer organizations to learn what they do, why they do it, and what their relationship is to the two national organizations (and strategies) I am interested in. To create the sample, I examined those organizations that had filed as a tax-exempt organization with the Internal Revenue Service with "breast" or "breast cancer" in the title and those that were categorized as cancer or women's health organizations, eliminating organizations that are not cancer-specific (e.g., breastfeeding groups), professional organizations (e.g., breast health specialists), and groups for which breast cancer is a small part of their overall mission (e.g., women's groups that focus less than half of their attention on breast cancer).

I selected a thirty-organization sample stratified by size:

- Small organizations have reported assets up to $24,999 (the minimum reporting requirement).
- Medium organizations have reported assets between $25,000 and $499,999.
- Large organizations have reported assets at $500,000 and above.

With the help of a research assistant, I tracked down the best contact information I could find for the organizations (looking first for an organizational website, tax records, and then to local phone directories). This exercise was instructive for data quality. Of the original thirty-organization sample, we could not find contact information (either a phone number or an email address) for six of the organizations (20 percent). Four of those organizations are characterized as small and two as medium. Our inability to locate these organizations squares with the anecdotal stories that respondents told about the creation and waning of groups associated with breast cancer. One organization was listed twice (two EIN, or tax ID, numbers). I called the remaining twenty-three organizations (up to four callbacks) and completed semistructured interviews with seventeen of them (74 percent response rate). Two organizations requested, and received, the questions by email.

All interviews followed the proposed questions for the organizational survey, but allowed organizational representatives to elaborate on their answers. I spoke with the head of the organization when there was either a very small paid staff (one or two people) or no staffers. When the organization was large enough to have a director of communications, I asked to speak with him or her. The interviews took place between October and November 2009, and they lasted anywhere between fifteen minutes and an hour. All respondents were promised neither they nor their organization would be identified. They are identified by the categories listed earlier (small, medium, large). These interviews do not figure prominently in this book, but they bolster the story told here.

COMPARATIVE CAUSES: CONTENT ANALYSIS

Because there is no comprehensive database of cause-marketing campaigns, organizations, or causes, with the help of a research assistant I created a database from articles. We searched for "cause marketing" and "cause branding" in *Advertising Age* between 1988 and August 2010 on Lexis-Nexis and on the *Advertising Age* online archive (adage.com, which includes their blog). We coded these stories following the same procedures that Baumgartner and Jones followed in their Policy Agendas Project. Between 1988 and 2010, we identified 381 cause-marketing stories. During nearly the same time frame (1988 and 2008) Congress held more than 32,000 hearings (19,943 in the House, 11,495 in the Senate, and 650 joint). The overwhelming majority of hearings lasted just one day, but some lasted as long as a week or more.

I compare those issues to which cause marketers devote their attention (as discussed in the database of causes generated for this project) and those issues that policymakers devote their attention to (as measured by hearings in the Policy Agendas Project). Neither of these sources provides a complete picture of what is being done and how it is being accomplished. The cause-marketing database contains cause-marketing campaigns found in news stories and press releases, while the hearings data are a complete accounting of all hearings. Further, the hearings are just one slice of the policy process. Still, I believe these two sources offer the most complete and representative sample of stories generated and told through cause marketing and the policy process. With respect to quantitative data, the number of hearings far surpasses the number of cause-marketing campaigns in part because there really are more hearings than national cause-marketing campaigns, but also because I have captured all hearings whereas I have made only the best attempt at capturing all campaigns. With respect to the qualitative data, the hearings are a richer source of information; therefore, I supplement what is found in the cause-marketing campaigns with material found on websites, social media, and articles.

For the qualitative analysis, I looked at the issue areas that are most prevalent in cause marketing, most prevalent in the policy process, and most prevalent in both. The top cases for cause marketing and for policy were selected at random using STATA from the subset of issues and matched for comparison. For example, the Agendas Project codes Government Operations into eighteen subtopic codes, and my random sample included one. With this strategy, the issues that were randomly selected are most likely, but not always, the subtopics to which the policy process devoted the most attention. In the case of Government Operations, my sample included appropriations, the second most common category. The case illustrated for comparison from cause marketing was chosen at random in the same category, unless there were too few cases from which to select.

In addition to the general landscape for cause marketing and policy, I mapped the specific case of breast cancer. In February 2014, I searched ProQuest Congressional for mentions of "breast cancer" and "lung cancer" in all fields (e.g., subject, source, title), except full text for congressional documents (legislative histories from 1969, bills and laws from

1987, committee prints from 1789, Congressional Record from 1985, hearings from 1824, House and Senate documents from 1789, and House and Senate reports from 1789 to the present). The search returned 1,377 items for breast cancer and 211 for lung cancer. I sorted them by relevance and chose the top 100 (most relevant) items for each.

LANDLINE INTRO

Hello, my name is _____, and I'm calling from the Abt SRBI Public Affairs Research Center on behalf of researchers at the University at Albany, State University of New York. We are conducting a brief telephone survey to talk with you about your attitudes and beliefs on some current issues. So that all types of people are represented in our survey, may I please speak to the person 18 years or older living in your household who had a birthday most recently? [GO TO BEGIN]

CELL INTRO:

Hello, my name is _____, and I'm calling from the Abt SRBI Public Affairs Research Center on behalf of researchers at the University at Albany, State University of New York. We are conducting a brief telephone survey to talk with you about your attitudes and beliefs on some current issues. We are not selling anything. As a small token of our appreciation, we will provide you $10 for participating in this study. Are you at least 18 yeas old?

(C1) If you are now driving or doing any activity requiring your full attention, I can call you back later.

    1 NO, NOT DRIVING → PROCEED

    2 YES, CURRENTLY DRIVING/NOT AVAILABLE → SCHEDULE CALLBACK

    8 DK [THANK AND END]

    9 REF [THANK AND END]

(C2) Just to verify, is this a cell phone?

    1 YES → PROCEED WITH INTERVIEW [GO TO 1.1]

    2 NO [THANK AND END]

    8 DK [THANK AND END]

    9 REF [THANK AND END]

[BEGIN]

Before we begin, we would like to assure you that the interview is confidential and completely voluntary. If we should come to any question that you don't want to answer, just let me know and we'll go on to the next question.

We'd like to start off by asking you some questions about your shopping habits.

I. *Consumer Habits:*

  (1) In general, how often do you shop at [INSERT ITEM, RANDOMIZE]. Would you say more than once per week, once a week, every other week, once a month, less often, or never?

    (a) Grocery stores

    (b) Shopping malls

    (c) Large general retail stores, like Wal-Mart or Target

      1. More than once per week

      2. Once per week

      3. Every other week

      4. Once a month

      5. Less often

      6. Never

8. (VOL) Don't know

9. (VOL) Refused

(2) In your household, how often are you responsible for purchasing **household goods (like groceries, small electrics,
or linens)?**

1. Never

2. Sometimes

3. Often

4. Almost always

8. (VOL) Don't know

9.(VOL) Refused

(4) (IF Q2 ≠1) When you are purchasing **household goods**,
which of the following considerations is most important in
your decision to purchase?

1. Price

2. Quality

4. Social or political considerations

8. (VOL) Don't know

9. (VOL) Refused

(4b) (IF Q2 ≠1) And which would you say is second most
important?

[CATI: Use same list, remove answer from Question 2]

II. *Political, Civic, and Market Behavior*

**Now, we're going to ask you some questions about political and civic
activities that you may or may not participate in.** We know that many
people are busy and move around often, making some or all of these
difficult to do. To the best of your knowledge,

(6) Did you vote in the November 2008 presidential election?

1. Yes

2. No

8. (VOL) Don't know

9. (VOL) Refused

(6b) [If Q6 ≠1]

Were you registered to vote for this election?

> 1. Yes
> 2. No
> 8. (VOL) Don't know
> 9. (VOL) Refused

(7) For each of the following, please tell me whether you have done an activity or not in the past month [RANDOMIZE, item j should always be followed by item k].

> (a) Contacted a government official at any level of government to express your opinion
> (b) Worked for a political party or candidate
> (c) Contributed money for a political campaign
> (d) Attended a political meeting, rally, or speech
> (e) Displayed a political button, sticker, sign
> (f) Signed an e-mail or written petition about a political issue.
> (h) Volunteered or participated in charity or public service projects
> (i) Contributed money to a charitable organization
> (j) Bought something from a company because you agree with the social or political values of the company that produces it
> (k) NOT bought something from a company because you disagree with the social or political values of the company that produces it.
> (l) Personally walked, ran, or bicycled for a charitable cause—this is separate from sponsoring or giving money to this type of event.
> 1. Yes
> 2. No
> 8. (VOL) Don't know
> 9. (VOL) Refused

(8) Please tell me if you agree or disagree with the following statements. [CATI: BLOCK ROTATION]

    a. When an individual contacts an elected official it has an effect on government policy

    b. When an individual contacts an elected official it has an effect on an individual's personal satisfaction

    c. When an individual volunteers or participates in charity or public service projects it has an effect on the local community

    d. When an individual volunteers or participates in charity or public service projects it has an effect on an individual's personal satisfaction

    e. When an individual buys something because he or she agrees with the political or social values of the company that produces it, it has an effect on companies' behavior

    f. When an individual buys something because he or she agrees with the political or social values of the company that produces it, it has an effect on an individual's personal satisfaction

    1. Agree

    2. Disagree

    8. (VOL) Don't know

    9. (VOL) Refused

(26) Many people put ribbons on their cars or wear them on their clothes in order to show their support for a social or political issue. Can you tell me what causes the following ribbons stand for?

    a. Yellow Ribbon (DO NOT READ)

        1. Support our troops/Veterans

        2. Suicide awareness

        3. Something else

        8. (VOL) Don't know

        9. (VOL) Refused

      b. Pink Ribbon (DO NOT READ)

      1. Breast Cancer

      2. Something else

      8. (VOL) Don't know

      9. (VOL) Refused

III. *Trust and Efficacy*

We'd like to know your thoughts on government and business.

(9) Which of the statements I read comes closer to your own opinion. You might agree to some extent with both, but we want to know which one is closer to your own views.

(9b) 1. ONE, we need a strong government to handle today's complex economic problems; OR

    2. TWO, the free market can handle these problems without government being involved.

    8. (VOL) Don't know

    9. (VOL) Refused

(10) How much confidence do you have in [INSERT ITEM, RANDOMIZE]? Would you say A great deal of confidence, Some confidence, Very little confidence, or No confidence at all?

    (a) U.S. Congress

    (b) Business and Industry

    (c) Government agencies

      1. A great deal of confidence

      2. Some confidence

      3. Very little confidence

      4. No confidence at all

      8. (VOL) Don't know

      9. (VOL) Refused

(11) How much influence do you think someone like you can have in solving

    (a) Local community problems, like traffic or homelessness?

(b) National problems, like the economy or foreign affairs?

    1. A lot

    2. Some

    3. Very little or

    4. None at all

    8. (VOL) Don't know

    9. (VOL) Refused

V. *Cause Marketing*

We want to ask now about private companies' attention to social problems.

(12a) In the past month, how often have you seen products that advertise some portion of the purchase price supports a particular cause?

    1. Never

    2. Sometimes

    3. Often

    8. (VOL) Don't know

    9. (VOL) Refused

(12b) [ASK IF 12a = 2–9]How often have you purchased a product that advertises some portion of the purchase price supports a particular cause?

    1. Never

    2. Sometimes

    3. Often

    8. (VOL) Don't know

    9. (VOL) Refused

[ASK IF Q12b = 2 or 3, ELSE SKIP TO Q16]

(13) To the best of your knowledge, what was the last product you bought where the portion of the purchase price supports a particular cause? [RECORD OPEN END]

(14) Can you tell me what cause the product supported? [RECORD OPEN END]

(15) Which of the following statements comes closest to explaining your motivation for purchasing this product?

1. I often choose products that support causes

2. I believe we should be doing more for this cause however possible

3. I would have bought the product regardless of whether or not some portion of the purchase price supports a cause

8. (VOL) Don't know

9. (VOL) Refused

Now, we'd like to ask about breast cancer in particular.

(15a) In the past month, have you donated money to a breast cancer charity?

1. Yes

2. No

8. (VOL) Don't know

9. (VOL) Refused

(16a) Many different organizations spend time working on the problems associated with breast cancer. In your opinion, which of the following should spend the most on **scientific research**? [RANDOMIZE]

1. The Federal government

2. Private corporations

3. Charitable Organizations

8. (VOL) Don't know

9. (VOL) Refused

(16b) Second most? [RANDOMIZE]

1. The Federal government

2. Private corporations

3. Charitable Organizations

8. (VOL) Don't know

9. (VOL) Refused

(17a) And in your opinion which of the following should spend the most time and money on breast cancer treatment and support? [RANDOMIZE]

1. The Federal government

2. Private corporations

3. Charitable Organizations

8. (VOL) Don't know

9. (VOL) Refused

(17b) Second most? [RANDOMIZE]

1. The Federal government

2. Private corporations

3. Charitable Organizations

8. (VOL) Don't know

9. (VOL) Refused

(18) The federal government spends money every year on research and education for a variety of diseases. Knowing that there are limited funds available, which of the following should be the federal government's top priority? [RANDOMIZE]

1. Breast cancer

2. Diabetes

4. Heart disease

8. (VOL) Don't know

9. (VOL) Refused

(18b) What should be the federal government's second priority? [CATI, REMOVE RESPONSE FROM Q18]

1. Breast cancer

2. Diabetes

4. Heart disease

8. (VOL) Don't know

9. (VOL) Refused

(19) Now, focusing on just the last week have you seen [RANDOMIZE A-C; if 19c = 'YES' FOLLOW UP WITH 19a]

(a) Pink products, a portion of the sale of which supports breast cancer research

(b) Walks, races, or runs in support of breast cancer research

(c) Stories about breast cancer

    1. Yes

    2. No

    8. (VOL) Don't know

    9. (VOL) Refused

(20) In the past week, have you purchased a product in the supermarket, shopping mall, large general retail stores or on the internet where a portion of the proceeds benefits breast cancer research?

    1. Yes

    2. No

    8. (VOL) Don't know

    9. (VOL) Refused

If R says yes:

(20a) Did purchasing this product

    1. Make you feel good

    2. Make you feel uncomfortable

    3. Make no difference

    8. (VOL) Don't know

    9. (VOL) Refused

(21) *(experimental question, random assignment)* Imagine you stopped by the supermarket to pick up a few items with only $10 in your wallet. One item you want to buy is a beverage, but there are two nearly identical products on the shelf. One product gives part of the purchase price to fund breast cancer research and cost [CATI RANDOMLY ASSIGN: $1.50, $2.00, $2.50]. The other does not and cost $1.00. Which one would you choose?

    1. $1.50/$2.00/$2.50

    2. $1.00

8. (VOL) Don't know

9. (VOL) Refused

(22) Have you or anyone close to you been diagnosed with breast cancer?

1. Yes

2. No

8. (VOL) Don't know

9. (VOL) Refused

(22a) [If Q22 = 1] Would that person be

    1. You

    2. an immediate family member

    3. an extended family member

    4. close friend, or

    5. Someone else?

    8. (VOL) Don't know

    9. (VOL) Refused

IV. *Knowledge*

We are going to ask you a few questions about government, current events, and shopping habits. Many people do not know the answer to these questions, so if there are some you don't know just tell me and we'll go on.

(23) What job or political office is now held by Joe Biden? (DO NOT READ)

1. Vice president

2. Something else

8. (VOL) Don't know

9. (VOL) Refused

(24) Which political party has the most members in the House of Representatives? (DO NOT READ)

1. Democrat

2. Republican

3. Something else

8. (VOL) Don't know

9. (VOL) Refused

(25) Compared to this time last year, has the number of U.S. soldiers in Iraq

1. Increased

2. Decreased

3. Stayed about the same

(27) Can you tell me what products the following companies make?

a. DeWalt (duh-WALT) (DO NOT READ)

1. Power tools

2. Something else

8. (VOL) Don't know

9. (VOL) Refused

b. Yoplait (YO-play) (DO NOT READ)

1. Yogurt/Dairy products

2. Something else

8. (VOL) Don't know

9. (VOL) Refused

(28) When is "National Breast Cancer Awareness Month"? (DO NOT READ)

1. October

2. Something else

8. (VOL) Don't know

9. (VOL) Refused

(29) Which of the following best describes a woman's risk of breast cancer?

1. 1 in 2 women will be diagnosed with breast cancer

2. 1 in 8 women will be diagnosed with breast cancer

3. 1 in 25 women will be diagnosed with breast cancer

8. (VOL) Don't Know

9. (VOL) Refused

(30) Which of the following organizations does **NOT** fund breast cancer research?

1. National Institutes of Health

2. Susan G. Komen for the Cure

3. Health Resources and Services Administration

8. (VOL) Don't know

9. (VOL) Refused

V. *Demographic Variables*

Finally, I have a few questions for statistical purposes.

(31) In what year were you born? [ENTER YEAR]

RANGE: 1900-1992, 9998, 9999

(32) What is your gender?

1. Male

2. Female

(33) Which of the following categories, best defines your race/ ethnicity (READ LIST)?

1. White

2. Black

3. Hispanic

4. Asian

5. Native American

6. Mixed

7. Other

8. (VOL) Don't know

9. (VOL) Refused

(34) What is the highest level of education that you have completed?

1. Less than high school

2. High school

3. 2-year college

4. Some college

5. 4-year college

6. Post graduate

8. (VOL) Don't Know

9. (VOL) Refused

(34a) How many adults age 18 or over currently live in your household, INCLUDING YOURSELF?
1-6 RECORD NUMBER [ENTER 6 IF 6 OR GREATER]
  8 DK (VOL)
  9 REF (VOL)

(35) We hear a lot of talk these days about liberals and conservatives. When it comes to politics, do you usually think of yourself as liberal, slightly liberal, moderate, slightly conservative, conservative, or haven't you thought much about this?
  1. Liberal
  2. Slightly liberal
  3. Moderate
  4. Slightly conservative
  5. Conservative
  8. (VOL) Don't know, haven't thought much about this
  9. (VOL) Refused

(36) Last year, that is in 2009, what was your total family income from all sources, before taxes? Just stop me when I get to the right category. [**READ**] [QID:INCOME]
  1. Less than $10,000
  2. 10 to under $20,000
  3. 20 to under $30,000
  4. 30 to under $40,000
  5. 40 to under $50,000
  6. 50 to under $75,000
  7. 75 to under $100,000
  8. 100 to under $150,000
  9. $150,000 or more
  10. [**VOL. DO NOT READ**] Don't know/Refused

ASK IF LL SAMPLE

(37) Now thinking about your telephone use, do you have a working cell phone?
  1. Yes, have cell phone

2. No, do not

8. DK (VOL)

9. REF (VOL)

ASK IF CELL SAMPLE

(38) Is this cell phone your ONLY phone, or do you also have a regular landline telephone at home?

1. Cell phone is ONLY phone

2. Have landline telephone at home

3. THIS IS A LANDLINE (VOL)

8. DK (VOL)

9. REF (VOL)

[IF CELL PHONE INTERVIEW:]

(39) So that we may send you your $10 check, may I please have your address?

1. RESP GAVE MAILING ADDRESS [GOTO 73]

2. RESP DOESN'T WANT MONEY (VOL) [GOTO END]

(40) CATI: USE ADDRESS TEMPLATE FOR COLLECTING:

FULL NAME

ADDRESS

CITY

STATE

ZIP[GOTO END]

Those are all of the questions I have, thank you very much for your time.

REFERENCES

Archibald, Matthew E., and Charity Crabtree. "Health Social Movements in the United States: An Overview." *Sociology Compass* 4, no. 5 (2010): 334–43.

Aschwanden, Christie. "Why I'm Opting out of Mammography." *JAMA Internal Medicine* 175, no. 2 (2014): 164–65.

Bachrach, Peter, and Morton S. Baratz. "Two Faces of Power." *American Political Science Review* 56, no. 4 (1962): 947–52.

Baldassare, Mark, and Cheryl Katz, "The Personal Threat of Environmental Problems as Predictor of Environmental Practices." *Environment and Behavior* 24, no. 5 (1992): 602–16.

Baralt, Lori, and Tracy A. Weitz. "The Komen–Planned Parenthood Controversy: Bringing the Politics of Breast Cancer Advocacy to the Forefront." *Women's Health Issues* 22, no. 6 (2012): e509–12.

Baron, David P. "Private Politics, Corporate Social Responsibility, and Integrated Strategy." *Journal of Economics & Management Strategy* 10, no. 1 (2001): 7–45.

Barone, Michael, Anthony D. Miyazaki, and Kimberly A. Taylor. "The Influence of Cause-Related Marketing on Consumer Choice: Does One Good Turn Deserve Another?" *Journal of the Academy of Marketing Science* 28, no. 2 (2000): 248–62.

Baum, Matthew A. "Sex, Lies, and War: How Soft News Brings Foreign Policy to the Inattentive Public." *American Political Science Review* 96, no. 1 (2002): 91–109.

Baumgartner, Frank R., and Bryan D. Jones. *Agendas and Instability in American Politics*. Chicago: University of Chicago Press, 1993.

Baumgartner, Frank R., and Beth L. Leech. *Basic Interests: The Importance of Groups in Politics and in Political Science*. Princeton, NJ: Princeton University Press, 1998.

Bayh, Marvella, with Mary Lynn Kotz. *Marvella: A Personal Journey*. New York: Harcourt Brace Jovanovich, 1979.

Beaumont, Elizabeth. "Promoting Political Agency, Addressing Political Inequality: A Multilevel Model of Internal Political Efficacy." *Journal of Politics* 73, no. 1 (2011): 216–31.

Beerman, Samantha. "Bye-Bye Betty." *Incentive* 180, no. 9 (2006): 1.

Behr, Roy L., and Shanto Iyengar. "Television News, Real-World Cues, and Changes in the Public Agenda." *Public Opinion Quarterly* 49, no. 1 (1985): 38–57.

Belkin, Lisa. "Charity Begins at . . . the Marketing Meeting, the Gala Event, the Product Tie-In: How Breast Cancer Became This Year's Cause." *New York Times*, December 22, 1996.

Bennett, Stephen, and William R. Klecka. "Social Status and Political Participation: A Multivariate Analysis of Predictive Power." *Midwest Journal of Political Science* 14, no. 3 (1970): 355–82.

Berglind, Matthew, and Cheryl Nakata. "Cause-Related Marketing: More Bank Than Buck?" *Business Horizons* 48, no. 5 (2005): 443–53.

Berinsky, Adam. 2002. "Silent Voices: Social Welfare Policy Opinions and Political Equality in America." *American Journal of Political Science* 46, no. 2 (2002): 276–87.

Bernays, Edward. *Propaganda*. New York: Ig Publishing, 2004.

Bernstein, Mary. "Celebration and Suppression: The Strategic Uses of Identity by the Lesbian and Gay Movement." *American Journal of Sociology* 103, no. 3 (1997): 531–65.

Berry, Jeffrey M. *Lobbying for the People: The Political Behavior of Public Interest Groups*. Princeton, NJ: Princeton University Press, 1977.

Black, Shirley Temple. "Don't Sit Home and Be Afraid." *McCall's*, February (1973): 82–83, 114–16.

Blee, Kathleen M. *Inside Organized Racism: Women and Men in the Hate Movement*. Berkeley: University of California Press, 2002.

Bloom, Paul N., Steve Hoeffler, Kevin Lane Keller, and Carlos E. Basurto Meza. "How Social-Cause Marketing Affects Consumer Perceptions." *MIT Sloan Management Review* 47, no. 2 (2006): 49–55.

Boehner, Ulrike. *The Personal and the Political: Women's Activism in Response to the Breast Cancer and AIDS Epidemics*. Albany, NY: SUNY Press, 2000.

Boorstin, Daniel J. *The Image: A Guide to Pseudo-Events in America*. New York: Vintage Books, 2012.

Breen, T. H. *The Marketplace of Revolution: How Consumer Politics Shaped American Independence*. New York: Oxford University Press, 2004.

Brinker, Nancy G. "When Society Meets Science." *Nature Medicine* 11, no. 10 (October 2005): 1040–42.

Brinker, Nancy G. *Winning the Race: Taking Charge of Breast Cancer*. Irving, TX: Tapestry Press, 2001.

Brody, Jane E. "Breast Cancer Awareness May Carry Its Own Risks." *New York Times*, October 7, 1997.

Brown, Phil, and Stephen Zavestoski. "Social Movements in Health: An Introduction." *Sociology of Health & Illness* 26, no. 6 (2004): 679–94.

Brown, Phil, Stephen Zavestoski, Sabrina McCormick, Brian Mayer, Rachel Morello-Frosch, and Rebecca Gasior Altman. "Embodied Health Movements: New Approaches to Social Movements in Health." *Sociology of Health & Illness* 26, no. 1 (2004): 50–80.

Bumiller, Elisabeth. "Focusing on the Home Front, Bush Signs Education Bill." *New York Times*, January 9, 2002.

Burns, Nancy, Kay Lehman Schlozman, and Sidney Verba. *The Private Roots of Public Action: Gender, Equality, and Political Participation*. Cambridge, MA: Harvard University Press, 2001.

Campion, Rosamond. "Five Years Later: No Regrets." *McCall's*, June (1976): 113+.

Campion, Rosamond. *The Invisible Worm: A Woman's Right to Choose an Alternate to Radical Surgery*. New York: Macmillan, 1972.

Casamayou, Maureen Hogan. *The Politics of Breast Cancer*. Washington, DC: Georgetown University Press, 2001.

Cohen, David K., and Susan L. Moffitt. *The Ordeal of Equality: Did Federal Regulation Fix the Schools?* Cambridge, MA: Harvard University Press, 2009.

Cohen, Lizabeth. *A Consumers' Republic: The Politics of Mass Consumption in Postwar America*. New York: Knopf, 2003.

"Cone Research Report: Cause Evolution and Environmental Survey." Boston: Cone LLC, 2007.

Cress, Daniel M., and David A. Snow. "Mobilization at the Margins: Resources, Benefactors, and the Vitality of the Homeless Social Movement Organization." *American Sociological Review* 61, no. 6 (1996): 1089–109.

Cress, Daniel M., and David A. Snow. "The Outcomes of Homeless Mobilization: The Influence of Organization, Disruption, Political Mediation, and Framing." *American Journal of Sociology* 105, no. 4 (2000): 1063–104.

Dahl, Darren W., and Anne M. Lavach. "Cause-Related Markets: Impact of Size of Cause-Related Promotion on Consumer Perceptions and Participation." In *1995 AMA Winter Educators Conference: Marketing Theory and Application*, edited by David W. Stewart and Naufel J. Vilcassim, 476–81. Chicago: American Marketing Association, 1995.

Downs, Anthony. "Up and Down with Ecology: The 'Issue-Attention' Cycle." *Public Interest* 28 (1972): 38–50.

Doyle, Kathleen. "Stamping Out Tuberculosis: The Story of Christmas Seals." *American History Illustrated* 24, no. 6 (1989): 66–68.

Edelman, Murray J. "Symbols and Political Quiescence." *American Political Science Review* 54, no. 3 (1960): 695–704.

Ehrenreich, Barbara. "The Pink Ribbon Breast Cancer Cult." Tomdispatch.com (December 2, 2009).

Ehrenreich, Barbara. "Welcome to Cancerland: A Mammogram Leads to a Culture of Pink Kitsch." *Harper's Magazine*, November 2001, 43–53.

Eikenberry, Angela M. "A Critique of the Discourse of Marketized Philanthropy." *American Behavioral Scientist* 52, no. 7 (2009): 974–89.

Elliott, Charlene. "Pink! Community, Contestation, and the Colour of Breast Cancer." *Canadian Journal of Communications* 32, no. 3 (2007): 521–36.

Ellul, Jacques. *Propaganda: The Formation of Men's Attitudes*. New York: Vintage Books, 1973.

Eno, Clara B. "The First Tuberculosis Christmas Seal Sale in Arkansas." *Arkansas Historical Quarterly* 6, no. 3 (1947): 300–301.

Finkel, Ed. "Keeping Her Word." *Modern Healthcare* 37, no. 12 (2007): H2–H8.

Finkel, Steven E. "Reciprocal Effects of Participation and Political Efficacy: A Panel Analysis." *American Journal of Political Science* 29, no. 4 (1985): 891–913.

Flavin, Patrick, and John D. Griffin. "Policy, Preferences, and Participation: Government's Impact on Democratic Citizenship." *Journal of Politics* 71, no. 2 (2009): 544–59.

Fowler, James H. 2006. "Altruism and Turnout." *Journal of Politics* 68, no. 3 (2006): 674–83.

Fowler, James H., and Cindy D. Kam. "Beyond the Self: Social Identity, Altruism, and Political Participation." *The Journal of Politics* 69, no. 3 (2007): 813–27.

Fung, Archon, Mary Graham, and David Weil. *Full Disclosure: The Perils and Promise of Transparency.* New York: Cambridge University Press, 2007.

Gamson, William A., and Andre Modigliani. "Media Discourse and Public Opinion on Nuclear Power: A Constructionist Approach." *American Journal of Sociology* 95, no. 1 (1989): 1–37.

Ganz, Marshall. "Resources and Resourcefulness: Strategic Capacity in the Unionization of California Agriculture, 1959–1966." *American Journal of Sociology* 105, no. 4 (2000): 1003–62.

Gardner, Kirsten E. *Early Detection: Women, Cancer, and Awareness Campaigns in the Twentieth-Century United States.* Chapel Hill: University of North Carolina Press, 2006.

Gaventa, John. *Power and Powerlessness: Quiescence and Rebellion in an Appalachian Valley.* Urbana: University of Illinois Press, 1980.

Gilliam, Franklin D., Jr., and Shanto Iyengar. "Prime Suspects: The Influence of Local Television News on the Viewing Public." *American Journal of Political Science* 44, no. 3 (2000): 560–73.

Glickman, Lawrence. *Buying Power: A History of Consumer Activism in America.* Chicago: University of Chicago Press, 2009.

Goerres, Achim. "Why Are Older People More Likely to Vote? The Impact of Aging on Electoral Turnout in Europe." *British Journal of Politics and International Relations* 9, no. 1 (2007): 90–121.

Goffman, Erving. *The Presentation of Self in Everyday Life.* Garden City, NY: Doubleday, 1959.

Gould, Deborah B. *Moving Politics: Emotion and ACT UP's Fight Against AIDS.* Chicago: University of Chicago Press, 2009.

Gray, Virginia, and David Lowery. "Reconceptualizing PAC Formation: It's Not a Collective Action Problem, It May Be an Arms Race." *American Politics Quarterly* 25 (1997): 319–46.

Greenberg, Cheryl. "'Don't Buy Where You Can't Work.'" In *Consumer Society in American History: A Reader,* edited by Lawrence Glickman, 241–73. Ithaca, NY: Cornell University Press, 1999.

Grimes, William. "Norman Brinker, Casual Dining Innovator, Dies at 78." *New York Times,* June 10, 2009.

Hacker, Jacob S. *The Divided Welfare State: The Battle over Public and Private Social Benefits in the United States.* Cambridge: Cambridge University Press, 2002.

Han, Hahrie. *Moved to Action: Motivation, Participation, and Inequality in American Politics.* Stanford: Stanford University Press, 2009.

Harvey, Jennifer A., and Michal Ann Strahilevitz. "The Power of Pink: Cause-Related Marketing and the Impact on Breast Cancer." *Journal of American College of Radiology* 6 (2009): 26–32.

Hilton, Matthew. "Consumers and the State since the Second World War." *Annals of the American Academy of Political and Social Science* 611 (2007): 66–81.

Hoeffler, Steve, and Kevin Lane Keller. "Building Brand Equity through Corporate Societal Marketing." *Journal of Public Policy & Marketing* 21, no. 1 (2002): 78–89.

Hojnacki, Marie. "Interest Groups' Decisions to Join Alliances or Work Alone." *American Journal of Political Science* 41, no. 1 (1997): 61–87.

Hojnacki, Marie, and David C. Kimball. "The Who and How of Organizations' Lobbying Strategies in Committee." *Journal of Politics* 61, no. 4 (1999): 999–1024.

Holmes, John H., and Christopher Kilbane. "Cause-Related Marketing: Selected Effects of Price and Charitable Donations." *Journal of Nonprofit & Public Sector Marketing* 1, no. 4 (1993): 67–83.

Huckfeldt, Robert, Jeffrey Levine, William Morgan, and John Sprague. "Accessibility and the Political Unity of Partisan and Ideological Orientations." *American Journal of Political Science* 43, no. 3 (1999): 888–911.

Iyengar, Shanto, and Donald R. Kinder. *News That Matters.* Chicago: University of Chicago Press, 1987.

Iyengar, Shanto, Mark D. Peters, and Donald R. Kinder. "Experimental Demonstrations of the 'Not-So-Minimal' Consequences of Television News Programs." *American Political Science Review* 76, no. 4 (1982): 848–58.

Jacobs, Meg. *Pocketbook Politics: Economic Citizenship in Twentieth-Century America.* Princeton, NJ: Princeton University Press, 2005.

Kam, Cindy D. "Who Toes the Party Line? Cues, Values, and Individual Differences." *Political Behavior* 7, no. 2 (2005): 163–82.

Kendrowski, Karen M., and Marilyn Stine Sarow. *Cancer Activism: Gender, Media, and Public Policy.* Urbana: University of Illinois Press, 2007.

King, Brayden G., and Nicholas A. Pearce. "The Contentiousness of Markets: Politics, Social Movements, and Institutional Change in Markets." *Annual Review of Sociology* 36 (2010): 249–67.

King, Samantha. "Pink Ribbons Inc.: The Emergence of Cause-Related Marketing and the Corporatization of the Breast Cancer Movement." In *Governing the Female Body: Gender, Health, and Networks of Power,* edited by Lori Reed and Paula Saukko, 85–111. Albany: State University of New York Press, 2010.

King, Samantha. *Pink Ribbons, Inc.: Breast Cancer and the Politics of Philanthropy.* Minneapolis: University of Minnesota Press, 2006.

Kingdon, John. *Agendas, Alternatives, and Public Policies.* Boston: Little Brown, 1984.

Klawiter, Maren. *The Biopolitics of Breast Cancer: Changing Cultures of Disease and Activism.* Minneapolis: University of Minnesota Press, 2008.

Klawiter, Maren. "Racing for the Cure, Walking Women and Toxic Touring: Mapping Cultures of Action within the Bay Area Terrain of Breast Cancer." In *Ideologies of Breast Cancer: Feminist Perspectives,* edited by Laura K. Potts, 181–204. New York: St. Martin's Press, 2000.

Klawiter, Maren. "Racing for the Cure, Walking Women, and Toxic Touring: Mapping Cultures of Action within the Bay Area Terrain of Breast Cancer." *Social Problems* 46, no. 1 (1999): 104–26.

Kolata, Gina. "Grant System Leads Cancer Researchers to Play It Safe." *New York Times,* June 27, 2009.

Kollman, Ken. *Outside Lobbying and Interest Group Strategies*. Princeton, NJ: Princeton University Press, 1998.

Kotler, Philip, and Nancy Lee. *Corporate Social Responsibility: Doing the Most Good for Your Company and Your Cause*. New York: Wiley, 2005.

Krishna, Aradhna, and Uday Rajan. "Cause Marketing: Spillover Effects of Cause-Related Products in Product Portfolio." *Management Science* 55, no. 9 (2009): 1469–85.

Krosnick, Jon A., and Donald R. Kinder. "Altering the Foundations of Support for the President Through Priming." *American Political Science Review* 84, no. 2 (1990): 497–512.

Kushner, Rose. *Breast Cancer: A Personal History and an Investigative Report*. New York: Harcourt Brace Jovanovich, 1975.

Lenz, Gabriel S. *Follow the Leader? How Voters Respond to Politicians Policies and Performance*. Chicago: University of Chicago Press, 2012.

Leopold, Ellen. *A Darker Ribbon: Breast Cancer, Women and Their Doctors in the Twentieth Century*. Boston: Beacon Press, 1999.

Lerner, Barron H. *The Breast Cancer Wars: Hope, Fear, and the Pursuit of a Cure in Twentieth-Century America*. New York: Oxford University Press, 2001.

Ley, Barbara L. *From Pink to Green: Disease Prevention and the Environmental Breast Cancer Movement*. New Brunswick, NJ: Rutgers University Press, 2009.

Lindblom, Charles. *Politics and Markets: The World's Political-Economic Systems*. New York: Basic Books, 1977.

Liu, Edison, Eleanor Nealon, and Richard Klausner. "Perspective from the National Cancer Institute (NCI)." *Breast Disease* 10, no. 5–6 (1998): 29–31.

Long, Esmond R. "Development of the Voluntary Health Movement in America as Illustrated in the Pioneer National Tuberculosis Association." *Proceedings of the American Philosophical Society* 101, no. 2 (1957): 142–48.

Lorde, Audre. *The Cancer Journals*. Argyle, NY: Spinsters, 1980.

Lorge, Sarah. "Is Cause-Related Marketing Worth It? Altruism Shouldn't Be the Only Reason to Support Charities." *Sales & Marketing Management* 150, no. 6 (1998): 72.

Lowery, David, and Virginia Gray. "Interest Organization Communities: Their Assembly and Consequences." In *Interest Group Politics*, edited by Allan J. Cigler and Burdett A. Loomis, 130–56. Washington, DC: CQ Press, 2007.

Luker, Kristin. *Abortion and the Politics of Motherhood*. Berkeley: University of California Press, 1985.

Lukes, Steven. *Power: A Radical View*. 2d ed. Hampshire: Palgrave Macmillan, 2005.

Lukes, Steven. *Power: A Radical View*. New York: Macmillan, 1974.

Luo, Xueming, and Chitra Bhanu Bhattacharya. "Corporate Social Responsibility, Customer Satisfaction, and Market Value." *Journal of Marketing* 70, no. 4 (2006): 1–18.

Manna, Paul. *School's In: Federalism and the National Education Agenda*. Washington, DC: Georgetown University Press, 2006.

Mansbridge, Jane. *Why We Lost the ERA*. Chicago: University of Chicago Press, 1986.

McAdam, Doug, and David A. Snow. "Social Movements: Conceptual and Theoretical Issues." In *Readings on Social Movements: Origins, Dynamics, and Outcomes*, edited by Doug McAdam and David A. Snow, 1–8. New York: Oxford University Press, 2010.

McCarthy, John D., and Mark Wolfson. "Consensus Movements, Conflict Movements, and the Cooptation of Civic and State Infrastructures." In *Frontiers in Social Movement Theory*, edited by Aldon D. Morris and Carol McClurg Mueller, 273–92. New Haven, CT: Yale University Press, 1992.

McCarthy, John D., and Mayer N. Zald. "Resource Mobilization and Social Movements: A Partial Theory." *American Journal of Sociology* 82, no. 6 (1977): 1212–41.

McCombs, Maxwell, and Donald Shaw. "The Agenda-Setting Function of the Mass Media." *Public Opinion Quarterly* 36, no. 2 (1972): 176–87.

McCormick, Sabrina. *No Family History: The Environmental Links to Breast Cancer.* Lanham, MD: Rowman & Littlefield, 2009.

Mehta, Jal. *The Allure of Order: High Hopes, Dashed Expectations, and the Troubled Quest to Remake American Schooling.* New York: Oxford University Press, 2013.

Metastatic Breast Cancer Alliance. "Changing the Landscape for People Living with Metastatic Breast Cancer." New York: Metastatic Breast Cancer Alliance, 2014.

Mettler, Suzanne. *Soldiers to Citizens: The GI Bill and the Making of the Greatest Generation.* New York: Oxford University Press, 2005.

Mettler, Suzanne. *The Submerged State: How Invisible Government Policies Undermine American Democracy.* Chicago: University of Chicago Press, 2011.

Michaelson, Marc. "Wangari Maathai and Kenya's Green Belt Movement: Exploring the Evolution and Potentialities of Consensus Movement Mobilization." *Social Problems* 41, no. 4 (1994): 540–61.

Michels, Robert. *Political Parties: A Sociological Study of the Oligarchical Tendencies of Modern Democracy.* Glencoe, IL: Free Press, 1949.

Miller, Anthony B., Claus Wall, Cornelia J. Baines, Ping Sun, Teresa To, and Steven A. Narod. "Twenty Five Year Follow-up for Breast Cancer Incidence and Mortality of the Canadian National Breast Screening Study: Randomised Screening Trial." *British Medical Journal* 348 (2014): g366.

Minkoff, Debra C. "The Emergence of Hybrid Organizational Forms: Combining Identity-Based Service Provision and Political Action." *Nonprofit and Voluntary Sector Quarterly* 31, no. 3 (2002): 377–401.

Minkoff, Debra C. "The Sequencing of Social Movements." *American Sociological Review* 62, no. 5 (1997): 779–99.

Minkoff, Debra C., and John D. McCarthy. "Reinvigorating the Study of Organizational Processes in Social Movements." *Mobilization: An International Journal* 10, no. 2 (2005): 289–308.

Mohai, Paul. "Men, Women, and the Environment: An Examination of the Gender Gap in Environmental Concern and Activism." *Society and Natural Resources: An International Journal* 5, no. 1 (1992): 1–19.

Myhre, Jennifer. *Medical Mavens: Gender, Science, and the Consensus Politics of Breast Cancer Activism.* PhD dissertation, University of California Davis, 2001.

Nelson, Barbara. *Making an Issue of Child Abuse: Political Agenda Setting for Social Problems.* Chicago: University of Chicago Press, 1984.

Newman, Benjamin J., and Brandon L. Bartels. "Politics at the Checkout Line: Explaining Political Consumerism in the US." *Political Research Quarterly* 64, no. 4 (2011): 803–807.

Nickel, Patricia Mooney and Angela M. Eikenberry. "The Hidden Costs of Cause Marketing." *Stanford Social Innovation Review* (Summer 2009): 51–55.

Nowak, Linda I., and Judith H. Washburn. "Marketing Alliances between Non-profits and Businesses: Changing the Public's Attitudes and Intentions towards the Cause." *Journal of Nonprofit & Public Sector Marketing* 7, no. 4 (2000): 33–44.

Nownes, Anthony J. "The Population Ecology of Interest Group Formation: Mobilizing for Gay and Lesbian Rights in the United States, 1950–98." *British Journal of Political Science* 34, no. 1 (2004): 49–67.

Nownes, Anthony J., and Patricia Freeman. "Interest Group Activity in the States." *Journal of Politics* 60, no. 1 (1998): 86–112.

Olsen, Marvin E. "Social and Political Participation of Blacks." *American Sociological Review* 35, no. 4 (1970): 682–97.

Olson, James. *Bathsheba's Breast*. Baltimore: Johns Hopkins University Press, 2002.

Olson, Mancur, Jr. *The Logic of Collective Action: Public Goods and the Theory of Groups*. Cambridge, MA: Harvard University Press, 1965.

Orenstein, Peggy. "Our Feel-Good War on Breast Cancer." *New York Times*, April 25, 2013.

Osborne, David, and Ted Gaebler. *Reinventing Government: How the Entrepreneurial Spirit Is Transforming the Public Sector*. New York: Plume, 1992.

Packard, Vance. *The Hidden Persuaders*. New York: Ig Publishing, 2007.

Patterson, James T. *The Dread Disease: Cancer and Modern American Culture*. Cambridge, MA: Harvard University Press, 1987.

Peterson, Linda. "A Promise Kept." *Biography* 7, no. 10 (2003): 60–91.

Piven, Frances Fox, and Richard A. Cloward. *Poor Peoples' Movements*. New York: Vintage Books, 1977.

Plutzer, Eric. "Becoming a Habitual Voter: Inertia, Resources, and Growth in Young Adulthood." *American Political Science Review* 96, no. 1 (2002): 41–56.

Polletta, Francesca. *Freedom in an Endless Meeting: Democracy in American Social Movements*. Chicago: University of Chicago Press, 2002.

Popkin, Samuel Lewis. *The Reasoning Voter*. Chicago: University of Chicago Press, 1991.

Putnam, Robert D. *Bowling Alone: The Collapse and Revival of American Community*. New York: Simon & Schuster, 2000.

Reich, Robert B. *Supercapitalism: The Transformation of Business, Democracy, and Everyday Life*. New York: Vintage Books, 2007.

Rich, Irene, Yvonne Andejeski, Isabelle Crawford Bisceglio, Erika S. Breslau, Lisa McCall, and Alex Valdez. "Perspective from the Department of Defense Breast Cancer Research Program." *Breast Disease* 10, no. 5–6 (1998): 33–45.

Riddle, Wayne C. "The No Child Left Behind Act: An Overview of Reauthorization Issues for the 110th Congress." In *CRS Report for Congress*. Washington, DC: Congressional Research Service, 2008.

Rockefeller, Margaretta, with Eleanor Harris. "If It Should Happen to You." *Reader's Digest*, May (1976): 131–34.

Rosenbaum, Marcy E., and Gun M. Roos. "Women's Experiences of Breast Cancer." In *Breast Cancer: Society Shapes an Epidemic*, edited by Anne S. Kasper and Susan J. Ferguson, 153–81. New York: St. Martin's Press, 2000.

Ross, John K. III, Mary Ann Stutts, and Larry Patterson. "Tactical Considerations for the Effective Use of Cause-Related Marketing." *Journal of Applied Business Research* 7, no. 2 (2011): 58–65.

Rosser, Sue. "Controversies on Breast Cancer Research." In *Breast Cancer: Society Shapes an Epidemic*, edited by Anne S. Kasper and Susan J. Ferguson, 245–70. New York: St. Martin's Press, 2000.

Rubin, Alissa J. "New Breast Cancer Research Funding Raises Old Questions About Priorities." *CQ Weekly Report*, May 29, 1993.

Runté, Mary, Debra Z. Basil, and Sameer Deshpande. "Cause-Related Marketing from the Nonprofit's Perspective: Classifying Goals and Experienced Outcomes." *Journal of Nonprofit & Public Sector Marketing* 21, no. 3 (2009): 255–70.

Salamon, Lester M. "The New Governance and the Tools of Public Action: An Introduction." In *The Tools of Government: A Guide to New Governance*, edited by Lester M. Salamon, 1–47. New York: Oxford University Press, 2002.

Sanchez, Gabriel. "The Role of Group Consciousness in Political Participation Among Latinos in the United States." *American Politics Research* 34, no. 4 (2006): 427–50.

Schattschneider, E. E. *The Semi-Sovereign People*. New York: Holt, Rinehart, Winston, 1960.

Schemo, Diana Jean. "New Law Is News to Many." *New York Times*, October 15, 2002.

Schlozman, Kay Lehman, and John T. Tierney. *Organized Interests and American Democracy*. New York: Harper & Row, 1986.

Schneider, Anne, and Helen Ingram. "Social Construction of Target Populations: Implications for Politics and Policy." *American Political Science Review* 87, no. 2 (1993): 334–47.

Shah, Dhavan V., Douglas McLeod, M., Lewis Friedland, and Michelle R. Nelson. "The Politics of Consumption / The Consumption of Politics." *Annals of the American Academy of Political and Social Science* 611, no. 1 (2007): 6–15.

Shah, Dhavan V., Douglas McLeod, M., Eunkyung Kim, Sun Young Lee, Melissa Gotlieb, Shirley S. Ho, and Hilde Breivik. "Political Consumerism: How Communication and Consumption Orientations Drive 'Lifestyle Politics.'" *Annals of the American Academy of Political and Social Science* 611, no. 1 (2007): 217–35.

Shaw, Daron R., and Bartholomew H. Sparrow. "From the Inner Ring Out: News Congruence, Cue-Taking, and Campaign Coverage." *Political Research Quarterly* 52, no. 2 (1999): 323–51.

Smith, Mark A. *American Business and Political Power*. Chicago: University of Chicago Press, 2000.

Snow, David A., and Leon Anderson. "Identity Work among the Homeless: The Verbal Construction and Avowal of Personal Identities." *American Journal of Sociology* 92, no. 6 (1987): 1336–71.

Snow, David A., and Doug McAdam. "Identity Work Processes in the Context of Social Movements: Clarifying the Identity/Movement Nexus." In *Self, Identity, and Social Movements*, edited by Sheldon Stryker, Timothy J. Owens, and Robert W. White, 41–67. Minneapolis: University of Minnesota Press, 2000.

Soss, Joe. "Lessons of Welfare: Policy Design, Political Learning, and Political Action." *American Political Science Review* 93, no. 2 (1999): 363–80.

Soule, Sarah A. *Contention and Corporate Social Responsibility.* New York: Cambridge University Press, 2009.

Staggenborg, Suzanne. "The Consequences of Professionalization and Formalization in the American Labor Movement." *American Sociological Review* 53, no. 4 (1988): 585–605.

Staudohar, Connie. "'Food, Rest, & Happyness': Limitations and Possibilities in the Early Treatment of Tuberculosis in Montana Part II." *Magazine of Western History* 48, no. 1 (1998): 44–55.

Steingraber, Sandra. "The Environmental Link to Breast Cancer." In *Breast Cancer: Society Shapes an Epidemic*, edited by Anne S. Kasper and Susan J. Ferguson, 271–302. New York: St. Martin's Press, 2000.

Stokes, Atiya Kai. "Latino Group Consciousness and Political Participation." *American Politics Research* 31, no. 4 (2003): 361–78.

Stolder, Mary Ellen. "Consumptive Citadel: The Crusade against Tuberculosis in Eau Claire County, 1903–1917." *Wisconsin Magazine of History* 77, no. 4 (1994): 264–94.

Stolle, Dietlind, Marc Hooghe, and Michelle Micheletti. "Politics in the Supermarket: Political Consumerism as a Form of Political Participation." *International Political Science Review* 26, no. 3 (2005): 245–69.

Stone, Deborah. "Causal Stories and the Formation of Policy Agendas." *Political Science Quarterly* 104, no. 2 (1989): 281–300.

Stone, Deborah A. *Policy Paradox: The Art of Political Decision Making.* Rev. ed. New York: Norton, 2002.

Storrs, Landon R. Y. *Civilizing Capitalism: The National Consumers' League, Women's Activism, and Labor Standards in the New Deal Era.* Chapel Hill: University of North Carolina Press, 2000.

Strach, Patricia. "Gender Practice as Political Practice: Cancer, Culture, and Identity." *Politics, Groups, and Identity* 1, no. 2 (2013): 250–52.

Streek, Wolfgang, and Kathleen Thelan. "Introduction: Institutional Change in Advanced Political Economies." In *Beyond Continuity: Institutional Change in Advanced Political Economies*, edited by Wolfgang Streek and Kathleen Thelan, 1–39. New York: Oxford University Press, 2005.

Strolovitch, Dara Z. *Affirmative Advocacy: Race, Class, and Gender in Interest Group Politics*, Chicago: University of Chicago Press, 2007.

Sulik, Gayle. *Pink Ribbon Blues: How Breast Cancer Undermines Women's Health.* New York: Oxford University Press, 2011.

Sulik, Gayle. "#Rethinkpink Moving beyond Breast Cancer Awareness SWS Distinguished Feminist Lecture." *Gender and Society* 28, no. 5 (2014): 655–78.

Sulik, Gayle, and Bonnie Spanier. "Time to Debunk the Mammography Myth." CNN. com, March 18 (2014).

Sulik, Gayle, and Edyta Zierkiewicz. "Gender, Power, and Feminisms in Breast Cancer Advocacy: Lessons from the United States and Poland." *Journal of Gender and Power* 1, no. 1 (2014): 111–46.

Taylor, Desiree. "CHAT Band Seeks Help." *Selma Times Journal*, September 27, 2011.

Taylor, Verta, and Nella Van Dyke. "'Get Up, Stand Up': Tactical Repertoires of Social Movements." In *The Blackwell Companion to Social Movements*, edited by David A. Snow, Sarah A. Soule, and Hanspeter Kriesi, 262–93. Malden, MA: Blackwell, 2007.

Thompson, Stephanie. "Raising Awareness, Doubling Sales; Idea Spotting: Pink Campbell Cans a Hit with Kroger." *Advertising Age*, October 2, 2006.

Till, Brian D., and Linda I. Nowak. "Toward Effective Use of Cause-Related Marketing Alliances." *Journal of Product & Brand Management* 9, no. 7 (2000): 472–84.

Tilly, Charles. "Social Movements and National Politics." In *Statemaking and Social Movements: Essays in History and Theory*, edited by Charles Bright and Susan Friend Harding, 297–317. Ann Arbor: University of Michigan Press, 1984.

US Congress, House of Representatives, Committee on Education and the Workforce, Subcommittee on Select Education. *Status of Financial Management at the U.S. Department of Education*, First Session, 2002.

US Congress, House of Representatives, Committee on Small Business, Subcommittee on Small Business Procurement, Exports, and Business Opportunities. *Private Sector Resources for Exports*, First Session, 1995.

US Congress, House of Representatives, House Foreign Affairs Committee and the House Armed Service Committee. *Beyond the September Report: What's Next for Iraq?*, First Session, 2007.

US Congress, House of Representatives, Select Committee on Aging, Subcommittee on Health and Long-Term Care. *Winning the Battles, Losing the War*, Second Session, October 1, 1992.

US Congress, Senate, Committee on Appropriations, Subcommittee on Labor, HHS, Education, and Related Agencies Appropriations. *Pandemic Influenza: Progress Made and Challenges Ahead*, First Session, 2007.

US Congress, Senate, Committee on Armed Services, Subcommittee on Military Readiness and Defense Infrastructure. *Department of Defense Authorization for Appropriations for FY95 and the Future Years Defense Program Part 3: Military Readiness and Defense Infrastructure*, Second Session, 1994.

US Congress, Senate, Committee on Energy and Natural Resources. *Energy Policy Act of 1992 and the President's Climate Change Action Plan*, Second Session, 1994.

US Congress, Senate, Committee on Finance, Subcommittee on Health Care. *Health Savings Accounts: The Experience So Far*, Second Session, 2006.

US Congress, Senate, Committee on Health, Education, Labor, and Pensions, Children of September 11: The Need for Mental Health Services, Second Session, 1992.

US Congress, Senate. Committee on Labor and Human Resources. *Breast Cancer*, Second Session, 1976.

Valentino, Nicholas. "Crime News and the Priming of Racial Attitudes During Evaluations of the President." *Public Opinion Quarterly* 63, no. 4 (1999): 293–320.

Varadarajan, P. Rajan, and Anil Menon. "Cause-Related Marketing: A Coalignment of Marketing Strategy and Corporate Philanthropy." *Journal of Marketing* 52, no. 3 (1988): 58–74.

Verba, Sidney, and Norman H. Nie. *Participation in America: Political Democracy and Social Equality*. New York: Harper and Row, 1972.

Verba, Sidney, Kay Lehman Schlozman, and Henry Brady. *Voice and Equality: Civic Volunteerism in American Politics*. Cambridge, MA: Harvard University Press, 1995.

Visco, Fran. "Message from Fran Visco: Beyond Pink." *Call to Action*, October 2006, 1.

Vogel, David. *Lobbying the Corporation: Citizen Challenges to Business Authority.* New York: Basic Books, 1978.

Vogel, David. *The Market for Virtue: The Potential and Limits of Corporate Social Responsibility.* Washington, DC: Brookings Institution Press, 2005.

Walker, Edward T. "Contingent Pathways from Joiner to Activist: The Indirect Effect of Participation in Voluntary Associations on Civic Engagement." *Sociological Forum* 23, no. 1 (2008): 116–43.

Walker, Edward T. *Grassroots for Hire: Public Affairs Consultants in American Democracy.* New York: Cambridge University Press, 2014.

Walker, Edward T., Andrew W. Martin, and John D. McCarthy. "Confronting the State, the Corporation, and the Academy: The Influence of Institutional Targets on Social Movement Repertoires." *American Journal of Sociology* 114, no. 1 (2008): 35–76.

Walker, Edward T., and Christopher M. Rea. "The Political Mobilization of Firms and Industries." *Annual Review of Sociology* 40 (2014): 281–304.

Walker, Jack L. *Mobilizing Interest Groups in America: Patrons, Professions, and Social Movements.* Ann Arbor: University of Michigan Press, 1991.

Walsh, Katherine Cramer. *Talking about Politics: Informal Groups and Social Identity in American Life.* Chicago: University of Chicago Press, 2003.

Weisman, Carol S. "Breast Cancer Policymaking." In *Breast Cancer: Society Shapes an Epidemic,* edited by Anne S. Kasper and Susan J. Ferguson, 213–43. New York: St. Martin's Press, 2000.

Weisman, Carol S. *Women's Health Care: Activist Traditions and Institutional Change.* Baltimore: Johns Hopkins University Press, 1998.

Weiss, Janet A. "Public Information." In *Tools of Government: A Guide to the New Governance,* edited by Lester Salamon, 217–54. New York: Oxford University Press, 2002.

Werner, Timothy. *Public Forces and Private Politics in American Big Business.* New York: Cambridge University Press, 2012.

Woloshin, Steven, and Lisa M. Schwartz. "How a Charity Oversells Mammography." *British Medical Journal* 345 (2012): e5132.

Wymer, Walter, and Adrian Sargeant. "Insights from a Review of the Literature on Cause Marketing." *International Review on Public and Non Profit Marketing* 3, no. 1 (2006): 9–15.

Yaziji, Michael, and Jonathan Doh. *NGOs and Corporations: Conflict and Collaboration.* New York: Cambridge University Press, 2009.

Zones, Jane S. "Profits from Pain: The Political Economy of Breast Cancer." In *Breast Cancer: Society Shapes an Epidemic,* edited by Anne S. Kasper and Susan J. Ferguson, 119–52. New York: St. Martin's Press, 2000.

Zukin, Cliff, Scott Keeter, Molly Andolina, Krista Jenkins, and Michael X. Delli Carpini. *A New Engagement: Political Participation, Civic Life, and the Changing American Citizen.* New York: Oxford University Press, 2006.

Abt SRBI, 199

accidental activists: CCS survey results, 52, 58–59, 64–66, 65*f*, 70, 119–120, 121, 122*t*, 131–33, 132–33*f*, 135, 135*f*; defined, 5, 19; participation drivers, 186–87*t*; summary conclusion, 181–82

ACT UP, 155, 157, 165–66, 179

Adelphi NY Statewide Breast Cancer Support Hotline, 143

Agendas and Instability in American Politics (Baumgartner and Jones), 43–44

agenda setting, 43–48

AIDS activism, 61, 63, 147, 155, 179

American Academy of Family Physicians, 111

American Airlines, 109, 147, 150

American Cancer Society (ACS), 16, 38, 111, 141, 143, 156

American College of Radiology, 111

American Heart Association, 13, 79, 172

American Society for the Control of Cancer (ASCC), 141

Arkansas Federation of Women's Clubs, 31

Atomic Energy Commission, 44

avian flu, 99–100

Awareness Bra, 107–8

awareness vs. information, 88–92, 120, 122*t*, 123–24*f*, 123–26, 126*f*, 182–83

Bachrach, Peter, 50

Bakken, Jeremy, 107

Baratz, Morton S., 50

Barnes and Noble, 170

Baton Rouge Breast Foundation, 144

Baumgartner, Frank R., 8, 43–44, 173. *See also* Policy Agendas Project (Baumgartner and Jones)

Bayh, Marvella, 37, 142–43

Belk, 106

Bernays, Edward, 11

Black, Shirley Temple, 37, 142

Black and Married with Kids (blog), 80–81

BMW, 11

Body Shop, 27

Box Tops for Education, 79–81, 84, 92–94

boycotts. *See* contentious politics and activism

Brady, Henry E., 68

breast cancer: debates over, 8–9; history of stigma of, 1, 14, 38, 139, 140; history of treatment of, 140, 142; metastatic, 41, 42; statistics on, 45n74, 168*f*

Breast Cancer Action, 170

Breast Cancer: A Personal History and Investigative Report (Kushner), 142

breast cancer cause marketing, overview: actions offer hope, 107–8;

CCS survey data, 63, 63*f*, 70–72, 71*f*;
      easy individual solutions, 107; focus
      on awareness vs. information, 107;
      and policymaking, 106–7, 109–16;
      promotion of positive imagery,
      108–9. *See also* Citizen Consumer
      Survey (CCS)
Breast Cancer Network of Strength, 143
Breast Cancer Research Foundation, 12,
      107, 113
Brillo, 107
Brinker, Nancy G.: corporate connec-
      tions of, 38, 151–52; declines inter-
      view, 201; as founder of Komen, 12,
      16, 63, 106, 144–49; on impact on
      breast cancer research, 167; political
      connections of, 37, 151–52. *See also*
      Susan G. Komen
Brinker, Norman, 37, 146–47
Brinker International, 147
Bush, George W., 82, 83, 152, 167–68
Bush, Laura, 37, 152, 167–68
buycotting, 26–29, 72–74, 73*f*

Campbell Soup Company, 120, 148–49
cancer, history of, 140
Cancer Care, 154
Casamayou, Maureen Hogan, 43
cause followers: CCS survey results,
      66–68, 67*f*, 119–120, 121, 122*t*,
      131–33, 132–33*f*, 135, 135*f*; de-
      fined, 5, 19; participation drivers,
      186–87*t*
cause marketing, overview: and breast
      cancer, 2; Cone Communications
      study on, 22, 78, 87; defined, 24–25;
      depoliticizing of issues, 19–20,
      77–78, 107; impact on attitudes,
      4–6, 9–13; practices of, 17–21; types
      of campaigns, 63–64, 63*f*. *See also*
      consensus politics and cause mar-
      keting; framing and cause market-
      ing; policymaking, distinguished
      from cause marketing
Centers for Disease Control, 152, 162

charitable activities, as model variable,
      186–87*t*, 188
Children's Miracle Network, 79
Christmas Seals, 31
Citizen Consumer Survey (CCS),
      117–137; awareness vs. information,
      120, 122*t*, 123–24*f*, 123–26, 126*f*;
      breast cancer awareness, 17; buy-
      cotting, 72–74, 73*f*; Cooperative
      Campaign Analysis Project
      (CCAP), 199–205; demographics
      of, 67*f*; duration of, 59; enablement
      and empowerment of individuals,
      130–33, 132–33*f*; individual vs.
      collective solutions, 127–130, 127*t*,
      129*f*; in mixed methods study,
      52–55; promotion of marketable
      emotions, 134–35*f*, 134–36; scope
      of, 18, 20, 119; script of, 206–20;
      summary conclusion, 136–37,
      177. *See also* accidental activists;
      cause followers; lifestyle buyers;
      methodology
citizen science, 26
Climate Change Action Plan
      (1994), 95–96
Clinton, Bill, 95–96, 101
Clinton, Hillary, 90, 92
Coca-Cola, 10, 13, 172
Cohen, Lizabeth, 30
Cold Stone Creamery, 78–79
collective solutions. *See individual vs.*
      collective solutions
Colorectal Cancer Awareness
      Month, 115
colored ribbons, 45, 121. *See also specific*
      ribbons
Color Me Co., 79
commemorative coins, 113
commercial social movements: compo-
      nents of, 40; criticisms of, 40–43;
      explanation of, 13–17; as policy
      monopolies, 169, 183–84. *See also*
      contentious politics and activism;
      Susan G. Komen

Computer Assisted Telephone
   Interviewing (CATI) survey,
   199–200
Cone Communications, 22, 78, 87
confidence in business, as model variable, 186–87t, 188
conflict of interest, 41
congressional hearings. *See* policymaking, distinguished from
   cause marketing; U.S. House of
   Representatives; U.S. Senate
connection to breast cancer, as model
   variable, 186–87t, 188–89
consensus politics and cause marketing, 20, 138–173; breast cancer
   as positive issue, 139–144; consequences of Komen's pink framing,
   166–172; health social movements,
   153–166; and Komen as commercial social movement, 144–153,
   168–69; methodology, 54; summary
   conclusion, 172–73
Consumer Union, 26
contentious politics and activism: avoidance of, 2–3, 4, 14–16; boycotts, 4,
   26, 56, 57; and corporate sponsored
   promotions, 26; history of, 22–23,
   26, 57–58; and marginalized people,
   27, 58; protests, 26, 56; purpose of,
   178; types of, 25–27. *See also* commercial social movements
Converse, 61
Cooperative Campaign Analysis Project
   (CCAP), 199
cooperative market mechanisms: core
   features of, 46–48; history of, 23;
   incidence of, 18–19; and intentional
   engagement, 27–29. *See also* consensus politics and cause marketing;
   cooperative market mechanisms,
   and survey data; framing and cause
   marketing; market mechanisms
   and politics
cooperative market mechanisms, and
   survey data, 56–74; on accidental

activists, 58–59, 64–66, 65f, 67f, 70;
   and breast cancer cause marketing,
   63, 63f, 70–72, 71f; on buycotting,
   72–74, 73f; on cause followers, 66–
   68, 67f, 70; demographics, 67f; and
   factors in political participation,
   68–70; gender patterns, 67–68, 67f;
   individual participation in cause
   marketing, 59–64, 60–63f; on lifestyle buyers, 66–68, 67f, 69; market
   activism and cooperative market
   mechanisms, 57–59; model variables, 185–89, 186–87t; participant
   age patterns, 66; and political ideology, 67–68, 67f; race patterns, 66–
   67, 67f. *See also* Citizen Consumer
   Survey (CCS)
corporate-marketing strategies and
   democratic politics, 174–184;
   awareness vs. information, 182–83;
   consequences of pink framing monopoly, 175; and corporate social
   responsibility, 175, 178; focus on
   sporting events, 179–180; frag-
   mentation of breast cancer activism, 176; individual vs. collective
   solutions, 183; issue frames vs.
   emotional frames, 179–180; market
   mechanisms and politics, 176–181;
   policy monopolies, 183–84; rise of
   private sector in politics, 174–76;
   shaping public opinion and policy,
   181–82; summary conclusion,
   182–84
corporate social responsibility, 10, 22–23,
   25, 175, 178
corporations: benefits of cause marketing, 24–25; corporate marketing
   and democratic politics, 21; corporate social responsibility, 10, 22–23,
   25, 175, 178; influence on policymaking, 47–51; policymaking vs.
   cause marketing, 78–84, 178–79. *See
   also specific corporations*
Cracker Barrel, 26

Dannon, 60
Defense Department: breast cancer initiatives, 100–101, 159–162, 167; Congressionally Directed Medical Research Program, 17; NBCC lobbies for increased funding, 43
Delaware Red Cross, 31
demographic controls, as model variable, 186–87t, 189
developing country initiatives, 103–4
Dickersin, Kay, 200–201
Diet Coke, 26, 46
disaster relief initiatives, 89–91
disease advocacy, 97–100, 108–9, 113–16, 155, 168, 172
Don't Buy Where You Can't Work, 4, 27, 29

Education Department, 95, 162
education initiatives, 79–84, 92–94, 96
efficacy, as model variable, 186–87t, 188
emotional frames. See issue frames vs. emotional frames
enablement and empowerment of individuals, 92–96, 130–33, 132–33f
environmental breast cancer movement, 6, 8, 39, 41, 46, 169
environmental initiatives, 94, 95–96
Equal Rights Amendment (ERA), 35
Ernst & Young, 166
Estée Lauder, 12, 115, 148
Every Student Succeeds Act (2015), 84

federal policy process. See policymaking, distinguished from cause marketing
Feeding America, 79
feminist activism, 7, 35, 54, 143–44, 155
Fit for the Cure, 107–8
Ford, Betty, 37, 140, 143, 152
Ford Motor Company, 26, 106, 148, 166
framing and cause marketing, 22–55; overview, 4–5, 7, 18, 22–23; and breast cancer activism, 32–34, 36–37; cause marketing, defined,

24–25; comparison of contentious activism with, 25–27; criticisms of pink framing, 40–46; historical practices distinguished from, 29–32; implications for power, influence, and equality, 48–51; Komen as commercial social movement, 37–43; methodology, 52–55; policy monopolies and agenda setting, 43–48; political consumerism distinguished from, 27–28; summary conclusion, 55; tactics and strategies of social movements, 34–37. See also pink framing

Gap, 61
Gaventa, John, 50
gay rights activists, 26, 27
General Mills, 11, 60, 79–81, 84, 92–94, 97
Gerberding, Julie, 99–100
Give Hope with Every Cup, 60
Glickman, Lawrence, 30, 57–58
Goodman, John, 98–99
Gore, Al, 152
Gore, Tipper, 152
Go Red for Women, 13, 61, 172
Gould, Deborah, 179
Government Accounting Office (GAO), 95, 110, 159
governmental policymaking. See policymaking, distinguished from cause marketing
Great American Cleanup, 94
Greater Washington Area Coalition for Cancer Survivorship, 154

Haley, Charlotte, 147–48
Hanes, 61
Harkin, Tom, 99–100, 159–160
Hayek, Selma, 104
Health and Human Services Department, 99
Health Care Finance Administration, 162

health savings accounts (HSAs), 98–99
health social movements, 6, 8, 33, 39, 41–42, 153–166
Heroes at Home, 101–3
Hester, Susan, 154
Home Depot, 25
Hope Shines On, 106
Hunger Awareness Day, 89
hunger relief initiatives, 88–89
Hunter, Duncan, 105

ICI Pharmaceuticals, 111
identity movements, 33
individual vs. collective solutions, 127–130, 127*t*, 129*f*, 183
information. *See* awareness vs. information
Inspector General's Office, 95
intentional participators, 27–29. *See also* cause followers; lifestyle buyers
interest groups, 36
Invisible Worm, The (Campion), 142
issue-attention cycle, 77–78
issue framing: and cause marketing, 19–20, 77–78, 107, 176–77; and media coverage, 100, 117–18; vs. emotional frames, 100–103, 179–180. *See also* framing and cause marketing; pink framing

Jacobs, Hollye, 108
Jacobs, Meg, 30
James, LeBron, 80–81
Jones, Bryan D., 8, 43–44, 173. *See also* Policy Agendas Project (Baumgartner and Jones)
Jones, Ivan, 79–81

Keep America Beautiful, 94
Kendrowski, Karen M., 43
King, Samantha, 8
Kingdon, John, 48, 82
Klawiter, Maren, 46
KNOW Hunger, 88–89

knowledge, as model variable, 185, 186–87*t*
Kohl's, 108
Komen. *See* Susan G. Komen
Kotler, Philip, 86
Kraft, 25, 89
K2, 170
Kushner, Rose, 142, 200–201

Lace Up for the Cure, 106
Lance Armstrong Foundation, 79
Langer, Amy, 154
Lantos, Tom, 105
Lasker, Mary, 141, 153
Lauder, Evelyn, 12, 16, 148
Lee, Nancy, 86
lifestyle buyers: CCS survey results, 66–68, 67*f*, 69, 119–120, 121, 122*t*, 131–33, 132–33*f*, 135, 135*f*; defined, 5, 18–19; participation drivers, 186–87*t*
Linda Creed Breast Cancer Foundation, 143
Loads of Hope, 89–90
lobbying, 10, 11, 36, 50
Long Island Women's Outreach Network, 143
Lorde, Audre, 143
Lose for Good, 89
Love, Susan, 153
Lukes, Steven, 50
lumpectomy, 142
lung cancer, 113–14, 168*f*
Lung Cancer Awareness Month, 114–15

Macy's, 13, 61, 79, 172
Major League Baseball, 109
Make-A-Wish Foundation, 78–79
mammograms, 6, 42, 110–13, 143, 151, 152, 162
Manzullo, Donald, 91
Marcus, Stanley, 12
market activism, history of, 57–58. *See also* contentious politics and activism

market mechanisms and politics, 1–21;
    activists with ties to industry, 2–3;
    cause marketing, 2, 4–6, 9–13,
    17–21; commercial social move-
    ment, 13–17; cooperative market
    mechanisms, 3–5, 8–10, 18–19; and
    corporate resources, 12–13; indus-
    try influence in politics, 7, 9, 10–11,
    21; issue definition, 9, 19; and pink
    framing, 6–7, 12–14, 16, 20; sum-
    mary conclusion, 21
Marvella: A Personal Journey
    (Bayh), 142–43
mastectomy, 140, 142
media coverage: compared to cause
    marketing, 17, 128–29; and issue
    framing, 100, 117–18; Kendrowki
    and Sarow on, 43; in methodology,
    53, 60; and policymaking, 77; and
    stigma of breast cancer, 140, 144–45
methodology: archival research, 200–
    201; Computer Assisted Telephone
    Interviewing (CATI) survey,
    199–200; Cooperative Campaign
    Analysis Project (CCAP), 199;
    development of database, 19–20,
    84–85, 203–5; interviews, 201–3;
    mixed-methods study, 52–55; re-
    gression analysis, 69, 124–25, 128,
    131, 132, 186-187*t*, 190–98*t*. *See also*
    Citizen Consumer Survey (CCS);
    specific aspects of survey
Minkoff, Debra, 36
Mitsubishi, 26
monopolies. *See* policy monopolies
Montana Tuberculosis Association, 31
Myhre, Jennifer, 15

National Alliance of Breast Cancer
    Organizations, 111, 156–57
National Breast Cancer Awareness
    Month, 110–13, 115, 122*t*. *See also*
    Citizen Consumer Survey (CCS)
National Breast Cancer Awareness
    Week, 111

National Breast Cancer Coalition
    (NBCC), 12, 20; Advocacy Training
    Conference, 162, 164; consensus
    framing, 165, 169; and corporate
    partnerships, 165–66; corporate
    partnerships with, 60, 170, 171;
    distinguished from Komen, 163–65,
    169–170; Do the Write Thing
    campaign, 157–58; formation of,
    154–55; governmental partner-
    ships and funding for, 43, 54–55,
    159–164; as health social move-
    ment, 32–33, 39, 155–165; image
    of organization, 157–58; Not Just
    Ribbons campaign, 170; Project
    LEAD, 161, 162–63, 164; and value
    of mammograms, 110
National Cancer Care Foundation, 111
National Cancer Institute (NCI), 110,
    111, 155, 159–161, 167
National Civic Engagement
    Survey, 28–29
National Consumers' League, 29
National Institutes of Health (NIH),
    1, 2, 17, 109–10, 125–26, 159,
    168*f*, 180–81
National Science Foundation, 52, 199
National Wildlife Foundation, 13
Neiman Marcus, 146–47
Nestlé Pure Life, 94
New Balance, 4, 106
Nickelodeon, 13
Nike, 22, 26, 79
No Child Left Behind Act (2001), 82–84
Not Just Ribbons campaign, 170
Nowak, Linda I., 64
nuclear energy framing, 8, 44

Obama, Barack, 80–81, 168
O'Leary, Hazel, 96
Orenstein, Peggy, 45–46, 172
outsider tactics, 34

Pallone, Frank, 110
Pampers, 46, 103–4

peach ribbons, 115, 147–48
Pentel, 107
Perry, William, 104–5
Pier One, 147, 150
pink framing: and corporate ties, 12–14; criticisms of, 40–46, 169–170, 171, 179, 180–81; effects of, 6–7, 16–17, 20, 166–172, 175, 179; impact on NBCC, 165; monopoly of, 61, 175
Pink Is Our Passion, 106
pink purchasers, 70–72, 186–87t
pink ribbon symbology, 11, 12, 16, 45, 115, 120–21, 125
Pink Warriors, 106
Pinky Promise, 107
Policy Agendas Project (Baumgartner and Jones), 19, 53, 85, 86, 87f, 203–4
policymaking, distinguished from cause marketing, 75–116; awareness vs. information, 88–92; and breast cancer cause marketing, 106–7, 109–16; comparison of issue definition, 86–88, 87f; and constitutional regulation, 87–88; and corporate partnerships, 78–84; difficult vs. easy solutions, 96–100; and education initiatives, 79–84, 92–94, 96; effects of market mechanisms on, 47–55; focus on controversy vs. consensus, 103–6; focus on limitations vs. enablement and empowerment of individuals, 92–96; issue frames vs. emotional frames, 100–103; methodology, 19–20, 52–53, 76, 84–86, 109; National Breast Cancer Awareness Month, 110–13; summary conclusion, 116, 177; symbolic action based on market-based frames, 113–16. See also U.S. House of Representatives; U.S. Senate
policy monopolies: and agenda setting, 43–48; Baumgartner and Jones on, 44; and breast cancer campaigns, 44–45; of commercial social movements, 169, 183–84; and corporate

resources, 12–13, 178–79; and nuclear energy, 43–44. See also commercial social movements; pink framing
Polimetrix, 199
political consumerism: and buycotting, 26–29; comparison to cause marketing, 28–29, 65–66, 65f; defined, 27; incidence of, 6, 28–29, 72; as intentional engagement, 56
political importance and awareness, 127–133, 127t
postal stamp, 7, 17, 113, 167
President's Cancer Advisory Board, 37
Proctor & Gamble, 11, 79, 89–90, 104
ProQuest Congressional, 109, 204–5
prostate cancer, 168f
Prostate Cancer Awareness Month, 115

Quayle, Dan, 152
Quayle, Marilyn, 152

Race for the Cure, 4, 12, 26, 36–37, 113, 145–152, 166
radical mastectomy, 142
Rainforest Action Network, 26
Reach to Recovery, 156
Reagan, Ronald, 174
Rebuilding Together, 101–3
red ribbons, 147
regression analysis results,186-187t, 190–98t
responsibility for household purchases, as model variable, 185, 186–87t
Revlon, 165–66
revolving door, 49
Rihanna, 80–81
Rockefeller, Happy, 37, 142
Rose, The, 143
Rosmond, Babette, 142, 143

Saatchi and Saatchi, 104
Sallie Astor Burdine Breast Foundation, 144
Sarow, Marilyn Stine, 43

Save Lids to Save Lives, 60, 97
Schattschneider, E. E., 9
Schlozman, Kay Lehman, 68
Schroeder, Pat, 157
Sears, 101–3
Self (magazine), 115
Selma Middle CHAT Academy, 79–81
Shah, Dhavan V., 28
Share Our Strength, 79, 88
Silver Lining: A Supportive and Insightful Guide to Breast Cancer, The (Jacobs), 108
Small Business Committee's Subcommittee on Procurement, Exports, and Business Opportunities, 91, 92
Smeal, Eleanor, 154
socially responsible purchases, 130–32
social media, 89, 102–3
social movements: Myhre on, 15; tactics and strategies of, 34–36. *See also* contentious politics and activism
softening up process (Kingdon), 82
Soule, Sarah, 27
Specter, Arlen, 160
Spielman, Stefanie, 113
spillover effects, 41–42
Starbucks, 10, 22
Stern, Caryl, 104
STOP ERA movement, 35
Stories of Hope, 16
Strolovitch, Dara, 24f
Stuart Pharmaceuticals, 111
Sulik, Gayle, 41
Sun Chips, 106
Susan G. Komen, 115; Advocacy Alliance, 110; and commemorative coins, 113; as commercial social movement, 16, 33, 37–43, 54–55, 144–153, 168–69, 171, 172, 175; corporate partnerships with, 4, 60, 79, 97, 107–8, 111, 138, 146–152, 166; establishment of affiliates, 166–67; founder of, 12; image of organization, 155; namesake of, 144; public awareness of, 1, 125–26,
126f; scope of, 33; statistics on, 138, 166–67; tactics and strategies of, 36–37, 167–69; volunteers, 167. *See also* Brinker, Nancy G.; pink framing; Race for the Cure

Target, 79
Think Before You Pink, 170
Tide, 89–90
Till, Brian D., 64
Toxic Tours, 46
Tyler, Lamar, 80–81
Tyler, Ronnie, 80–81
Tyson, 88–89

UNICEF, 79, 103–4
unintentional activists. *See* accidental activists
U.S. House of Representatives: Committee on Armed Services, 104–5; Committee on Education and the Workforce Subcommittee on Select Education, 95; Committee on Foreign Affairs, 104–5; Committee on Government Operations, Subcommittee on Human Resources and Inter Governmental Relations, 109–10; Energy and Commerce Committee, Subcommittee on Health, 110; Joint Congressional Committee on Atomic Energy, 44. *See also* policymaking, distinguished from cause marketing
U.S. Senate: Appropriations Subcommittee on Labor, HHS, Education, and Related Agencies, 99; Committee on Armed Services Subcommittee on Military Readiness and Defense Infrastructure, 100–101; Committee on Energy and Natural Resources, 95–96; Committee on Health, Education, Labor, and Pensions, 90; Joint Congressional

Committee on Atomic Energy, 44; Labor and Human Resources Aging Subcommittee, 151, 152; Subcommittee on Healthcare, 98. *See also* policymaking, distinguished from cause marketing

vaccines, 99, 103–4
Verba, Sidney, 68
Veteran's Administration, 162
Visco, Fran, 164, 169, 170, 201

Wacoal, 107–8
Walker, Edward, 50
Walmart, 89
Weight Watchers, 89
Weisman, Carol, 43

Wilson, 16, 170
Wisconsin Anti-Tuberculosis Association, 31
Wolfe, Thad A., 101
Women's Cancer Resource Center, 144
Women's Community Cancer Center, 144
Women's Field Army, 141
Women's International League for Peace and Freedom, 81–82

yellow ribbons, 121
Y-Me, 143, 154
Yoplait, 60, 97, 148, 150

Zukin, Cliff, 28–29, 68

Printed in Australia
AUHW012013211119
320301AU00002B/10